THEATRICALITY

Theatricality

*A study of convention
in the theatre
and in social life*

Elizabeth Burns

LONGMAN

LONGMAN GROUP LIMITED
London

Associated companies, branches and representatives
throughout the world

First published 1972

ISBN 0 582 50034 6

Printed in Great Britain by
Cox & Wyman Ltd, London, Reading and Fakenham

Contents

Acknowledgements

I would like to thank Violet Laidlaw who undertook the typing of this book, little realising how much of her time it would consume. Her work in helping me to put the manuscript into a publishable form has been arduous for her but invaluable to me.

I have referred several times in this book to my husband's published work. But these references constitute only a small part of the contribution that he has made both to the original conception and to the development of the theme.

ELIZABETH BURNS

The publishers are grateful to the following for permission to reproduce copyright material:
Arnold Simmel for extracts from Das Individuelle Gesetz by G. Simmel, trans. Elizabeth Burns; British Broadcasting Corporation for an extract from *Cultural Bureaucracy* by Tom Burns (unpublished). A study of Occupational Milieux in the B.B.C. undertaken in 1963/64; Cambridge University Press for an extract from *Adventure of Ideas* by A. N. Whitehead; David Caute for an extract from 'Actor's Theatre' by David Caute from *The Listener* 3/6/71, Volume 85; author's agents for excerpts from *The Groucho Letters* by Groucho Marx, published by Michael Joseph Ltd., proprietors—Simon and Schuster Inc.; Dr S. Messinger for an extract from 'Life as Theatre' by S. Messinger, Sampson and Towne from *Sociometry* 1962; *Theatre Quarterly* for extract from 'Finding a Style for Farquhar' an interview with William Gaskill, *Theatre Quarterly No. 1*, Jan-Mar 1971, reproduced by permission of the Editors of *Theatre Quarterly*; The New York Review of Books for an extract from 'Pintermania' by Nigel Dennis, reprinted with permission from *The New York Review of Books*. Copyright © 1972 NYREV Inc.

1

Sociology and the theatre

I have considered our whole life is like a play: wherein every
man forgetful of himself is in travail with expression of another
... though the most be players, some must be spectators.[1]

The idea of the world as a stage, of men as actors assuming and
discarding different roles, and of the world of social reality becoming
a play contrived by hidden, superhuman or impersonal forces, has
been familiar in literature as long as it and drama have existed. Latterly the so-called behavioural sciences, sociology and social psychology, have taken up the similitude and exploited it as a device for
analysing social behaviour.

Yet despite the apparently inexhaustible resource of ideas the similitude has provided and continues to provide, it remains suspect as
an analogy. 'The concept of role', writes Peter Worsley, 'is the central concept in the social sciences. Its analytical utility is immediately obvious ... As in the theatre—from whence the metaphor is
taken—the script is written for the actor: he does not invent the role.
Yet it is precisely at this point that the limits of the analogy reveal
themselves. Too often the social role is conceived of as absolutely
fixed.'[2] More singularly, Erving Goffman, whose elaboration of this
similitude in his best known work takes him through chapter after
chapter dealing with 'performances', 'team-play', 'front-stage' and
'back-stage', 'performers and audience' in real life 'settings' and 'situations', refers in his preface to the 'obvious inadequacies' of the 'perspective employed in this report'. In his final pages, added to the
second edition of the book, he writes, as a 'final comment':

In developing the conceptual frame-work employed in this

---

[1] Ben Jonson, *Discoveries*, in *Works*, ed. W. Gifford (London, 1816) ix, p. 191.
[2] Peter Worsley, *The Distribution of Power in Industrial Society*, Soc. Review Monograph 8 (Keele 1964), p. 15.

report, some language of the stage was used. I spoke of performers and audiences, of routines and parts; of performances
coming off and falling flat; of cues, stage-settings and backstage;
of dramaturgical needs, dramaturgical skills and dramaturgical
strategies. Now it should be admitted that this attempt to press a
mere   analogy   so   far   was   in   part   a   rhetoric   and   a
manoeuvre.[3]

My central purpose in this book is to explore the significance and
the meaning of the 'mere analogy' itself.

Implicit in all analogy lies the 'shock of recognition'—the elementary poetic or musical experience. In drama, this experience, the
immediate 'coming to recognise' an unexpected feature of natural or
social reality, is doubled. First, drama is a special kind of activity
which consists in composing a plausible semblance of human action
of an important or consequential kind. Secondly, we use the terminology and conceptual apparatus (the social technology) which makes
this special kind of activity possible as a means of understanding
human action itself.

This two-way process is a universal social fact. It is at the same
time ritualistic and heuristic. It has been observed and exploited by
social anthropologists in their interpretations of ritual performances.
Ritual serves in a multitude of ways as a store of otherwise inarticulate understandings of the formalities and observances, constraints and obligations, rights and privileges which are observably
present and more or less unquestioningly maintained. Myth similarly
may be interpreted as presenting a key not merely to primitive cos-
mologies but to the way in which such systems of belief are quarried
out of the physical realities and behavioural possibilities present and
available, a key to the peculiarities of the selective process by which
the *socially* real world is constructed,[4] and to the way in which the
realities excluded from the 'socially real world' may yet have their
existence acknowledged.

> Mythical speculations ... do not have anything to do with the
> reality of the structure of Tsimshian society, but rather with its
> inherent possibilities and its latent potentialities. Such specu-
> lations, in the last analysis, do not seek to depict what is real,
> but to justify the shortcomings of reality, since the extreme
> positions are only imagined in order to show that they are un-
> tenable.[5]

Many literary critics have directed their criticism to revealing the

[3] Erving Goffman, *Presentation of Self in Everyday Life* (Anchor Books, 1959), p. 254.
[4] Cf. A. Schutz, *The Phenomenology of the Social World*, trans. S. Walsh and F. Lehnert
(Northwestern University Press, 1967).
[5] C. Lévi-Strauss 'The story of Asidwal' in *The Structural Study of Myth and Totemism*,
ed. E. Leach (Tavistock, 1967), p. 30.

principles of selection and construction which seem to govern the individually created fictive worlds of writers—poets, novelists and playwrights.[6] A perceptive study of the principles on which literary fictions are constructed is made by Frank Kermode in *The Sense of an Ending*. He sees literary fictions by virtue of their conscious falsity as the most potent means of ordering our universe:

> They [literary fictions] find out about the changing world on our behalf; they arrange our complementarities. They do this for some of us perhaps better than history, perhaps better than theology, largely because they are consciously false; but the way to understand their development is to see how they are related to those other fictional systems.[7]

Sociologists, for their part, seem mostly to have treated literature as source material for 'historical' reconstruction of social realities of the past, much as Weber recreated the *Protestant Ethic* from the writings of sectarian divines (and usually with as little regard for chronology), or as a library of corroborative evidence for their own observations and *aperçus*. There is, however, a partial sociology of the drama and a programme for a more extensive one. There is also a substantial body of writing which could be entitled, collectively, a 'sociology of literature'; the first is largely French, the latter more cosmopolitan, but certainly European.

Although these various sub-disciplines are relevant to the present exploratory study, and reference will be made to them, it should be emphasised that I am not attempting a synthesis either of the several 'approaches' or of the appropriate insights which students of ritual, myth, literary and dramatic criticism and the sociology of the drama have so far revealed. Instead I intend to explore what I have called the double relationship between the theatre and social life, 'theatricality' itself, by examining the varieties of theatrical convention that can be observed in the development of drama in the English theatre.

It is through the analysis of conventions to which actions conform inside and outside the theatre, in drama and in everyday life, that I hope to be able to express the nature of 'theatricality' inherent, to varying degrees, in all human action. Just as the theatrical metaphor arises out of the ambiguous vision of life as a stage, and of the stage as a representation of life, and of social life as 'unreal', so too the understanding of theatricality depends on the perception of the two-

---

[6] Outstanding amongst such critical works are Northrop Frye's study of Blake's mythology in *Fearful Symmetry* (Beacon Press, 1962) and F. R. Leavis's examination of Dickens's construction of the social world of *Hard Times* in *The Great Tradition* (Chatto & Windus, 1948).
[7] Frank Kermode, *The Sense of an Ending—studies in the theory of fiction* (Oxford University Press, 1967), p. 64.

way process whereby drama in performance is both formed by and helps to re-form and so conserve or change the values and norms of the society which supports it as against the alternative realities which lie outside the currency of any particular social reality. Inside the theatre this is part of the recognized creative process. Outside the theatre, where there is neither dramatist nor script, the same creativity in the field of ordinary behaviour is commonly unrecognised, or, when recognised, regarded as bizarre, perhaps disreputable, presumptuous, in any case deviant. The moral value placed on spontaneity and sincerity in personal relations has produced a dichotomy between 'natural' and 'theatrical' behaviour.

It is difficult to avoid examining the varieties of theatrical convention in historical sequence although there are disadvantages to this method. The historical frame of reference, where I have adopted it, is used for convenience only and I hope to avoid the implication that chronology denotes progress and that the history of the theatre is a history of increasing sophistication. For historical change has not meant the replacement of one kind of convention by another but the accumulation of a repertoire of conventions which are themselves related to corresponding social conventions. Thus the theatrical tradition is not merely the transmission of a code of rules to which players, playwrights—and audiences—should conform, but a store of possible modes of representing social action which accumulates over the generations. In the modern theatre the adoption of the round or open stage, the abandonment of scenery and use of direct rhetorical devices, derived from the Renaissance theatre, does not mean that there is any return to the modes of thought or behaviour of an earlier period. It does mean, however, that we have extended our awareness of the implications of these conventions and of their value as indices as well as expressions of meaning. It is with this body of conventions, in the present, that I wish to deal. But they can be most easily identified by referring to their origin as innovations, and their development through history cannot be neglected.

On the other side this book treats the theatre as a social institution, comprising performance and performers, spectators and critics, drama and dramatists, plays, actors and producers. The viewpoint therefore will not be identical with that of the traditional literary critic any more than it will be identical with that of the sociologist.

There is of course no hard and fast distinction between the kind of insights which literary critics seek and those which the sociologist (or historian, for that matter) tries to derive from the same material. But the emphasis, the centre of gravity, the purpose are different, as are the concepts, the universe of discourse and sometimes the methods employed. For the sociologist, the theatre is a social milieu, an institution in itself. It is also part and parcel of the world of social behaviour and of the structure of society as a whole. It is, thirdly, a 'theatre' of social action and social values—an arena, among many, in which it is possible to study manifestations of the social values, forms and conventions of society, and also the images of social reality which people of different kinds and at different times have constructed for themselves.

The content of the book draws on three separate and established fields: first, the history of the drama and the theatre on which the inexhaustible scholarship of Allardyce Nicoll and of many others, prominent amongst whom are Glynne Wickham, M. C. Bradbrook and Richard Southern, has worked to provide a thorough reconstruction of past conditions and their social implications. The second is one which might be termed micro-sociology, but is known more widely among sociologists as the 'Chicago school tradition', of which Robert Park and Herbert Blumer were the main creators, and Everett Hughes, Howard Becker and Erving Goffman its most distinguished exponents. The third, and most recent, is a sub-discipline, the sociology of the theatre.

This last needs some brief expository reference, as being even less known in Britain and America than the rather tenuous thread of sociological writings on literature which are connected with the names of Georg Lukács, Ernst Auerbach, Lucien Goldmann, Robert Escarpit, Umberto Eco, and Eduardo Sanguineti.

Apart from the illuminating but incomplete writings of Simmel and Lukács, the sociology of the theatre has been wholly the concern of French scholars. Their interest over the last decade coincides with the new function of the theatre in England, Germany and France as a cultural catalyst in which social change of a more or less political nature has been explored or reflected.

In 1955, Georges Gurvitch summarised in an article the findings of a Conference on Theatre and Society, held at Royaumont. Following the usual procedure of such conferences the outcome was a programme for future research. The suggested studies were:

1. The nature and diversity of the public on which the theatre depends; its cohesion and division into structured groups; the organisation of spectators within this society.
2. The relationship of plays, styles of production and theatrical tradition with the contemporary social setting; the correspondences and contrasts between society as it is and as it is represented in the theatre.
3. The acting profession, its organisation, structure and relationship with other professions and with the class structure of society.

4. The relationship of the content, the theme, of plays, with different types of social structure and different ideologies.
5. The different interpretations that these themes are given at different times and in different societies, according to the basic social assumptions of the time.
6. The function of the theatre in the social life of its period, e.g. as a form of ritual in the Middle Ages; as a form of intellectual education and justification of the social hierarchy during the sixteenth and seventeenth centuries, and, in modern capitalist society, as a form of diversion seized upon and exploited as a commercial enterprise, or, in contrast, as an organ of protest against the established social structure.[8]

The late Georges Gurvitch published no further writings on these lines. But Jean Duvignaud, in his two books, *Le Sociologie du Théâtre* and *L'Acteur*,[9] developed some of Gurvitch's ideas, especially those in paras. 4, 5, and 6. In his *Sociologie du Théâtre* he concentrated specifically on changes in the setting of the action (the church, the court, the public and later the private theatres), changes in the functions of the theatre (as a means of expanding religious experience, a leisure pursuit for the aristocracy, an amusement for a public drawn from all classes) in accordance with changes in the social structure, and changes in the concept of the person.

In *L'Acteur* he dealt with questions arising from the relationship of the actor to the society of which he is a part, and the creation by actor, dramatist and spectators of the personality and actions of a fictional character, a creation that corresponds to the process whereby 'character' is composed by the constraints and pressures of social life. His approach to these questions is, for the most part, broadly historical. His main concern is with the political transformations of society which the theatre, as an institution, reflects.

In this book my primary concern is with the phenomenon of theatricality as it is manifested in the theatre and in social life. I shall first examine the process by which the theatre emerged from ritual, as the language of dramatic convention, product of a consensus of performers and spectators became the essential mode of expression in the theatre. Such conventions comprise the many forms of rhetoric which create a theatrical world and the devices which contribute to the *illusion* of authenticity.

I shall then consider the ways in which the actor uses these conventions and is himself seen in conventional terms, as presenter, interpreter and created character.

[8] G. Gurvitch, 'Sociologie du théâtre', *Les Lettres Nouvelles* xxxv (Paris, 1956), 202–4 (my translation, E.B.).
[9] J. Duvignaud, *Sociologie du Théâtre*, Presses Universitaires de France, 1963; *L'Acteur* (PUF, 1965).

The actor as creator has his counterpart in ordinary life, as the individual who assumes roles and foresees and develops sequences of actions. Similarities and differences between these two kinds of part playing display significant changes throughout the period of theatrical development.

Other aspects of the theatre as an institution: acting as an occupation, the growth in importance of the producer, the role of the audience and the emergence of the professional critic, will be considered in relation to change in the larger society which sustains the theatre.

Finally, meaning and themes in the drama will be related to the rituals which underlie thought, and which organise action, in everyday life.

2

The theatrical metaphor: the world as a stage, and the theatre as paradigm

The part played by the theatrical metaphor as a compelling image in Western literature makes explicit the continuing presence both of theatricality, and of our awareness of it.

Plato made frequent use of the 'play' metaphor. In *Philebus*[1] he spoke of the 'great stage of human life' where comedy and tragedy take place. In the *Laws*[2] he developed the stage imagery in the moral fable of the human puppets, whose strings, representing conflicting impulses of fear and confidence, are manipulated by the gods. The implication is first that it is not the individual alone who is responsible for his own actions but an unseen (or undefined) producer of the whole dramatic action, and second that other possible social worlds exist outside that which is currently accepted as real. This problem of the relationship of man to his roles is one that is constantly evoked by the theatrical metaphor. Yet the more obvious aspect of the metaphor, the equation of 'stage acting' with action in the world, was the one most commonly employed by later Greek and Latin writers. Petronius's *Totus mundus agit histrionem*[3] was one of many versions of the same idea, and is believed to have been used as an inscription on the Globe theatre.

During the Middle Ages the stage metaphor was less prominent in literature although the world was frequently presented dramatically as a 'dream' in a tradition that stretched from *Le Roman de la Rose* to Langland's *Piers Plowman* and Chaucer's *Hous of Fame*. The involuntary nature of the dream, in which the dreamer is both actor

---

[1] Plato, *Philebus, Dialogues of Plato*, trans. and ed. B. Jowett (4th edn. Oxford University Press, 1953), iii, p. 609.
[2] Plato, *The Laws*, trans. A. E. Taylor (Dent, Everyman, 1934), p. 33.
[3] It is possible that this motto was taken directly from John of Salisbury's *Policraticus* where Petronius's idea is paraphrased and extended. See E. Curtius, *European Literature and the Latin Middle Ages*, trans. W. Trask (Bollingen Series, Routledge, 1953), p. 138.

and spectator, also characterises early stages of drama so that the dream can be seen as a rudimentary private drama. The 'dance' image interpreted as 'The Dance of Death' in both literature and the plastic arts also carried a strong theatrical connotation. Each man played a part in an action animated by a personification of death. Man was still thought of and presented as an 'actor', acting in the eye of God.

By the sixteenth century the *Theatrum Mundi* metaphor had become so popular that its commonplace quality was sometimes exposed. Cervantes allows Sancho to deflate his master's elaborate use of the play image, the comparison of life with the stage: 'A fine comparison' said Sancho, 'although not so new that I haven't heard it on various occasions before—like the one of the game of chess.[4]

Frances Yates describes the way in which this *topos*—the concept of the theatre of the world as an emblem of the life of man—was expressed not only in literature but also in engravings such as De Bry's '*Theatrum vitae Humanae*', an illustration to Boissard's verses.[5] The moral/religious conception of the classical theatre as a representation of the human drama seems to have persisted even while religious and secular theatres were becoming popular as places where theatrical performances were taking place. Thus when the play metaphor was used in the drama as it so often was in the sixteenth and seventeenth centuries[6] it referred not only to the stage as it was seen but also to the centuries-old idea of the stage as the paradigm of human life, and of the artificial boundaries placed on feasible behaviour and on the actualities of social existence. Most people were aware of this and were accustomed to connect the theatre, in this literary, traditional sense, with a moral and critical view of humanity. When Jaques makes his well-known speech in *As You Like It* in which he elaborates the *topos* in order to emphasise the *meaninglessness* of life, he is both more and less than a player. Man and actor cancel each other out on a stage which represents the unreality of the world. This bleak demonstration of the way in which the metaphor really works is repeated by Macbeth and by Antonio in *The Merchant of Venice*:

> I hold the world but as the world Gratiano—
> A stage where every man must play a part,
> And mine a sad one. (I, i)[7]

But Shakespeare does not only use this metaphor to conjure up

---

[4] Miguel de Cervantes, *Don Quixote*, trans. J. M. Cohen (Penguin, 1950), p. 539.
[5] F. Yates, *The Theatre of the World* (Routledge, 1969), pp. 165 ff 5–27.
[6] Curtius (*op. cit.*, pp. 140–2) gives many other examples from European literature including an epilogue of Ronsard and Calderon's play *La vida es sueno*.
[7] *The Merchant of Venice*, ed. A. Quiller Couch and J. Dover Wilson, Cambridge University Press, 1926.

the idea of the theatre as a moral emblem. With the knowledge and insights of a player as well as a dramatist he is acutely aware of the fabricated nature of conduct both on and off the stage. Hamlet, who uses the players' performance as a means of manipulating events is shocked by the ability of a player to feel and express emotion: 'But in a fiction, in a dream of passion', in contrast with his own deficiency in feeling and enterprise for a real cause. His immediate decision to take action through the staging of a play, 'The Murder of Gonzago', suggests that he as much as the King has to see the scene acted before it becomes real—shockingly recognisable—to him.

Shakespeare's varied and developing use of the play metaphor has been examined by Ann Righter who suggests that he carries the implications of the metaphor to their furthest limits until the play itself, his final play, *The Tempest*, becomes a play within a play. Both men and players are characterised as 'such stuff/As dreams are made on'. Shakespeare transformed the *topos*: 'Gradually the association of the world with the stage fundamental to Elizabethan drama built itself deeply into his imagination, and into the structure of his plays. . . . In his hands something individual and characteristically brilliant emerged from a theatrical commonplace of the age.'[8]

Shakespeare's dramatic use of the metaphor transformed it from a simple allegorical figure into a complex imaginative mode of expression. Yet people continued to use theatrical terms to describe conduct long after the idea of the theatre as a moral emblem representing man as creature and creator of a world of artifice had been lost. This idea did not so far as we can tell survive the closing of the theatres. The new Restoration theatres belonged exclusively to the world of pleasure and entertainment, to the secular sector of life. Attention was focused less on the fundamental conception of life as dramatic invention, more on the histrionic aspects of ordinary public and private behaviour. Interest in the theatre was stimulated by the comparisons that could be made between acting on the stage and acting in ordinary life, a comparison later stereotyped by Richard Steele:

> The player acts the world, the world the player;
> Whom still that world unjustly disesteems,
> Though he alone professes what he seems.

The overt satirical aim of so many dramatists of this period was directed not so much against vices and abuses in general as against those of particular kinds of people, often against individuals who might be easily recognised by the coterie audiences who frequented the theatres. This was a continuation of the use made of the play as a weapon in the battles of the wits earlier in the century. The drama

---

[8] A. Righter, *Shakespeare and the Idea of the Play* (Penguin, 1962), p. 81.

was operating on a level at which the manners and style of conduct of the dramatic characters were very close to that of the greater part of the audience, the spectators who came from the Court and the town, plus their servants and hangers-on.

From this time the idea of the world as a theatre where the drama of human life is acted descended from the transcendental to the social plane. The stage was regarded as a mirror of the actual rather than the spiritual world, the plays as the 'abstracts and brief chronicles of the time'.

Shakespeare had seen that in drama we are confronted with a version of humanity in one version of the world. From this it is only a short step of vulgarisation to perceiving our actions and setting outside the theatre in theatrical terms. This perception is derived not from a view of life directed by God, Providence or some less anthropomorphic spiritual force, but from a growing awareness of the way in which people compose their own characters, contribute to situations and design settings. As we have seen, the perception is not new to the late seventeenth century but it *is* more apparent, from this time until the present, as the frame of reference for most people in formulating their attitudes has become secular rather than religious. The image of the mind as a theatre came easily to Hume in his consideration of identity: 'The mind is a kind of theatre where several perceptions make their appearance; pass and repass, glide away and mingle in an infinite variety of postures and situations.'[9] But the commonplace analogy is of the world itself as a place where people, like actors, play parts, in an action which is felt obscurely to be designed by 'social forces' or the natural drives of individual men. The emblematic character of theatre has become secularised.

The 'theatrical commonplace', as it is accepted by ordinary people today has lost much of its moral and cosmic significance. It has been replaced by the self-consciousness of the actor. The theatrical quality of life, taken for granted by nearly everyone, seems to be experienced most concretely by those who feel themselves on the margin of events either because they have adopted the role of spectator or because, though present, they have not yet been offered a part or have not learnt it sufficiently well to enable them to join the actors. The spectators are to be found observing a ceremony of any kind from a coronation to a funeral, or watching a street fight or spying on a private quarrel taking place in an uncurtained room. The 'partless actors' are those who for neurotic reasons feel themselves outside life, those who have not yet learnt the conventions of a foreign country, or those who find themselves suddenly in a situation in which they had never envisaged themselves, in a hospital bed or prison cell. It is the common experience of first entry into the en-

[9] D. Hume, *Treatise concerning Human Nature* (1739; Penguin, 1969), p. 301.

closed and unfamiliar world of work. On such occasions people often stress their sense of unreality by saying that they feel they are in a dream or watching a play. This comment was made after interviewing a number of executives in one organization:

> What was very apparent in the interviews which form the basis of this study, and what indeed appears in many of the passages quoted, is that people can observe themselves in situations which require them to use their intelligence, skill and knowledge to the full, can feel an 'I' which remains critical and detached from engagements and commitments ... In many of the quoted passages from interviews there is a clear implication of detachment not only from the roles which are being acted out but from the self which is being, or has been, formed in order to act out the roles effectively, a detachment familiar to everyone at times when an 'is this really me?' question thrusts itself on us and divests the situation and one's presence and actions in it of reality.[10]

The feeling is particularly acute when one is called upon to play an unfamiliar role for a very short time. A member of a jury, on which I served for a three-day murder trial, declared that she could not believe that it was she herself who was really sitting there in the court. Back in the jury room she, along with the other members, seemed to feel that she had recovered 'her own identity'.

People's performances are assessed; they are accused of 'overplaying' or 'underplaying' a part, of making a good or bad 'entrance' or 'exit', or of knowing how to hold the 'stage' (usually in a pejorative sense). Their acts take place in a 'scene' which is 'set'. Such language, commonplace as it has become in many contexts, is still used to distinguish action of a more or less theatrical nature. Most people like to think that sometimes they behave naturally, as 'themselves', while confessing that sometimes they 'put on an act'. The presumption is that there is an approved 'normal' level of behaviour very difficult to define which is neither too expressive nor too inexpressive.

Behaviour can be described as 'theatrical' only by those who know what drama is, even if their knowledge is limited to the theatre in their own country and period. It is an audience term just as the θέᾱτρον was originally a place for viewing, an audience place. Behaviour is not therefore theatrical because it is of a certain kind but because the observer recognises certain patterns and sequences which are analogous to those with which he is familiar in the theatre. It is with the contrivance and composition of these sequences that the actor in ordinary life as much as the stage actor is con-

---

[10] Tom Burns, 'Cultural Bureaucracy: a study of occupational milieux in the BBC' (unpublished report, 1964), p. 63.

cerned. The spectator inside the theatre sees them as the product of dramatist, producer, and actor, while the observer in the world outside, partly involved himself, is less conscious of the processes that produce action. He guesses not only at motives and intentions but also at sources and degrees of power and at what really constitutes accident. He is aware of a process which forms action into coherent and consequential sequences although he cannot always distinguish the forces that are in control.

Theatricality is not therefore a mode of behaviour or expression, but attaches to any kind of behaviour perceived and interpreted by others and described (mentally or explicitly) in theatrical terms. These others are more aware of the symbolic than of the instrumental aspect of any behaviour which they feel that they can describe as theatrical. In this way outsiders *place* the bearing of the upper-class Englishman, the mourning cries of Greek peasant women, or the grimaces of Japanese wrestlers. There is of course always a social norm to which such people adhere and of which people in another society may be unaware, so that degrees of theatricality are culturally determined. But theatricality itself is determined by a particular viewpoint, a mode of perception.

People inhabit many social worlds, each of which is a construct, arising from a common perspective held by the members of that world. The behaviour that takes place in any of these worlds can appear theatrical to those observers who are not participants or to those newcomers who are just learning the rules. They are acutely aware of the element of composition in the management of sequences of action, which the participants may feel to be spontaneous.

The perception of the expressive aspects of ordinary action as significant in themselves and interesting to observe is independent of the realisation of drama as a form of art. This perception emerges in the history of the individual when the child realises that what happens in the world about him is not under his control. Events which affect him or have significance for him are caused by other people, known or unknown. A child is aware of the dramatic when he observes an episode in which he is not a direct participant though he may at first attempt to take part in the scene. Small children are not aware of the boundaries that surround strangers or people who are not concerned with them until they are pulled away or rebuffed by adults. Gradually they learn that there are many episodes, even some concerning their own family, in which they are not expected to take an active part. On such occasions they become spectators, confronted with action which can only be understood if it is 'interpreted' or explained in words.

The word *drama* means 'action' but denotes imitative action which is primarily symbolic, that is, it refers to something which already has or could have taken place. This of course belongs to the theatre. Yet in ordinary life people create drama both by their interpretations of behaviour and through the effect which their presence (and the awareness that they are 'interpreting') has on the behaviour of participants. 'Behaviour', indeed, becomes 'action' when it is recognised as expressing intention. Often enough, intention has to be read into human behaviour in order to give it meaning; there is a generative grammar of behaviour as there is of speech, which enables us to comprehend a pat on the head as sometimes signifying approval, sometimes reproof. Such 'reading in' of intention is an essential factor in the legal process. (Whether or not the reported remarks and actions of the defendants at the Chicago trial in 1969 could be 'read' as intending revolutionary action was the central issue at stake.) In addition, of course, participants are themselves necessarily aware of the way in which others may be 'filling out' their behaviour by reading in intentions. So a demonstration, a street fight, a wedding or even a family quarrel glimpsed through a window becomes a show for those who watch, and, although the acts which are, for those who are involved, instruments directed at accomplishing an immediate objective, that accomplishment is often only complete if the full meaning and intention of their actions is apprehended by others. It is only then that the *consequences* they wish to achieve can in fact be accomplished.

Although all forms of fiction are imitative, dramatic representation of action is the most complete as it rests on the assumption that the peopled dramatic world is autonomous and represents a temporary reality equivalent in its significance—its consequentiality—to that of the social world outside the theatre. By being acted out here and now it claims to belong to the present rather than the past.

Dramatic representation is, however, a construct of perceptions and interpretations. Instrumentality is lost. The perception of a possible dramatic construction of action and theme by the dramatist is interpreted by the producer who projects his interpretation to the actors who in turn project it to the audience. The spectators then see something which has moved a long way from the dramatist's original perception and which they severally perceive according to their own experience and perspectives derived from their participation, at first or second hand, in the groups, communities and society in which they have lived their lives. This multiplicity of perceptions introduces an element of illusion into every performance. People see what they expect to see, and the performers play up to these expectations as far as they are able.

In relation to the theatre, reality and illusion are shifting terms. They do not denote opposites. Everything that happens on the stage can be called real, because it can be seen and heard to happen. It is perceived by the senses and is therefore as real as anything that happens outside the theatre. On the other hand there is an agreement between all those who take part in the performance, either as actors or spectators, that the two kinds of real event inside and outside the theatre are not causally connected. Dislocation is ensured both because nobody really believes the actors to be the people they represent and because action that significantly alters the state of the situation, such as murder, death by other causes, copulation and birth, are always simulated.[11]

How does the actor define the level of reality at which the spectator is supposed to place the action which he sees on the stage? It can be defined by a direct appeal to the audience: 'Here be I, St George. An Englishman so stout—' of the medieval mummers,[12] by ostensible and elaborate disregard of the audience in the developed 'realistic' theatre of the late nineteenth century or, as in contemporary improvisations, by involvement with the audience. The first of these says: 'let's pretend this is reality'; the second 'this is a plausible alternative, reality closely akin and possibly alternative to the one you accept in your particular lives'; the third 'let us together make this a reality that overrides any other possible reality' ('we can then go out naked into the streets or make a revolution', which is part of the message of the Living Theatre).

Each of these versions of reality becomes an exercise in illusion on the stage. The completeness of the illusion depends less, however, on the sophistication of techniques involved than on the consensus attained by actors and audience, the agreement about which of these three levels of reality or 'definitions of the situation' is being used.

Definition of the situation in everyday life has been explained sociologically as a process arising out of a parallel consciousness of the emergence and relativity of social behaviour. McHugh uses the term 'emergence' to describe the discovery and interpretation of patterns that are 'documented' by the agent 'in his immediate ongoing

---

[11] Neither of these statements is now true of the new theatre. Groups such as the La Mama and the Living Theatre often try to act out their own private problems on the stage—to be in fact the same people off-stage as on. There is also some pressure from such groups to be allowed to show copulation on the stage. This is not the first time that the theatre has attempted to present rather than represent such acts. Under the Roman Emperors sexual displays were a common form of entertainment and 'executions' were often carried out by substituting for the actor a condemned criminal (see W. Beare, *The Roman Stage*, Methuen 1950, p. 238). It does not seem likely that the Romans would have defended such performances as 'artistically valuable'. They were entertainments and were regarded by the literate minority as symptomatic of the degradation of the theatre.

[12] This formula was retained by the mummers until the end of the last century—the chief character changing to King Billy or King George.

situations', thus allowing him 'to integrate temporarily discrete
events by giving them a baseline of meaning'.[13] To take part in any
social occasion, to assume membership of the relationships which go
with it, the participants accept an initial commitment to keep things
going, 'to keep within bounds'. There has therefore to be a common
perception of those bounds, an acceptance of a definable normality
of conduct, purpose and intent which Anselm Strauss has labelled
'concord'.[14] It is this perception and the acceptance of the constraints which one's presence at a social occasion imposes, with its
concomitant acceptance of specific values and meanings (as against
others) of this version of the causes and effects of actions rather than
any other, of one shared belief in the probability of these consequences and outcomes rather than others, which Goffman terms all-
inclusively 'involvement in the situation'.[15] McHugh suggests that
concord and involvement in the situation are not so much given
constraints on action (like the notices of by-laws and regulations
which stand at the entrance of public parks) as part of an emergent
process which takes place during the course of interaction on any
occasion. In so far as this process, by which appropriate norms,
values and rules 'emerge', is successfully accomplished, they are also
seen as connected with norms, values and rules prevailing on previous other occasions. They are perceived, that is, as relative. 'Emergence' and 'relativity' are two dimensions of the process which
enables social action as it is ordinarily conceived, to take place. The
actor sees, then he interprets and then he acts.

Although this analysis of the mechanism of understanding, intention and action in ordinary life may seem (as it does in the experiments devised to test it)[16] oversimplified, it approximates to the
model of action presented by the dramatist and accepted by the
audience as valid—at least, when it is successful. At the same time
the audience's understanding of the play depends on the emergence
of meaning and the ability of the audience to relate it to their own
experience, their knowledge of norms, roles and the rules of conduct
in a contemporary or past social milieu.

The fact that the theme of a play is in most cases (except in improvisations) already part of a predetermined pattern and that the
action is only animated by the actors means that a selection has
taken place which constrains the possible forms of action which may
emerge. This is the point at which illusion first arises. The level of
reality is chosen—the pretend, the alternative, or the overriding re-

[13] Peter McHugh, *Defining the Situation* (Bobbs Merrill, 1968), p. 35.
[14] Anselm Strauss *et al.*, *Psychiatric Ideologies and Institutions* (Collier-Macmillan,
1964): p. 14—'Concord includes those bedrock agreements about the most generally accepted goals of the organisation'.
[15] E. Goffman, *Behavior in Public Places* (Free Press, 1963), p. 37.
[16] McHugh, *Defining the Situation*, pp. 83–103.

ality—and is maintained by the attitude of the actors both to the characters in the play and to the audience.

But illusion is only a specifically theatrical term for a process inherent in all social interaction. It is the process of confining attention to those involved in a specific situation, of limiting activities, given that situation, to what is appropriate or meaningful or consequential, and of observing a defined level of reality. The process is essentially that of providing a frame for action. The important thing is to signify the degree of seriousness or fatefulness that is to be attached to an event. At a party people are aware that the purpose of the event is enjoyment and that as Simmel says: 'One does as if all were equal, as if one honoured each of them in particular.'[17] Not only is the 'as if' of equality a temporary fabrication—an illusion; so also are the 'as if' of the importance of the occasion, the necessity to 'keep things going' until the end, to prevent awkward silences, open hostility or sheer boredom which may cause people to leave. The 'self-contained play forms' of sociability are deliberately maintained by those who take part on such an occasion. Even in ordinary life a level of reality is selected though it may not be possible to maintain it if people fail to conform to the constricting rules on which its maintenance depends. These levels of reality approximate to three perceived levels of reality, accepted in the theatre, the 'pretend' reality of games, sports, parties, ceremonies, the 'alternative' reality of occupational worlds and ritual, or the 'overriding' reality concerned with the deliberate efforts to change or defend definitions of the situation, the 'rules of the game'.

These three levels of reality in the social world do not of course differ in any absolute sense. Each is constructed on the basis of certain agreed rules about the possible outcomes of action. The idea of 'overriding reality' itself may be regarded as a fiction by the sceptic but for the committed it denotes a dimension in which irreversible action can take place, action moreover which affects the whole person and his future behaviour. Although only the biological facts of birth, copulation, and death are regarded by most people as belonging to this concept of the 'real', the concept is commonly extended to contain a much larger range of events selected by the individual as constituting his biological and social career. In fact the 'real' self and the 'real' activities of the self are usually defined by a vague dialectical opposition to the unrealness of 'make-believe' or 'alternative reality'. A person subtracts from his life those activities in the realm of politics, career, domestic or social life, which he regards as play. Perhaps there seems to the observer to be nothing left, but to the individual sanity may depend on the belief in this residual reality against which all his false selves and false actions

[17] *The Sociology of G. Simmel*, ed. K. H. Wolff (Collier-Macmillan, 1950), p. 49.

can be tested. So the world of 'unreal' action lends support to a personal rationale according to which he organises his 'real' life.

The support—validation, almost—for this personal preserve of reality lies in the institutionalisation of play (make-believe) or innocuous (alternative) action in the society to which he belongs. Or, rather, it is a mirror image of the institutionalisation of the three levels in society.

The elaborate game of love and gallantry, the game of wooing the 'Faerie Queene' played at the court of Queen Elizabeth and at the country residences of her courtiers was played on a level of 'pretend' or 'as if' reality. But there too the reality of the Queen's power and her use of it in bestowing and withholding favour meant that the game was played against a background of overriding reality as and when it was so defined by the people concerned. The Queen and Essex both recognised the play element in their relationship but the Queen's anger was not simulated and Essex's fate was to lose his head in earnest. Staying in favour or staying alive in this period depended to a large extent on the ability to recognise the signs that play was about to be abandoned in favour of action that was instrumental as well as symbolic. And for the other players in the games which involved political power the execution of Essex had its symbolism too.

Social life at the end of the nineteenth century in upper-class circles in England, the life of the London season and country house party, was maintained by hosts and hostesses who deliberately contrived settings and situations to provide leisure time activities which appeared to take place on a level of alternative reality but which, because of the inevitable overlapping of the public and private domains when men in public positions meet, could relapse dangerously into the realm of overriding reality. Social encounters were used if not to discuss matters of politics or business or sexual intrigue at least to evaluate people in these spheres. So much is clear from the novels of Trollope and Henry James. Those involved often placed more value on their leisure activities than on those in their occupational world, but their actions were more heavily constrained by the latter. Today the occupational world has become, for many people, more important as a place for both work and leisure activities and often provides the 'alternative' to the domestic or outside world.

Informal relationships between friends which are intended to manifest spontaneity and to avoid ceremony are supposed to steer clear of the levels of pretend and alternative reality and to adhere to the level of overriding reality. Everything that happens in informal encounters is supposed to be related to the other (absent) aspects of the participants' characters and behaviour. Such an ideal relationship is, of course, seldom achieved or maintained. But sensitivity to changes from one level of reality to another is commonly developed.

Perception of reality is of course more complicated and more difficult to identify than these illustrations may suggest. Schutz, in discussing the 'natural attitude' of the ordinary man to everyday life described the way in which an agreed level of reality is maintained. Following Husserl[18] he used the term *epoché* to denote 'bracketing' the ad hoc frame put around a particular kind of situation and action and hence the suspension of belief in the reality of the world and events external to the occasion so framed. For the man within the 'natural attitude' the *epoché* of the 'natural attitude' is the exclusion of any doubt that the world and its objects might be otherwise than they appear to him.[19]

The same device can be applied to the audience's interpretation of the significance of the dramatic world within the theatre although in this case the *epoché*—the frame of action—is declared and temporary. The world of the play becomes an alternative and frangible reality; hence there is a temptation to make play, as Pirandello did, with the shifting boundaries between the theatrical and the ordinary world. He is able to express doubt in reality without breaking the illusion of reality because he works always within a world that is bracketed as unreal. The mirror world can mirror endless images but is never broken. In this he is different from those contemporary dramatists or producers who try to break the circle of illusion and merge the real and theatrical worlds. They do not, however, escape the dilemma of definition. By drawing the audience into the action they substitute 'theatricality' for theatre.

The traditional theatre offers a play world (however serious) in which the spectators' anxieties about results and outcomes can be relaxed and in which both consequentiality of action and the intrusion of accident, are clearly spelt out. In happenings or improvised theatre the brackets which contain the unreal world are spaced more widely apart so that doubt enters in concerning the outcome, for players and audience alike, of the action in the ordinarily enclosed world of the theatre, of what goes on, and of what they will do, outside it. The converse of this process in ordinary life is the perception of and sometimes the insistence on theatricality as acceptable in ceremonial and ritual of both a religious and secular nature, because it is believed by enough people to serve some purpose, even if it is not its original purpose. (Some who search for a reason for the splendid and expensive coronation ceremonies suggest

---

[18] E. Husserl, *Ideas*, trans. Boyce Gibson (Allen & Unwin, 1931).
[19] See A. Schutz, 'Dimensions of the social world', in *Collected Papers* ii (The Hague, Nijhoff, 1964).

that it means 'an act of solidarity',[20] an emotional outlet or merely pleasure—anything but its original purpose, a declaration of the power and authority of the crown.)

The more easily overlooked ceremonies and rituals of ordinary life (demonstrations, exchanges of gifts, the ritual transformations of identity for entry into hospital, prison, the armed forces, or even a new job, and rituals of the political process, of sexual behaviour, and so forth) can suddenly betray themselves as patterns of behaviour that seem to have escaped from their brackets, scenes of unreality in the midst of reality, which call for a new hard look at what is commonly regarded as ordinary (untheatrical) behaviour. The line drawn between the two kinds of behaviour, theatrical and untheatrical, depends on the selectivity of moral vision which is conditioned by the process of socialisation in a particular social milieu, at a particular time. It is not simply a matter of degrees of demonstrativeness. The controlled behaviour of a group of upper-class English people at a formal function can appear to observers just as theatrical as the demonstrative behaviour of an Italian family greeting each other with kissing and hand-shaking.

The terminology of the stage is freely used in common discourse and has become an essential part of the professional language of journalists. It is also common in biographical writing where the writer is observer rather than creator of characters, for example: 'The young student [Trotsky] ... who had at any cost to play a role found his place in the army of Marxism—in the drama of progress, on the stage of earth, conceived in a certain way.'[21] This kind of language can become a substitute for analysis although it can also be used critically.

Few people like to believe that they are acting all the time. This seems to be perceived as a charge of insincerity and even a denial of identity. Heuristically, sociologists are prepared to assume that the self is unknowable and that all that can be observed can be described in a meaningful way by using what they call role theory, an elaboration of the terminology of the stage.[22] Kenneth Burke, who is concerned primarily not with social action but with the basic forms of thought which underlie it and which, 'in accordance with the nature of the world as all men necessarily experience it, are exemplified in the attributing of motives'[23] also uses 'dramatism'

[20] E. Shils and M. Young, 'The Coronation', *Sociological Review*, i, no. 2 (1953), 63.
[21] Edmund Wilson, *To the Finland Station* (Doubleday Anchor, 1953), p. 428.
[22] Cf., for example, R. Dahrendorf 'Homo Sociologicus', in *Essays in the Theory of Society* (Stanford University Press, 1968): 'Sociology necessarily takes social roles as its elements of analysis; its subject matter is the structure of social roles. But by reconstructing man as *homo sociologicus* in this manner Sociology creates for itself once again the moral and philosophical problem of how the artificial man of its theoretical analysis relates to the real man of our everyday experience'.
[23] K. Burke, *A Grammar of Motives* (University of California Press, 1945), p. xv.

(employing the key categories act, scene, agent, agency, purpose) as a method of analysis. Most sociologists have concentrated on the agent or actor and used the other categories of act, scene, agency, persona, motive and purpose as they are related to him. The emphasis put on the concept of 'role' comes from the fact that it provides the essential link between the social reality of the patterned world of institutions and the changes they undergo on the one hand, and the human reality of the individual consciousness and individual behaviour on the other.

3

From ritual to drama

In the theatre itself both spectators and performers are involved in the recognition and display of consequential behaviour. At the beginning of the published book of his play *Les Nègres*, Genet has written a note concerning production:

> This play written, I repeat, by a white man is intended for a white audience, but if, which is unlikely, it is ever performed before a black audience then a white person male or female should be invited every evening. The organiser of the show should welcome him formally, dress him in ceremonial costume and lead him to his seat, preferably in the front row of the stalls. The actors will play for him. A spotlight should be focused upon this symbolic white throughout the performance. But what if no white person accepted? Then let white masks be distributed to the black spectators as they enter the theatre. And if the blacks refuse, then let a dummy be used.[1]

This is an extreme example of what is expected of the spectator. In Genet's play the significance of the actions of the black actors only becomes clear if the context of a white society, in which they act, is stressed. Genet, however, is only safeguarding his play in case of certain contingencies. Every dramatist assumes the presence of a certain kind of audience made up of people who recognise not only common values and norms of behaviour but also similar expectations of sequences and consequences of action and common interpretations of character. The dramatist assumes that however critical they may be of these norms, values and outcomes they recognise them as 'making sense'.

Difficulty arises when a play is performed at a later period, when norms, values, even the meanings of words and other signs have changed. Thus the connotations of Othello's race and colour at the

[1] J. Genet, *The Blacks*, trans. B. Frechtman, Faber and Faber, 1960.

time when the play was first performed could not be the same in the nineteenth century theatre or again on the contemporary stage. In the same play the meanings of political power, authority, duty, honour and jealousy have also been modified throughout its history. Such difficulties of interpretation stress the part played by the audience in the realisation of the play. Genet's desire to focus a spotlight on the spectator only makes explicit what has always been implicit in the theatre.

Unlike all other forms of literary art a play is remade every time it is performed. The remaking occurs through the performance in which dramatist, producer, actors and audience all participate. This situation has for so long been taken for granted that the importance and nature of the conventions on which theatrical performance rests is easily overlooked, all the more easily because these conventions are for the most part implicit. The spectators are not as a rule told how to behave or what to expect when they go to the theatre. Conventions are learned in and through the performance. Yet drama has emerged in both Eastern and Western countries from religious ritual and the performance of religious ritual depends, by contrast, on rules or prescriptions that regulate the movements, actions, gestures and speech of those involved. The efficacy of ritual depends on its rightness. If certain rites are omitted or wrongly performed the ritual is usually regarded as ineffective and is often performed again.

The conventions governing theatrical performance are something new, but this newness can only be appreciated if one considers the transitional stage when dramatic forms were beginning to develop in the Church within the liturgy. In England, in the Christian liturgy, priests, cantors and congregation took part as one cohesive whole. Although their roles differed in importance, although their understanding of what was supposed to be happening could be slight or profound, no one can have been entirely ignorant of the purpose and symbolism of the rites. Moreover the priest had no more direct access to God than any one of the communicants. In considering religious ritual it is important to remember that it is not only symbolic. In defining ritual E. R. Leach writes 'every human action has a technical aspect which does something and an aesthetic communicative aspect which says something'.[2]

Dramatic action is an intrinsic part of magical rites. When Malinowski describes the behaviour of a Melanesian sorcerer pointing the magic dart to bring about the death of his victim, he is careful to explain that the essence of the act lay in the miming of fury, hatred and the passion of violence.[3] In Christianity, too, the instrumental

---

[2] E. R. Leach, 'Ritual' in *The International Encyclopaedia of Social Sciences* (Macmillan and Co. and The Free Press, 1968).
[3] B. Malinowski, *Magic Science and Religion* (Free Press, 1948), pp. 70–84.

nature of the Mass has always been stressed: 'When the Mass is celebrated something happens, something is actually done, a real transaction is completed between earth and heaven.'[4]

Yet the same cannot be said of the dramatic tropes, which were
introduced into the service during the ninth century. These tropes
had originated a century earlier as musical embellishments of the
liturgy, sung antiphonally by cantors and congregation. The distribution of parts to identifiable characters, the representation of
action by movement and gestures and the identification of different
parts of the church with places where the biblical episode was set are
now recognisable as specifications for dramatic performance.[5] The
most highly developed of these tropes, the Easter 'Quem quaeritis in
sepulchro', usually took place in the chancel where a sepulchre was
installed on the north side. The choir represented the assembly place
of the disciples from which the Maries and Peter and John set out on
their journey to the empty tomb. Thus for the duration of the performance the congregation's attention was given to observation of
expressive action rather than to worship or prayer, which are forms
of communication with God. The tropes were not essential in order
to make 'something happen' between the congregation and God.
They made something new happen between the performers and the
spectators.

In this way began the long slow process of structural division
between actors and audience which seems to be essential before
drama can develop as a separate art.[6] The *introit* play, performed in
Latin within the church by clergy or monks, continued to develop
between AD 950 and 1250. The purpose of the plays remained de-
votional and instructional but, because they were expressive representations rather than acts of devotion, the secular element was
inescapable. Their full dramatic development was only hampered by
the use of a language not fully understood by all the spectators, and
by the constraints of the church.

By the time the religious plays had moved out of the church in the
early fourteenth century to become parts of or episodes in the
Corpus Christi procession the division between performers and spec-

[4] A. B. Macdonald, *Christian Worship in the Primitive Church* (Clark, 1934), p. 9.
[5] See Hardin Craig, *English Religious Drama* (Oxford University Press, 1955), pp.
31ff.
[6] The same process seems to have occurred in Ancient Greece: 'We know from
tradition that in Athens ritual became art, a *dromenon* became the drama, and we
have seen the shift symbolised and expressed by the addition of the theatre or
spectator-place to the orchestra or dancing place': J. Harrison, *Ancient Art and
Ritual* (Oxford University Press, 1913), p. 136. The attempt to revive audience participation in the modern theatre occurred only *after* the development
of the Western theatre, at a time when traditional forms seemed to be resisting
the innovations which could only come through the interaction of actors and
spectators.

tators was becoming clearer. Although the actors, as members of a Guild, were not professional, their responsibility to the Church and their prestige as members of the Guild demanded a considerable degree of professional competence in carrying out the skills required for the performance. More important for the development of the drama, the spectators now recognised the actors as independent of any office within the Church. The performance, in spite of its religious content, provided a completely different kind of experience from that provided by the church services of which it had once formed an integral part.

There were of course other influences that contributed to the making of the drama. Secular pageantry was an important part of medieval life. On all public occasions, at court and civic ceremonies, royal entries, Lord Mayors' shows, tournaments and common ridings the emblematic tradition, a blend of religious and heraldic symbolism, provided form and content, aesthetic satisfaction as well as significant action.[7] But on these occasions too there seems to have been no rigid distinction between performers and spectators. The important figures who held the stage—kings or queens, nobles or civic dignitaries—had formal ties with the people and were often their spokesmen. It is important to remember, however, that this tradition of semi-dramatic performances continued to flourish well into the seventeenth century, preparing and sustaining spectators for the fully realised drama.

The historical transition from religious ritual to drama is something more, or something other, than a simple process of institutional evolution. The causal factors are problematic, but certainly include the features, common to institutional development in relatively stable societies, of accumulation and differentiation which lead to complexity and the division of social and economic tasks. But one must also see the development as one which, like similar historical trends towards institutional dominance, incorporates aspects of living which are part and parcel of everyday human behaviour and interaction into components of the growing institutional form. Just as entrepreneurship and industrial organisation has grown by incorporating more and more skills, information and activities within itself during the past century, and has also extended to cover more and more activities, from scientific research to pastimes, sports and entertainment, so the emergence of drama can be seen as a process of incorporating pre-existing aspects of everyday life, of extension, and innovation. Acting antedates drama. Ordinary

---

[7] For an extensive study of the emblematic tradition in public pageantry see Glynne Wickham, *Early English Stages* (Routledge 2 vols 1959, 1963), ii, pt. 1.

conversation often incorporates the representation of other people's words, attitudes and gestures. There are anecdotes and stories, reported speech, interpretations of 'what really happened'. This capacity, inherent in spontaneous interaction, is a prerequisite source from which fresh embodiments of convention can be contrived to develop the institutional form of drama. It is the same capacity, of course, which makes ritual itself possible. Children early discover the art of mime in play with others and, as adolescents, often show a high degree of skill in acting out amusing, impressive, or even frightening roles before their peers or before adults.[8]

When people take part in religious ritual (whatever their level of sophistication) as medieval May-day mummers, Andaman islanders or priests and cantors in the Catholic Church they step out of themselves to take on the part of persons distinct from their everyday selves. They may take that of a supernatural being, or discard their normal persona in order to achieve a relationship with the supernatural, as the priest does in the Mass in acting as mediator between the congregation and God.[9] A sacred office demands acting, the ability to present oneself to others or in a role that can be recognised as appropriate.

Acting requires the presence of others. When an actor practises before a mirror he creates a simulated situation in which his reflection represents himself as actor while he himself represents an audience, capable of criticising and assessing the performance. In religious ritual other people are continuously involved in the ceremony although their roles may vary in importance. Everyone has some part to perform even if it is only singing the responses, clapping in time to a dance or weeping at appropriate points in the ceremony. 'Responses', clapping and weeping are performed as part of the ceremony. They are not the reactions of outsiders.

But whereas acting is intrinsic to ritual as well as drama, the separation of audience from actors which accompanied the development of drama gradually produced changes in the nature of acting. The actor was required not only to realise an imagined

---

[8] Children's street games also preserve many features of early dramatic and semi-dramatic forms. Beatrice White, in her introduction to F. Warren's edition of *The Dance of Death* (Lydgate's translation of the French verses) suggests a connection between the *Dance* which was performed at least once at the court of the Duke of Burgundy and the children's game played in Switzerland and Germany: 'Who's afraid of the Black Man?' Its counterpart in this country seems to be 'Dead man, dark scenery', played in the streets of East London within the last forty years. (*Dance of Death*, Oxford University Press, 1931).

[9] 'The Church as a body offers sacrifice through the priests . . . At the climax of the sacrifice it is Christ who is the real agent and the ordained priest is the sole co-operator'; L. Eisenhofer, *The Liturgy of the Roman Rite* (Freiburg Nelson and Herder, 1961), p. 2.

character but also to present this character to spectators who did not feel themselves compelled to believe in its existence outside the special occasion of performance, nor to feel involved in its creation. Spectators and performers were learning to assume different, though, at times, interchangeable roles.

Yet they still shared a common purpose, the realisation of the play. This realisation depended upon the development of a new set of conventions, conventions distinguishable from those exercised either in ordinary social life or in the church service. These were the conventions that had been slowly emerging, or being incorporated, from recognisable aspects of the social realities of everyday life in the dramatic episodes introduced into the liturgy.[10]

[10] For a detailed discussion of the staging of the Corpus Christi plays see Wickham, *Early English Stages*, i, 124.

4

Conventions of performance

The process of separation between actors and spectators was completed in England by the time the first full-time theatre, James Burbage's *Theater* near Finsbury Fields, was built in 1576. What marks the change, amongst other things, is the emergence of a set of conventions specific to occasions of theatrical performance. The literature on the nature of conventions, in philosophy, sociology and literary and dramatic criticism, is far too extensive to be reviewed here, dating as it does in England alone from the eighteenth century. But there are certain salient features which have been stressed in recent years and which are relevant to my present purposes.

In the first place a convention is simply a mutual understanding about the meaning of action, which includes gestures and speech. Such an agreement is clearly essential if people are to understand each other's actions, gestures and words. Mutual understanding may and often does extend to an entirely tacit agreement (e.g. to continue a present regular arrangement, a series of meetings or relationship). The use of overt signs itself constitutes a language, of which the verbal parts are officially codified in dictionaries and grammars. But there are also a great many sounds and signs that never find their way into dictionaries or any other kind of written code. The language and gestures one learns at home, at school and in groups to which one later belongs in the context of work or recreation, are derived from tacit agreements constantly renewed or adjusted about the constancy and modification of meanings.

Secondly, the terms of agreement which constitute conventions derive from norms accepted by those involved. But whereas norms are shaped by the values of a society, conventions impose constraints which range from the strongest moral force to a completely amoral pressure. Flouting conventions can therefore denote, at one end of the scale, 'deviance', at the other approved unconventionality or less approved eccentricity. Thirdly, these tacit or explicit mutual under-standings are not merely a convenient shorthand. Conventions re-move the load of 'knowledge of intent' from the individual (the infinite regression of 'I know that you know that I know etc.') by imputing this awareness to the social system of which conventions are a part. Through familiar conventions syntheses of meanings are easily established.

Finally there need be no realisation or understanding that an agree-ment has been entered into. It is enough that one should learn by experience or observation that one's expectations of the expecta-tions of others will result in a 'co-ordination equilibrium'[1] for a regu-larity of conduct to emerge. It is this regularity of repeated conduct that becomes convention.

The language of conventions does not of course remain static. As people find themselves in new situations, supplied with new infor-mation, new agreements are automatically made. The kind of be-haviour that does not take account of this kind of change is often called merely 'conventional', implying that it is empty of meaning. But in practice social life is inescapably conventional. Without con-ventions it would be impossible to interpret the words or actions of others. This accounts for the initial difficulties that people encounter in an alien culture. H. Morsbach[2] has described the difficulties that beset friendship between English and Japanese in Japan. The sense of obligation that underlies all relationships in Japan means that presents, services or even love from one person must be conscientiously repaid by the other by its exact equivalent. The value put on generosity in the West can be easily misunderstood as a desire to put someone else under too heavy an obligation. Even English and Americans, who speak the same language, have to learn to understand each other's conventions. In spite of their friendly openness most Americans are taken aback by the Englishman's assumption that if you have a friend in town you will expect to stay with him rather than in a hotel.

When people find themselves in special situations, related to other people in such a way that the language of ordinary behaviour is not applicable, a special language often develops. This happens most fre-quently in situations where groups of people with different interests but a purpose common to the occasion confront each other, when the more powerful ritualise their separateness from the less powerful at a royal or civic ceremony, when Government and Opposition confront each other in the House of Commons[3], even when opposing

---

[1] See D. K. Lewis *Convention* (Harvard University Press, 1969) for a detailed exami-nation of the working of convention (pp. 36–51).
[2] H. Morsbach, lecture given in University of Edinburgh, 1971.
[3] For an examination of the ritualisation of political processes, and of its significance in the 'realities' of politics, see Abner Cohen 'Political anthropology: the analysis of the symbolism of power relations', *Man* iv, no. 2 (1969).

armies are drawn up for battle. On all such occasions certain forms of address, certain words and gestures are used which are only meaningful in the specific context.

One of the most clearly defined forms of this type of encounter is that which takes place in the theatre between actors and spectators. The actors' pretence that they inhabit a different world from the spectators, the world of the play, creates a need for a new language of conventions which can expand, emphasise and orchestrate the conventional language of the play so that its meaning becomes clear to the spectators.

This conventional language can only exist if there is an underlying consensus between dramatist, actors and audience, about the way in which the occasion in which they are all involved is defined. In ordinary life situations are often defined in different, even contradictory, ways by those involved. A few years ago a daylight bank robbery took place in a busy London street. A passerby who witnessed it took no action because, as he said at the trial, he thought he was watching a scene that was being filmed.

Consensus is therefore a term which implies a common definition of the situation in the sense in which W. I. Thomas uses it.[4] For this personal effort of definition to carry weight and convey meaning to others the bond of consensus has to imply some kind of social pressure. Consensus depends not on mere acquiescence but on a conviction that certain words, acts or gestures ought to have certain meanings which enable them to be related to each other. Thus consensus and common definition of the situation are not in themselves necessarily spontaneous or voluntary.[5] Consensus is a requirement laid on people (a requirement which they may of course fail or refuse to meet) who are present together in a space definable as a social setting.

The behaviour patterns which are set in train once a definition of the situation is established are limited in number (although in a sophisticated society the number of definable situations and modes of behaviour within them may be very large) and are by convention meaningful in terms of feelings, attitudes, cognitive states, motives and intentions.

On all social occasions conventions are detectable in behaviour, but become explicit and even obtrusive on occasions regarded as to

---

[4] W. I. Thomas, *Primitive Behavior* (McGraw-Hill, 1937) (see below, p. 88).
[5] Norman Birnbaum, in *The Crisis of Industrial Society* (Oxford University Press, 1960), pp. 66–7, has called attention to the way in which political scientists have taken the common unthinking acceptance by ordinary people of the political, economic and social constraints of the society into which they are born as 'consensus' in the sense of positive consent or agreement. Similarly, for Englishmen there is no alternative to the use of some recognisable form of English language if they are to participate in any kind of interaction with their fellows, or to sustain themselves at all.

some extent theatrical, such as weddings, civic ceremonies, academic functions, formal conferences and receptions. On these occasions the expressiveness and persuasiveness of behaviour are stressed though the action performed or celebrated is at the same time instrumental. There is a fictive, prepared, style for an actual non-fictional content. Recognised conventions are used to express, often over-express, solemnity at a state funeral, but the fact remains that a person has died. No conventions are essential to make this real. In fact the intention of such a performance often seems to be to stress unreality, to divert attention from the fact that the chief actor is missing. The action takes place, implicitly, at two levels.

When, however, a play is staged the social occasion is explicitly doubled. There is first the social occasion proper, the 'going to the theatre', which requires an appropriate setting, the establishment of a clearly defined social distance between actors and playgoers, appropriate mutual expectations and a common definition of the situation.

Within this social occasion occurs the realisation of the play in which fictitious characters take part in fictitious situations in a fictitious world. On one level actors and spectators see each other for what they are, disguised or undisguised, related to each other according to the demands of the occasion. On another level the spectators see the characters in the play while the actors 'in character' behave as if the spectators were invisible. Audience participation, of course, violates this convention and sets up a third type of relationship—that between characters in the play and spectators who are themselves encouraged to act 'outside themselves'—to act fictionalised characters too.

Dramatic performance is thus concerned with two distinct but related modes of interaction—interaction between performers and spectators, and interaction between the characters in the play—each making use of different sorts of convention. Between actors and spectators there is an implicit agreement that the actors will be allowed to conjure up a fictitious world, that their actions and words will be meaningful and affective (not instrumental and effective) within arbitrarily defined bounds of place, time, situation and character. This agreement underwrites the devices of exposition that enable the audience to understand the play. These conventions of which the dramatist takes account in writing the play, the producer in directing it and the actors in performing it can be described as *rhetorical*. They are the means by which the audience is persuaded to accept characters and situations whose validity is ephemeral and bound to the theatre.[6]

[6] In so far as ordinary social conventions are rhetorical they are represented as such on the stage 'authentically'; however, their rhetoric is directed at other characters in the play, not directly at the audience, e.g. the rhetoric of Antony's speech in *Julius Caesar* or the Inquisitor's speech in Shaw's *Saint Joan*.

The second set of conventions are those which prevail for the interaction of the actors as characters in the play. They 'model' social conventions in use at a specific time and in a specific place or milieu. The modes of speech, demeanour and action that are explicit in the play have to carry conviction and imply a connection with the world of human action of which the theatre is only a part. These conventions suggest a total and external code of values and norms of conduct from which the speech and action of the play are drawn. Their function is, therefore, to *authenticate* the play.[7]

Rhetorical and authenticating conventions in the theatre bear an obviously complementary relationship to each other. The actor has to try to convince the audience rhetorically that this is the way in which he, given such a situation, at such a time, could behave and at the same time to transmit to the audience the conviction that such behaviour is taking place in a coherent, credible world and is socially authentic.[8] The two processes are, in practice, inseparable.

Rhetorical conventions rely on what Aristotle, in *The Rhetoric*, called 'the very body and substance of persuasion', the use of the *enthymeme* to play on the spectators' share in a 'stockpile of attitudes, of expectations, of scruples and conventions, of truisms and commonplaces'.[9] But in drama, as distinct from oratory, authenticating conventions are also necessary to specify the particular set of attitudes, expectations and assumptions to which the rhetoric of the performers is addressed. This adds a further dimension, as it does to all performing arts, in that new authenticating devices must be continually invented to substantiate the essentially rhetorical effort.

There is, of course, an arbitrariness about distinguishing two *sets* of conventions. It is in practice extremely difficult to draw a line between the two, as between, say, the music and the libretto of an opera or even between content and form in literature or the message and the medium. What is more important is to perceive that both together, whether we regard rhetorical and authenticating conventions as two different kinds of rules or as two dimensions or aspects of convention, constitute a grammar of theatrical presen-

---

[7] Inauthenticity becomes apparent in unsuccessful attempts to update productions of older plays. In the National Theatre's production of *The Dance of Death* (1968) Kurt's and Alice's passionate love-making with blouse-tearing in the drawing-room conflicted grotesquely with the rest of their correct nineteenth-century behaviour. As a result it was difficult to accept as a convention of the time Alice's command that Kurt 'kiss her foot'. Passion was implicit in the whole of the play but was surely not intended to destroy the audience's belief in the characters' strong sense of public propriety.

[8] It is to emphasise this co-operation of actors and spectators in the making of a play that Brecht says, 'It is not the play but the performance that is the real purpose of all one's efforts': *The Messingkauf Dialogues* (Methuen, 1965).

[9] E. Black, *Rhetorical Criticism* (Macmillan, 1965), p. 125.

tation,[10] a grammar implicit in the practical composition of drama.

For drama is not a mirror of action. It is a composition. In composing words, gestures, and deeds to form a play, dramatist and performers operate within the constraints (or generate drama according to the grammar) of both kinds of convention. Together the constraints amount to a code of rules for the transmission of specific beliefs, attitudes and feelings in terms of organised social behaviour.

'Theatricality' in ordinary life consists in the resort to this special grammar of composed behaviour; it is when we suspect that behaviour is being composed according to this grammar of rhetorical and authenticating conventions that we regard it as theatrical. We feel that we are in the presence of some action which has been devised to transmit beliefs, attitudes and feelings of a kind that the 'composer' wishes us to have.[11] Where the rhetoric itself is familiar or subject to non-theatrical constraints, empty of precise meaning or even illegitimate (in the sense of being directed to feelings as against the rationale required for the consequential action which is called for) authenticating conventions become dominant.

Joe McGinnis's raw description of the running of the Nixon campaign in 1968 is primarily concerned with the deliberate use and balance of the two kinds of conventions in the television coverage.

Harry Treleaven, who became the 'creative director of advertising' for Nixon had won his reputation working for George Bush on his congressional campaign in Houston in a district from which no Republican had ever been elected:

> The fact that Bush was behind, Treleaven felt, was good. 'We can turn this into an advantage', he wrote, 'by creating a "Fighting underdog" image. Bush must convince voters that he really wants to be elected and is working hard to earn their vote. People sympathise with a man who tries hard: they are also flattered that anyone would really exert himself to get their vote. Bush therefore must be shown as a man who is working his heart out to win.'

[10] The notion of implicit rules guiding the generation of utterances, which stem from Chomsky's paradigmatic revolution in linguistics, already receiving considerable attention in the social sciences and in philosophy, seems likely to provide the clue to a sizeable number of hitherto unresolved puzzles. Among other things, it bridges the gap between art as a technique and art as communication of which aestheticians have made such heavy weather; see R. G. Collingwood, *Principles of Art* (Oxford University Press, 1938), chs xi-xiv.

[11] There is of course the special theatrical duplicity of openly confessing to 'putting on an act' which may be used to disarm possible suspicion of 'theatricality', or to lay claim to the prestige of expertness as a performer, or to disavow to some the commitment to action which we desire others to accept at face value (cf. Tom Burns, 'Friends, enemies and the polite fiction', *American Sociological Review*, 1953, p. 18).

And he was. Over and over again, on every television screen in Houston George Bush was seen with his coat slung over his shoulders; his sleeves rolled up; walking the streets of his district; grinning, gripping, sweating, letting the voter know he cared. About what was never made clear.[12]

The connection between behaviour in the socially real world and dramatic performance is a double link. Much of everyday social behaviour and socially consequential action is itself composed, and often in a fashion which is recognised at the time as 'theatrical' or is revealed as such afterwards. When we construct special buildings or settings for ritual occasions of many kinds, from judicial proceedings to love-making, when we set scenes and dress up or dress down for a social occasion there is a resemblance, which may not be admitted even to ourselves, to the enactment of composed theatrical performances by professional actors. Tacitly or explicitly we constantly draw on symbolic references and typifications shared by playwright, actors and audience. This is the basis of the adoption of dramaturgic terminology by social scientists and of its elaboration in the 'mere analogy' of the analysis of social behaviour as more or less skilled performance, by Erving Goffman, and as 'symbolic interaction' by Blumer, Becker and others.

The second connection runs, so to speak, the other way. Drama is a presentation of *interpretations* of everyday social behaviour and of consequential action which are, or are offered for, good currency. Moreover, because, as the audience, people can be shown more of the course, causes and consequences of action than they can ever know in the socially real world, the theatre provides usable paradigms for conduct. The excellence of the playwright as composer of theatrical action lies in this. The emergence of modern drama from religious ritual by way of Miracle plays and Moralities is not simply a fact of inconsequential chronology. First, in the Miracles there was the presentation in straightforward terms of the superhuman mechanics which formed human destinies, next in Moralities and Interludes the presentation of 'ideal types' of conduct, good, evil, wayward, mundane or spiritual, in confrontation, and eventually representation of stereotype figures working out recognisable or plausible strategies of action in order to engage themselves in or disengage themselves from recognisable or plausible social relationships or situations; all these constitute an evolutionary or epigenetic pattern familiar enough in the interpretation of contemporaneous historical changes.

All social structures maintain themselves by means of an apparatus of institutional forms[13] which provide individual members of

---

[12] J. McGinnis, *The Selling of the President* (Penguin, 1970), pp. 39–41.
[13] Arnold Gehlen's work is perhaps the main reference point for the study, now becoming a central concern of sociology, of the processes by which institutions are

the society with codes of behaviour and grammatical rules for reading the behaviour of others. Institutionalised behaviour is merely the formal patterning of conduct which relieves us of the otherwise overwhelming task of deciding our every conscious act as though it were entirely unprecedented and fraught with consequentiality (as indeed it might be – the injunction to live each day as if it were our last means no less). Every separable element of this institutional apparatus is tested, repaired, strengthened or weakened every time it is invoked and put to use; and it grows or diminishes as its usefulness becomes more or less apparent, more or less proved. Institutional forms which prove their utility in one area of life, tend, therefore, to extend, to become more prominent and well articulated, more sophisticated and characteristic of a particular social order.[14]

The emergence of modern theatre, construed in these rather functional terms, presumes an instrumental usefulness for the theatre: it 'performs a service'. This service is identifiable by its origins in religious ritual, however strained and tenuous the connection has ultimately become, as a public portrayal of approved and of reprobate behaviour and of the consequentiality of intended and unintended action—a consequentiality of which we have to be made freshly aware from time to time if the normative order of society is to be preserved.

To regard the same evolutionary pattern as part of the process of secularisation is to shift to a perspective which is significantly but not qualitatively different. Secularisation as a process by which publicly sacred institutions, formal religious practices and observances, and Church organisation gradually empty of authority, regular and sanctioned performances diminish, and acknowledged membership declines, has its counterpart in the sanctification of secular life. This double process of the secularisation of the sacred, and the sanctification of secular life in the historical period (the sixteenth century) with which we are centrally concerned at this point occurs clearly enough in the humanist movement and at the height of the Reformation. It has been documented and discussed fully enough. To suggest that the emergence of the theatre in its recognisably modern form is part of this process is paradoxical only in the context of the

---

created (see P. L. Berger and H. Kellner, 'Arnold Gehlen and the theory of institutions', *Social Research*, 1965 pp. 110ff.; see also H. Trevor-Roper for an account of the birth, growth and death of a particular institution, the bureaucratised court, in Renaissance Europe: 'The general crisis of the seventeenth century', in *Religion, the Reformation and Social Change* (Macmillan, 1967) pp. 46ff.).

[14] The epigenic pattern is visible in the institutionalisation of many disparate phenomena: of the Christian Church, of modern industrialism, of research and development, of drug taking, party system politics, nineteenth-century dandyism, and institutionalised fashion change in clothes.

concurrent war between puritanism (in Roman Catholic as well as the reformed churches) and the stage. The central preoccupations with human destiny, with the forces of good and evil, with legitimate authority and compliance with illegitimate power and subservience, and with the morality of ends and means are all there; so too is the implicit reference to a normative and eventually providential social order, an order which ritually appears in explicit form at the close of plays, as it did at the close of Church ceremonies and rituals.

The 'compositional' quality of the theatre is both what distinguishes it from everyday life and from consequential action in society *and* what renders it structurally relevant to society.

Just as the detection of composition in ordinary conduct deflates and devalues it, so the detection of elements which are not 'composed' in the theatrical action deflates and therefore devalues dramatic performance. Groucho Marx makes the point pungently and well:

> I have become a regular fan of the theatre and I think it's a great idea. I don't know if you've witnessed any of it, but you know how we go to a picture theatre and see pictures of the actors on the screen? Well, you won't believe it, Arthur, but here in New York they have real people up there on the stage. Why, you could almost talk to them! It's uncanny. I don't think it'll ever replace the movies, but it certainly strikes a new note in American Art.
>
> For example, I saw *I Am a Camera* last night, the John Van Druten play, and we sat in the first row. And Julie Harris (she plays I guess they call it 'the lead' in the theatre), you could see the scratches on her legs. At first we thought this had something to do with the plot and we waited for these scratches to come to life. But Arthur, it was never mentioned in the play and we finally came to the conclusion that either she had been shaving too close or she'd been kicked around in the dressing room by her boy friend. Now honestly, could anything like this happen in the movies? Think of it—here you see a girl's real scratches! It was great fun.[15]

Rather less fun is the secret composition of behaviour in social life when it is ordinarily assumed that behaviour among associates (*a*) is governed by publicly known rules and grammatical codes, (*b*) admits of tolerance (e.g. the 'bracketing out' of scratched legs as irrelevant to the action), and (*c*) involves mutual understanding of symbolic exchanges (spoken and others) and consensus about the definition of the situation. Edwin Lemert gives an expert account of the gener-

[15] Groucho Marx, letter to A. Sheepman, *The Groucho Letters* (Michael Joseph, 1967), p. 199.

ation of paranoia by an actual, half-conscious, conspiracy among colleagues:

> Staff members huddled around a water cooler to discuss an un-wanted associate ... and employed symbolic cues in his pre-sence such as humming the *Dragnet* theme song when he approached the group ... Much of the behaviour of the group at the time is strategic in nature, with determined rules as to 'what we will do if he does this or that'. In one of our cases a member of the board of trustees spoke of 'the game being played' with the person in controversy with them. Planned action may be carried to the length of agreeing upon the exact words to be used when confronted or challenged by the ... individual.[16]

People (such as the 'staff members') in such situations justify their behaviour by regarding it as part of a necessary role which they must sustain in their professional lives. They regard this role as some-thing which determines their actions, their very self, while at the same time a more real part of the self is disengaged from this role. So Sartre speaks of 'bad faith'—the refusal to be what one is, 'The basic concept which is thus engendered utilizes the double property of the human being who is at once a facticity and a *transcendence* ... bad faith does not wish either to coordinate them nor to surmount them in a synthesis. Bad faith seeks to affirm their identity while pre-serving their differences.'[17]

It is not the playing of a part that Sartre distinguishes as 'bad faith'—parts must be played—but it is in the consciousness of the individual that the choice can be made between the goal of sincerity and the goal of 'bad faith'. There is a sociological dispute that has not taken account of this distinction. In criticizing the 'drama-turgical approach' of other sociologists Messinger, Sampson and Towne claim that there is a non-acting level of behaviour.

Messinger quotes a statement of Sammy Davis Jr, who, as an actor, is acutely conscious of subtle shifts in part-playing: 'As soon as I go out of the front door of my house in the morning, I'm on Daddy, I'm on'; and Bernard Wolfe: 'Negroes in our culture spend most of their lives "on" ... every Negro is to some extent a performer.' To illus-trate this they go on to make the point that mental patients feel impelled to be 'on' for the benefit of the physicians and nurses watch-ing their behaviour for any departure from 'the normal':

> 'I have to pretend every day I am here. That I'm gay and happy in order to stay out of the isolation ward. So I laugh and pretend to be gay'; and
>
> Mr Yale told the interviewer that a nurse had told him his wife

---

[16] E. Lemert, 'Paranoia and the dynamics of exclusion', *Sociometry*, xxv (1962), 12.
[17] J. P. Sartre, *Being and Nothingness*, trans. M. E. Barnes (Methuen, 1951), p. 56.

was much improved. As a mark of 'improvement' the nurse
cited the fact that Mrs Yale was playing Scrabble a great deal.
The next day, after some hesitation about confidentiality, Mrs
Yale confided to the interviewer that she and her friends had
recently taken to playing Scrabble as a means of impressing the
staff with their ability to think clearly and be sociable.[18]

But having made this point, the authors are equally clear about the
co-existence, even with these same speakers, of another level of
social reality which is *not* composed, e.g.

Sammy Davis: But when I'm with the group [of intimate
friends] I can relax. We trust each other.

Bernard Wolfe: At other times 'relaxing among themselves'
negroes will mock the 'type' personalities they are obliged to
assume when they are 'on'.

During the balance of the interview Mrs Yale expressed a great
deal of concern over whether she was 'really' better or had
merely misled personnel.[19]

The issue here, it seems to me, is the question not so much of some
ontological difference between 'theatre' and 'real life', being 'on' or
being 'relaxed', but the degree to which *composition* is conscious or
unconscious, important or unimportant, recognisably present or invisible—and, most important of all, socially defined as 'normal' or
'deviant'.[20] This is revealed by the instance which Messinger,
Sampson and Towne use to clinch their case for defending 'ordinary
social life' as real for ordinary people even though it may be regarded as theatre by sociologists;

A dramaturgic analysis of a theatrical performance would presumably ... [consider] how stage actors manage to keep the
audience continually convinced that the play they are wit-
nessing is *a play*. Such an analysis might point out for example
that, by altering segments of time within which events can
'really' be accomplished, actors provide the audience with a
sense of 'play' as distinguished from 'reality'. It might document
the gestures actors employ on stage which *interrupt* the audience member's sense of emerging character, which remind the
audience that 'character' and actor are not the same. It might be
that returning for bows after the curtain has fallen not only
services actors' egos but also functions to remind the audience

---

[18] S. Messinger *et al.*, 'Life as Theater', *Sociometry* 1962, pp. 103, 101, 99.
[19] Messinger *et al.*, pp. 99, 101.
[20] *Ibid.* The question is not so easily resolved, as the writers on whom I have drawn
seem to think, by treating as a kind of existential absolute the difference between
the dramaturgic analyst's view of behaviour and the way his subjects view the
world. Even sociologists are people, and 'dramaturgic analysts' share the same
language, logical rules, norms of feeling, emotions and beliefs as their subjects.

that there *is* someone behind the 'appearance' they have been attending, for example, that the 'appearance' of the dead man was 'merely an appearance'. Such an analysis might inquire as to which members of the audience, children under certain ages, for example, cannot retain the sense of the play as a play.[21]

An actor is just as much 'on' when he is *in propria persona* taking a bow at the end of a performance as when he is playing a part; the degree and manner of composition are different, of course, as is the role. Similarly Mrs Yale when she played Scrabble for the sake of the impression of herself it might usefully implant in any of the medical staff who happened to notice her was composing her behaviour in a more self-conscious and explicit way than when she spoke to the interviewer. But it would be an extremely naïve interviewer who would for long remain unaware of any attempt, in that situation, to create the impression of the normality shared by the patient with the researcher in relation to the abnormal world inhabited by psychiatrists, just as it would be a simple-minded playgoer who took the bows, smiles and fluttering hands of actors as the expression of spontaneous acknowledgement of totally unexpected applause.

The differences between theatre and social life are of three kinds. First, there is the matter of the special double occasion (see above, p. 31). The performance is bounded in time and in consequences so that what happens on the stage may affect the audience at the time but cannot otherwise have any effective connection with their lives. Secondly, there is the acceptance in the theatre and the rejection outside of composed behaviour as normal. Thirdly, the performance in the theatre displays paradigmatic values which cannot be distinguished in the midst of action in ordinary life, where too much or too little is known about motives, intentions or consequences.

These differences keep the fictive world distinct from the socially real world and enable us to accept the deceptions of play-acting without the encumbrance of moral judgment. We are left free to connect, reject or transform for our own use in our own socially real world the motives and purposes for action presented on the stage and to recognise the rationales of strategies and actions in particular situations and the pattern of consequences which either inevitably or probably derive from them.[22]

[21] *Ibid*, p. 106.
[22] In tragedy inevitability is often stressed, in comedy chance or accident (see below, p. 220).

5

Rhetorical conventions: defining the situation

In both the fictive world of the theatre and the real, socially consequential world, we know action for what it is because it consists of behaviour and deeds into which meaning is read. Social action therefore encodes information, which has then to be interpreted. The rules by which this is done are conventions. Rhetorical conventions in the theatre govern the interaction between actors and audience. They are concerned with defining the situation—with establishing what, among all that is presently visible and audible, is relevant to the business in hand. They define the values and moral codes which apply to the motives and intentions of acts and characters. As in the real world, the Wittgensteinian language—'rules of the game'—appropriate to a situation, has to be established and maintained. In the theatre rhetorical conventions also relate to the establishment of the boundary between the fictive world presented through the stage actions and the world of social reality, from which both actors and audience come, to which they will return, and of which they possess knowledge in common.

Rhetorical conventions are not definitional in any masterful arbitrary sense; indeed the notion of convention is somewhat at odds with that of definition which seems to imply imposition or control. Even agreement is not a prerequisite. 'We can', writes Lewis 'do without agreement by choice if we find ourselves already satisfied with the content and strength of our mutual expectations.'[1] Conventions are, in short, common ways of arriving at coordination of social behaviour without going through the procedure of explicit or tacit agreement. 'Definition' enters in because the conventions applying to specific theatrical occasions are generally imposed and generated by playwrights, producers, actors (the presenters of theatrical action) and acceptance is expected of the audience.

[1] Lewis, *Convention*, p. 35.

Rhetoric, which, as one of the seven liberal arts, dominated art and education in the ancient and medieval worlds, is now commonly recognised as a term designating artificial, overelaborate, tendentious language. There are, however, literary critics—amongst them I. A. Richards, Wayne C. Booth and Edwin Black—who have tried to restore its original meaning to it without insisting on its formal terms. Richards redefines it as the 'study of verbal understanding and misunderstanding',[2] and Peter Dixon, in a recent study, extends this meaning to cover 'the whole complex business of communication through language, the intricate network of relationships which connects a speaker or writer with those he addresses'.[3]

In calling the conventions that obtain between performers and audience rhetorical I am reviving its original application to speech (the art of the orator) and extending the meaning further to cover both verbal and non-verbal forms of communication, including the demeanour, gestures and movements of the actors as well as staging, settings and timing—all those things that contribute to understanding of the whole dramatic situation. The term rhetoric stresses the persuasive intention of action in the theatre and can be equally well applied to communication between people in ordinary life.

This chapter is concerned with a fundamental conventional order of rhetoric: the ways in which understanding 'what is supposed to be going on here' is set out in the theatre and in social life.

Medieval drama took place in streets, in the market place, at court or in the hall of a lord's house, not in a theatre intended for such a performance. Thus at the very beginning one finds dramatists having to deal with the problem of defining the play as a play, of separating it from the current of ordinary living by what amounts to proclamation—a ceremonially composed pronouncement introducing this special sort of event and calling for silent, or at least sympathetic attention for its interruption of the flow of the audience's own lives. Fifteenth-century Interludes and Morality plays started with an introduction, often provided by an intermediary—a Presenter, later by a Prologue who defined the bounds of stage illusion and established the characters as fictions that the actors would interpret.[4] There was no attempt to deceive the spectators into believing the characters and actions to be real. They were 'mere figments'. Nevertheless, this very escape from the world of everyday reality could give such 'people'

[2] I. A. Richards, *Philosophy of Rhetoric* (Oxford University Press, 1936), p. 23.
[3] P. Dixon, *Rhetoric* (Methuen, 1971), p. 3.
[4] E. Welsford, in *The Court Masque* (Cambridge University Press, 1927) described the appearance of the Presenter in the fifteenth-century sword dance. He 'introduces each dancer with descriptive verses; or sometimes there may even be rough dialogue, and then the performance merges insensibly into that kind of folk-drama which survives in our St. George and mummers' plays' (p. 25).

and 'actions' a significance which underlined, by challenging, the reality and significance of the people and actions of ordinary life, and could also be used to project the insignificance and essential unreality of mundane existence. The Messenger's introduction to *Everyman* implies the precarious nature of worldly reality, and of life in this world:

> I pray you all give your audience
> And hear this matter with reverence,
> By figure a moral play,
> The *Summoning of Everyman* called it is
> That our lives and endings shews
> How transitory we be all day.[5]

Forms of offering by a Presenter were retained in the masque as late as the mid-seventeenth century. The blurring of distinction between actors and spectators in the court masque made the part of Presenter just as necessary as in the religious plays two centuries before.

In early secular plays an introduction was often made by pre-senting characters who were half in, half out of the play world—a sign that the validity of a secular performance was easily accepted. One of the first of these, Medwall's *Fulgens and Lucres*, moves be-tween the outer world of ordinary life to which the spectators be-longed and the enclosed world of the play in conscious exploitation of their relationship which bespeaks a sophisticated audience for this kind of occasion. The function of presenting was assigned to two anonymous characters, who, as retainers in a great hall, heralded the arrival of a troupe of players. They then addressed the spectators, specifying the role they were expected to play as a theatrical audi-ence:

> A for goddis will
> What mean ye syrs to stond so still?
> Have not ye etyn and your fill
> And payd no thinge therefore
> Here ye stond musynge
> Whereabout I cannot tell.[6]

Having imposed in the first place this circumstantial definition of the situation between themselves and the audience, they introduce the play proper, giving a detailed description of the setting and plot before it begins. Beyond this, they are soon involved in the selfsame plot, acting the parts of servants to the two main characters. They retain their ambivalence, stepping out of the play to comment on it from time to time, and implying some control over it:

[5] *Everyman* ed. A. C. Cawley (Dent, Everyman, 1956) C. 1–6.
[6] H. Medwall, *Fulgens and Lucres*, ed. Boas and Reed (Oxford University Press, 1926).

A. ... Pece let be
Be God thou wilt distroy all the play.

B. Distroy the play, quod a? nay, nay,
The play began never til now.

They also comment on the conclusion of the play in spite of their involvement in it.

As drama developed into an art independent of traditional story-telling it often dispensed with these presenting devices. Yet many dramatists used the Induction, occasionally, in order to direct the mood of the audience or to distance the play and supply satirical comment. In *The Knight of the Burning Pestle* Beaumont and Fletcher elaborated the *Fulgens and Lucres* convention to such an extent that a double play was created in which the outside charac-ter, the apprentice, could be introduced into the play proper, while his master and mistress constantly interrupted to comment on his performance or on the progress of the play. Finally they refuse to leave until Ralph has been allowed the honour of ending the play with a heroic death, parodying the speech of Andrea's Ghost in *The Spanish Tragedy*. The contrast between the grocer and his wife and the heroic style (of Kyd's tragedy and other popular sensational dramas) gave scope for fairly obvious satire, but at the same time exploited both the counter-reality and counter-artificiality of the world to which these 'citizens' belonged.[7]

Jonson's use of the Induction is different both in apparent inten-tion and effect although he also employs it only in comedy. The elaborate Induction to *Every Man out of his Humour* is used to discuss the merits and possible criticisms of the play and the evils of critics. Jonson himself appears as the playwright/producer with Cor-datus, the author's friend, and Mitis, a person of 'no character'. These characters intervene between the scenes to discuss the play and pro-vide a constant reminder that the play world is only sustained by illusion and a more subtle suggestion of the transitivity between the play world and the world from which the spectators came and to which they will return. The Inductions to *Bartholomew Fair*, *The Staple of News* and *The Magnetic Lady* are used in much the same way to satirise not only theatrical fashions, but manners and public taste. In the process Jonson reveals his and what is presumably the spectators' recognition of the two levels of theatrical interaction, the presentation of the play and the play itself. The same characters are allowed to move from the Induction into the play and to suggest a shifting perspective.

[7] Shakespeare also attached an elaborate Induction to *The Taming of the Shrew*, but only as a comic introduction to a comic play. He did not involve the characters of the Induction in the play, which can be acted without it.

Ben Jonson's appreciation of the possibilities of the Induction probably derived from his constant use of presenting techniques in the masque, in which they were essential; the masque often took place in the midst of non-theatrical recreation at a banquet or amongst dancing. It drew in as performers both players and courtiers. The art of presentation of masque and interlude had reached its most brilliant form in the courtly game played between Queen Elizabeth and her courtiers at court and on her country progresses to their estates.[8] The masque continued as a game and was presented as such at the courts of James I and Charles I. The fact that many of the courtiers joined in the masque meant that actors and spectators were presented together as in a dream in which all joined to conjure up a world of illusion.

Although the Induction, which afforded so much scope to the satirist, was retained by writers of comedy in the first half of the seventeenth century it was usually dispensed with in tragedy. Its place was sometimes taken as in *Romeo and Juliet* by an explanatory Prologue. The Prologue and Epilogue as set pieces increased in popularity during the eighteenth century but became extratheatrical means by which the dramatist could boost himself, forestall criticism or make a straightforward plea for a fair hearing. They became apologiae rather than acts of presentation, or sometimes polished pieces written by other writers for a particular actor or actress.

The Jonsonian mode of presentation was used again, though less elaborately, for Sheridan's *The Rivals*. In *The Critic* Sheridan, like his predecessor Buckingham in *The Rehearsal*, played with the idea of theatrical illusion and its relation to reality with an overtly satirical purpose. 'Presentation' had become so plainly a theatrical device that it was recognised as a means of directing the audience's interpretation of the play.

A further elaboration of presentation is found in the play-within-the-play, which appears very early in the history of English drama. In *Fulgens and Lucres* and *The Knight of the Burning Pestle* it was a straightforward form of presentation. But in the late sixteenth and early seventeenth centuries it came to be used in three ways: as an instrument directly affecting the action, as a means of bringing a special sort of pressure to bear on the characters, or of preparing or arousing the audience for certain kinds of events. An example of the first is found in *The Spanish Tragedy* where real murder is disguised as acted murder and the same device is used in *The Revenger's Tragedy* though in the form of a masque rather than a play. Shakespeare uses the second method in *Hamlet* as a device affecting the

[8] See M. C. Bradbrook, *The Rise of the Common Player* (Chatto & Windus, 1962) for a description of the elaborate masquing at the Summer Welcomes—'Drama as offering', p. 243ff.

characters and precipitating events. The 'Murder of Gonzago' is a means of exposing the King and at the same time of laying Hamlet's cards on the table. The third method is used by Marston in *Antonio and Mellida*, where he presents the dumb-show as a presage of future events intended to heighten the sense of horror and dread for the audience.

Although the play-within-the-play was discarded in the nineteenth and early twentieth centuries by most serious dramatists who regarded it as an artificial device that interfered with realism, it was never completely abandoned. When it was used it was often adapted to a special purpose. Shaw, in *Fanny's First Play* (1911) uses it as a satirical device to mount his attack on prejudice. In the Induction and Epilogue, he is able to satirise critics and playwrights, even himself, without losing the necessary sense of distance:

> VAUGHAN: Well at all events you can't deny that the characters in this play [Fanny's] are quite distinguishable from one another. That proves it's not by Shaw, because all Shaw's characters are himself: mere puppets stuck up to spout Shaw. It's only the actors that make them different.
> BANNAL: There can be no doubt of it: everybody knows it. But Shaw doesn't write his plays as plays. All he wants to do is to insult everybody all round and set us talking about him.
> TROTTER: And naturally here we are all talking about him . . .

Here the technique is developed so that the outer and inner plays have a quite explicit ambivalence.

So the rhetorical device of presentation, employed in the first place to mark the beginning of a theatrical occasion in an *ad hoc* fashion in places and at times when other kinds of public action could have continued uninterrupted was preserved for three centuries after the building of theatres. There is now, of course, a multiplicity of places and buildings designed and reserved as appropriate for differing sorts of activities. They themselves announce 'what is supposed to be going on here', but only in rather broad terms. It is up to the authors of the occasion—hosts, teachers, waiters, salesmen, actors, announcers, chairmen—to define the social situation in more specific terms; for if they do not, the pupils, guests, diners, customers and audience may conceivably define it in their own terms.[9]

Presentation, therefore, in the sense in which I have discussed it here, is not confined outside the theatre to formal ceremonies such as

[9] W. F. Whyte, *Human Relations in the Restaurant Industry* (McGraw-Hill, 1948): 'One of them [a waitress] gave these instructions to a new girl. "Get a clean cover on the table, give them the water, take the order and then leave if necessary. Once they have a feeling that you have taken charge they will be all right". Apparently it is up to the waitress to seize the initiative in customer relations—to set the pattern for the relationship. This she achieves by the things she does, the things she says, the way she uses her voice and the expression on her face' (pp. 110–11).

weddings, funerals and receptions. In the classroom, at a family
meal, in a large office or on the shopfloor people can become aware
that with or without any imposition by authority the situation has
been conventionally predefined. The rhetorical conventions in such a
situation relate to forms of address, to spacing and positioning of
persons, and to costume, manner, gestures, and timing of speech.

Although the dominant person, teacher, host or parent may
appear to act as presenter and therefore control definition, definition
is sustained when they are not present. Pupils, guests or children
behave when these people are absent for a short time as if they were
still there although they may eventually break down the conventions. But these are deliberate acts which show them to be aware
of and sensitive to the original definition. The persistence of conventional definition is seen in the tolerance of 'wild' behaviour by
students at an official 'rag' or on the occasion of a Scottish 'Rectorial'
Address when soot and flour may be thrown at the speaker, who is
usually a celebrity of some kind. This can be contrasted with the
intolerance of much quieter behaviour at an unofficial 'sit-in'. The
former have been defined by all parties in such a way that violent
behaviour is seemly whereas the latter are being newly defined by
the students and therefore replace the previously accepted conventions. There seems to be a growing tendency now for the 'sit-in'
situation to be accepted by many of those in authority so that in
time it may be rendered as conventionally innocuous as the Rectorial, thereby losing its instrumental force.

Thus the conventions through which situations are defined are not
resistant to change. They can be changed when one or some of those
involved causes a deliberate breakdown by refusing to respond as
expected to given cues, or when all those involved are conscious of a
loss of meaning in the situation. Grace before meals has been allowed
to disappear in all but the most religiously orthodox households (and
in Oxford and Cambridge colleges) so that the presentation of the
meal is left to the discretion of those involved. Similarly school
'prayers' have in some schools been abolished as a daily ritual, in
others secularised by replacing prayers with poetry readings and
hymns with secular music. In the latter case ritual is still observed
but is of a kind that is derived from 'high culture' as a makeshift
substitute for religion.

Just as in the orthodox theatre, presentation in the overt, manifest
sense can be dispensed with, so in buildings and settings designed for
other specific occasions, the formalities of presentation have often
dropped into disuse, and the ordered conduct of affairs is left to the
'good sense' (the conventional wisdom) of those present. To a considerable extent, this development has been stimulated by the increase, over the past century or so, of a regard for public order which

has been inculcated in the more or less universal process of socialisation and formal education, essential to the maintenance of the
complex institutional processes of advanced industrial societies.

Nevertheless, as I have tried to show, the rhetorical device of presentation has itself developed, and persists, in the theatre, building on
the accumulated audience awareness of the convention so as to
renew the deeper significance attaching to the ambiguous relationship between the play-world and the world outside the theatre, an
ambiguity resting on the representation in complete, comprehensible, bounded terms of the social realities from which the
members of the audience may be presumed to have emerged, and to
which they will return, and on the implicit or explicit reference to
other possible social realities. A similar cumulative evolutionary development is discernible in the innovations which have occurred in
presentational devices in classrooms, in meetings, teach-ins, orderly
demonstrations and picketing, and in the curious development of
'human relations' techniques within the authoritatively ordered
definition of industrial situations.

What are involved here are switching devices, by which we seek
to remedy the erosion of conventional acceptance of a particular
definition of the situation (e.g. in classroom or workshop) and the
emergence of disorder or of attempts (by students or workers) to
redefine the situation. A clue to this particular social device is provided by Pirandello's deliberate restructuring of the conventional
definition of the relationship between play-world and audience. In his
three plays which deal directly with the theatre, *Sei Personnagi in
cerca d'autore* (*Six characters in Search of an Author*), *Questa sera si
recita a soggetto* (*Tonight We Improvise*), and *Ciascuno a suo modo*
(*Each In His Own Way*) he examined the relationship between reality and illusion and questioned the right of the ordinary world to
be considered more real than the fabricated world of the play. At the
same time he emphasised the rhetorical conventions that maintain
the theatrical world. By including a 'pretend' audience in *Questa sera*
he presented the theatrical world as complete and autonomous. It is
a performance within a performance instead of just a play within a
play. This treatment of presentation has the effect of minimising the
part played by the real actors and audience. The social occasion
could be said to be trebled: the theatrical occasion encloses a fictional
situation (the play) which itself encloses a theatrical occasion, all of
equal weight. This manipulation of conventions whereby reality is
perceived as a series of Chinese boxes enables Pirandello to demonstrate that theatricality is not confined to the stage but is only an
emphasised exercise of the rhetorical conventions employed in
social life. Pirandello worked out these ideas so thoroughly in all
his plays that there was little incentive for subsequent playwrights

to take them further. He did, however, arouse interest in other possibilities of rhetorical conventions as alternatives to the over-authenticating conventions of the 'realist' theatre. If the dramatist wishes to qualify the reality of 'real life' he has scope to play with the many assumed levels of reality.

Brecht, who experimented with many forms of rhetorical convention in an attempt to make the audience cast a fresh eye on what the theatre can say if it is recognised as theatrical, revived the straightforward use of the Induction in *The Caucasian Chalk Circle*. But he integrated the play-within-the-play more deliberately than his predecessors by presenting a fictional moral problem which solves an analogous moral problem for the peasants in the Induction. They themselves represent an important sector of society. They, and therefore the audience, are made to see where rights and obligations lie, whether they are concerned with a plot of land or a child. This device is also a means of 'alienating' the play although Brecht does seem to demand some degree of identification with the class point of view of the peasants in the Induction, if not with the peasants themselves. Brecht made less use of the Induction in his other plays where he emphasised other rhetorical devices. This may have been because he realised that presentation strengthens rather than weakens the boundary between the play-world and social reality while it was his explicit aim to destroy illusion.

There have been few subsequent experiments with the 'presented' play or the play-within-the-play. The devaluation of 'occasion' in a formal sense and the preference for unceremonious behaviour in modern life are symptoms of a condition of mind antagonistic to formal presentation. Yet the assumption that everybody 'acts all the time' which implies that unceremonious behaviour is as carefully prepared as ceremony seems to be more easily accepted now (it is less censurable) and enables the dramatist to make use of different frames of action in order to express his theme. In *Le Balcon* and *Les Bonnes* Genet's characters conduct charades which cannot be clearly excised from the main themes of the play. The 'ceremony' which Claire and Solange act out in *Les Bonnes* cannot be distinguished as true or false in contrast with their ordinary scenes with Madame. In *Les Nègres* every character and each set of characters have double parts and are engaged in ceremonial within the play. In a more traditional presentation of the play-within-the-play Peter Weiss in *Marat/Sade* used the device to stress the persistence of historical ideas and the interfusion of different kinds of reality—past and present, sanity and insanity, acting and reality, rather than merely to double illusion. As the characters are the inhabitants of an asylum their 'acting' is a part of their personalities, and patients as actors and patients as patients are hardly differentiated.

Sometimes the device of setting some characters on the margins of the play is used more simply in order to emphasise the theatricality of the play. Thus Ann Jellicoe's *The Sport of my Mad Mother* opens with a drummer who watches the action as theatre, commenting on the oddities of acting convention, wondering why an actress lets herself be hit on stage. He is joined by an American who watches the action as action. Both are of course watched as actors by the spectators. This seems to be a study in the levels of spectating which also belong to ordinary life where realisation of the different view-points from which events are watched creates an appreciation of the artificiality of their interpretation.

In more recent avant-garde plays and improvisations there is no formal distinction between different levels of performance which blur and fade into each other. When the spectators themselves are expected to take part the outer edges of the theatrical world dissolve. Within its matrix many separate or related performances can continue at the same time. Total theatre demands that everything which occurs in the theatre is in the nature of a theatrical event. This kind of performance can only be successful if it is based on a very deep level of involvement, what Grotowski calls 'an act of collective introspection'. When this is achieved Grotowski claims to be able to produce gestures and intonations which conjure up specific images (e.g. an actor stops in the middle of a race and takes the stance of a cavalry soldier charging) which he regards in somewhat Jungian terms as rooted in the collective imagination.[10]

In this concept of the theatre the world of social reality is fused with or drowned in the theatrical presentation. Actors and spectators are both offered up, in some sacrificial way, to the theatrical experience. But the fusion could also be regarded as a contradiction of the aim of theatrical presentation which is to define *and by definition* to *relate* two kinds of experience, that of the familiar commonsense world and of the theatrical world, in such a way that they illuminate each other.

Whichever is the true explanation the fact that fusion of the two worlds is now seen as in any degree possible does indicate that presentation occurs, consciously or unconsciously, outside as well as inside the theatre. In fact the difficulty that many people find in audience participation arises because they expect inside the theatre to cast off their social roles, to remain passive and unpresented. Moreover, the role that they are offered is not as a rule a fully understood theatrical role which can replace their traditional audience role, or even their 'outside' selves. They are in fact asked to be props for the actors—neither themselves nor 'characters', involved wholly neither in a theatrical nor in a real life situation.

[10] See Eugenio Barba on Grotowski's Theatre Lab, *Tulane Drama Review*, 19, 1968.

Rhetorical conventions concern not only the mode of behaviour expected and *allowed for* on a social or theatrical occasion and the limitations of space and time regarded as appropriate or relevant. They are also concerned with the content of the occasion. In social life this relates to the disclosure or concealment of 'what is really happening' and sometimes of what has happened in the past. In any group special relationships between some of its members can be indicated by hints, private references, even tones of voice that ensure that other members of the group feel shut out not only from the relationship but from knowledge of a situation that has, perhaps, significance for the past, present and future.

On occasions when the attention is ostensibly focused on impersonal information and decisions at, say, committee meetings of a business, or of a political, academic or other nature, there are usually members who have more information about the facts and history of a particular problem than others who are either newcomers or have never been fully accepted by those 'in the know'. There are also those commitments to outside relationships and to interests other than those which are 'on the agenda'. Even if an attempt is made to 'put them in the picture' the 'picture' is bound to be incomplete and to lack elements that could only be observed in its making.

Each person's definition of the situation is therefore subject to private amendment according to the information at his disposal. He makes this available to others sometimes to impose his own definition (point of view), but also as a way of expressing the relationship to himself. In this way power hierarchies founded on the differential distribution of relevant information are created in even the smallest groups.

In social life exposition of private information of this kind is treated as rather a dark subject. Those who are anxious to reveal as much as possible about themselves, their motives, intentions and experiences, and those who are eager to find out as much as possible about others, are regarded with some suspicion. But both activities are to some extent practised by all people who have any contact with others. This kind of information is the currency of friendship and, when betrayed or distorted, the currency of enmity. As gossip it can entertain even those who have the very slightest acquaintance with those who are being gossiped about. As public revelation, it can substantially redefine the whole situation.

When information takes on a form of discourse, separable from the person, as confidence, confession, revelation or gossip, it comes very close to theatrical performance. Situations are altered and redefined as they are on the stage, and in both cases rhetorical conventions are at work. The difference lies in the use made of such rhetorical devices in the theatre, where, as I have said, action is 'composed'—i.e. preconceived—and is accepted as such. Composition of the same kind happens in ordinary life, but if seen as such it is regarded as suspect, or deviant, as designating 'theatrical' behaviour.

A dramatic situation displays 'the state of play' at a given moment in the drama. At such moments the relationships between the characters, their motives and goals are disclosed to the audience. The dramatist, through the actors, controls the output of information which the audience needs not only to understand the play but also to experience the emotional impact of the dramatic action.

The handling of dramatic action has changed since the days of the religious drama as much as the handling of acting space. It too has depended on consensus between performers and spectators, their agreement about what constitutes a dramatic situation and the ways in which it should be expressed. The understanding of dramatic situation depends upon a *regulated* supply of information to the audience. In pre-Shakespearian drama the most usual mode of supplying information was through the *set speech*. The set speech, in which both eloquence and style were cultivated, was part of the rhetorical tradition, a tradition which governed oratory and poetry. Its use in English drama seems to have been derived mainly from Seneca,[11] who used it as a substitute for direct action. These speeches could be used to report action that had already occurred or was occurring off-stage, to describe or deliberate on plans for future action and to disclose the innermost thoughts as well as the emotional condition of a character's mind: 'It is not the immediate event, not life lived in the present moment that are put before us, but what has gone before and what is still to come.'[12] This substitution of speech for action is found in *Gorboduc*, Hughes's *Misfortunes of Arthur*, and many other early semi-classical plays. Later in Kyd's *Spanish Tragedy* and in the plays of Greene and Peele vigorous action is introduced and the set speech is used as only one of the means of exposition. It was still retained by Marlowe and even by Shakespeare for occasional use, but was transformed by them from a mere expository device into speech which seems to come naturally to specific characters in specific situations.

The value of the set speech and of those conventional devices (soliloquy, aside, etc.) which are related to it, lies in the directness by which information can be conveyed. When the actor uses the *direct address* he steps out of his role to explain motives and intentions

---

[11] The conjecture that Seneca's plays were intended for reading rather than acting would explain the value of this device. It can seem clumsy in the *acted* Elizabethan plays which were so much influenced by his. See T. S. Eliot, 'Seneca in Elizabethan translation', in *Elizabethan Dramatists* (Faber, 1968).

[12] W. Clemen, *English Tragedy before Shakespeare* (Methuen, 1961), p. 24ff.

which are supposed to be concealed from the other characters. As an actor he discloses the nature of the character he is representing to the audience. It is difficult to portray hypocrisy on the stage without appearing to betray it to other characters. A real hypocrite would be unlikely to give himself away even to a confidant. Therefore the hypocrisy of Shakespeare's Richard III or Iago, or of Molière's Tartuffe is more convincingly expressed by allowing such a character to stand alone on the stage and reveal himself. At such points in the play both actor and spectator take a step towards each other; the actor by explaining his role 'alienates' it in Brecht's sense; the spectator by taking the part of the 'other' in relation to this one character becomes partially involved in the fabricated world of the play. A producer always has to choose between allowing a character to appear to speak directly to the audience whose presence he recognises, and letting him seem to think aloud. The latter effect is necessary in the case of the soliloquy but need not be aimed at in the expository speech that is a necessary explanation of the action.

In *Othello* Iago's speeches to the audience set him apart from the other characters. He is presented as the only person who knows what is happening, not only because he is manoeuvring much of the action himself but also because it has been necessary for him to discover all the weak points of the other characters: Othello's free and open nature, 'That thinks men honest that but seem to be so', Roderigo's infatuation and Cassio's malleability. His exposition of his motives is vague and changeable, but his statement of his intentions is explicit. He gives the audience all the information they need about the events of the play and the construction that will be put upon them. It is the task of such double characters, which also include Richard III and Edmund in *King Lear*, to act as informers, explaining the action and the other characters but hiding their own selves in a split role. Such a character is part presenter, part instigator of action.

The aside is only another abbreviated version of the direct address. Other actors are on stage within earshot and the actor speaks past them to the audience. The rather crude use of this device in pre-Shakespearian drama, and later in nineteenth-century melodrama, where the credulity of the audience was strained by long parentheses and digressions, has somewhat obscured its value as a skilful expository device. Shakespeare and Jonson used it to expose character and situation, and at the same time underline the falsity of apparently honest interaction between characters. The aside in *Volpone* is a third voice in all the conversations between Volpone, Mosca, and the hopeful inheritors:

VOLTORE: I'm sorry,
          To see you still thus weak.

MOSCA (*aside*): That he's not weaker.

CORBACCIO: I know thee honest.
MOSCA: You do lie sir (*aside*).

Shakespeare uses it constantly in tragedy, often to reveal the double part that is played by villainous characters. He also uses it in a more complex way in *Macbeth* where Macbeth reveals his immediate reactions to the witches' prophecies. These brief asides in the presence of Banquo lie somewhere between direct address and soliloquy. They expose at the same time Macbeth's state of mind and his plans for future action. His first aside, after the witches' greeting as 'Thane of Cawdor' has been proved right, expresses only amazement and bewilderment:

> Glamis, and thane of Cawdor:
> The greatest is behind . . .

The next aside expresses all the dreadful possibilities that are aroused in his mind:

> My thought whose murder yet is but fantastical,
> Shakes so my single state of man that function
> Is smothered in surmise, and nothing is
> But what is not.

The next two express a sense that his future actions are predetermined:

> If chance will have me king, why, chance may crown me,
> Without my stir.

and a resignation to fate:

> Come what come may,
> Time and the hour runs through the roughest day. I. iii.

Although the aside flourished as a comic device in Restoration and eighteenth-century comedy, its use in tragedy became awkward and absurd, and was parodied by Sheridan in *The Critic*. Later the picture stage of the nineteenth century was unsuitable for it, as it was impossible for the actor to step forward and take the audience into his confidence. Since then realist and naturalistic playwrights have avoided all such devices. But on the revived open stages many experimental playwrights have included it in a repertoire of rhetorical devices. Once more, in the 'placeless' theatre the actor stands in the midst of the audience and can address it directly as he did in the sixteenth century. Yet the flexibility with which conventions are used in experimental productions means that it is no longer necessary to create the illusion that certain people present on the stage cannot hear what is being said. The actor's public and private speech in such plays as Foster's *Tom Paine*, Van Itallie's *America Hurrah* and plays of Megan Terry and Rosalyn Drexler, is not usually addressed to any specific person in the play. Dialogue has to a large extent been replaced by public or private declarations which are sometimes related to other declarations, but which are as often isolated.

The soliloquy, a device through which the character can expose more than his immediate motives and intentions by exploring his own consciousness, can appear to be a true thinking aloud. Hamlet's soliloquies are of this nature, expressing as they do, not only his state of mind but also his moral view of the universe. He is not addressing the audience nor does the presence of the audience seem to be necessary for the effectiveness of such speeches. In fact the full implications of these soliloquies are better grasped in reading. It is for this reason that they present the actor with such difficulties. It is almost impossible for an actor to eliminate his consciousness of an audience.

The soliloquy gives depth to the dramatic situation by exposing the kind of considerations that are taken into account before a situation is defined by a character and before interaction can take place. A dimension is expressed which is lacking in the modern 'realistic' play where such considerations are either omitted or lose their force by being made explicit in conversation. A contrast can be seen here between the anomic melancholy expressed by Hamlet and by Oswald in Ibsen's *Ghosts*. Hamlet can make this feeling seem authentic while appearing to speak only to himself. He can then maintain his role in a variety of situations in which his behaviour is at variance with this feeling. Oswald can only express a similar state of mind through confessions that seem to be at variance with it.

These devices—the direct address, the aside and the soliloquy—were less prominent during the nineteenth century, though they were all freely used in melodrama. But they were still familiar and often the simplest means of supplying information. Again it is Ibsen who consciously seeks to alter conventions. In 1869 when he wrote *The League of Youth*, he was, in dispensing with these aids, a conscious innovator. He wrote to Georg Brandes: 'I have accomplished the feat of doing without any soliloquies, and in fact without a single aside.'[13] This he wrote at a time when he had determined to discard verse in favour of prose for the sake of realism.

In attempting to present dramatic situations realistically so that 'the reader (spectator) would feel that he was looking at

13 Ibsen's *Letters*, ed. E. Sprinchorn (MacGibbon & Kee, 1965).

something that had actually happened' Ibsen was obliged to supply the audience with all the information it needed to understand the play, through the actions and interactions of the characters. Since motives and intentions provided keys to the action in all his plays it was inevitable that they should be disclosed on occasions and in circumstances in which the character involved would be least likely to reveal them of his own accord. Thus, for the sake of verisimilitude, Ibsen relied on informers, confidants, friends or enemies from the past suddenly reappearing to provide the necessary information that would cast a new light on present action or instigate future action. Kroll is the investigator in *Rosmersholm*, who, by stirring up memories of Rebekka's past and shaking her confidence, is able to draw from her her wretched confessions. Kroll's motive is perhaps vengeance, but other motives can be implied. In *The Wild Duck* the part of informer is played by Gregers Werle who believes in honesty but also seems to be impelled by a desire for power. But the motives of these secondary characters are not of first importance as the function of the informer in these plays is to expose the motives of the main characters so that their actions can be completely understood by the audience. The chance arrival of old friends who, like Kristina in *A Doll's House*, can play the part of confidante, the lengthy recapitulations of the past, indulged in by people who know each other as well as Mrs Borkman and Ella in *John Gabriel Borkman*, are in themselves rhetorical devices intended to create empathy for the right characters and antipathy for others. At the same time the audience is supposed to feel that all this is happening by accident, that they are discovering the truth about situations portrayed by chance.

The illusion of 'realism', the illusion that a real world has been conjured up, depends on the dramatist's pretence that the characters are acting only for each other and not for the audience. But Ibsen knew that this was indeed a pretence and realised that he had to compensate the audience by careful attention to authenticating conventions. His skill in his later plays is emphasised if they are contrasted with his first realist play, *The League of Youth*, where exposition is neglected for the sake of action which is often obscure. Fjeldbö's mysterious joy in Act I is only accounted for in Act V when his engagement to Thora is announced as having taken place during Act I. There are other obscure allusions in the play that suggest that Ibsen thought that it was unnecessary to provide any bridge between the play and the audience. The political nature of this play and the fact that it was regarded, perhaps wrongly, as a *pièce à clef* ensured a stormy reaction from the audience, which pleased Ibsen. But he must have been aware of its shortcomings, for by the time he wrote *The Pillars of Society* in 1875 his technique had developed so much that in spite of the complications of the plot he was able to keep the audience fully informed and often better informed than other characters in the play, without straining credulity. He could therefore use sophisticated techniques such as dramatic irony and prospective irony, rhetorical devices which intensify the audience's emotional reactions without falsifying the authenticity of character or situation.

Dramatic irony depends on the audience having information about past or future actions that belie the words of an innocent or ignorant character. Ibsen uses this device frequently, usually by reference to past actions. In *A Doll's House*, after the audience has been fully informed of Nora's deception of Torwald, the latter, still unaware, refers to the dreadful consequences of dishonesty (in reference to Krogstad):

> TORWALD: . . . an atmosphere of lies like that infects and poisons the whole life of a home. In a house like that every breath that the children take is filled with the germs of evil.

> NORA: Are you certain of that?

> TORWALD: Oh, my dear as a lawyer I've seen it so often; nearly all young men who go to the bad have had lying mothers.

The irony here lies in her husband's complete faith in his rightness and in Nora's innocence of any such fault. In the same play he uses irony that the audience can only appreciate long after the event. This can be called *prospective irony*. In the first Act, before the audience knows anything about Nora's real character or her past actions, Torwald speaks of the horror of borrowing and getting into debt:

> TORWALD: . . . There's something constrained, something ugly even, about a home that's founded on borrowing and debt. You and I have managed to keep clear up to now, and we shall do so for the little time that is left.

> NORA (*going to the stove*). Very well Torwald, if you say so.

It is impossible for the audience to realise at this stage that every word in this scene is loaded with another meaning although Nora's sudden constraint of manner should suggest that something is wrong. Later in the play the spectators realise that they are in possession of more information than they realised. The play is dense with hidden meanings and implications.

Nearly all Ibsen's dramatic situations are defined in terms of a time-span in which the characters' past is as important as the present and future. Often the most significant incidents have occurred before the play begins, such incidents as Beate's death in *Rosmersholm*, Alving's miserable and hypocritical married life, and John Gabriel

Borkman's disgrace and imprisonment. The carefully timed disclosure of these incidents and the events surrounding them produce the tensions out of which new situations develop. The spectator's eye is constantly turned to the past so that he may see the present more clearly.

Through conventions of indirect exposition, the overheard conversations (Rebekka eavesdropping on Rosmer and Kroll), the unexpected visits from the past, the recapitulating conversations and the coincidental incidents (Oswald embracing Regina in his mother's dining-room) the spectator can be as fully informed about what is going on as he can by the conventions used in direct exposition, soliloquy, aside, or direct address. Yet Ibsen's assumption that the indirect method would persuade the spectators that what happened on the stage was more real than what happened in a play in which the rhetorical conventions declare themselves for what they are, as they did in the sixteenth and seventeenth centuries, is not altogether convincing. The illusion of reality was much more dependent on the authenticating than on rhetorical conventions, on the content of the play than on the style of presenting it. Before turning to this I would like to consider some of the ways in which rhetorical and authenticating conventions have been used since Ibsen's new style of presentation was introduced to the English stage with the production of Quicksands (Pillars of Society) in 1880.

Shaw was attracted more by the type of situations that Ibsen portrayed than by his way of presenting them. He too was interested in the relationship between the private and public person, and in the interest and emotional content of intellectual conflict. But he did not follow Ibsen in playing down rhetorical conventions. Even in what is supposed to be an intimate conversation his characters often seem to be addressing the audience rather than each other. Shaw never pretended to forget the audience. He was prepared to use the conventions of any genre, imitating Chekhov's impressionistic style in Heartbreak House, melodrama in The Devil's Disciple and the domestic problem play in Candida. He used any convention that enabled him to convey ideas to the audience and involve them in the theme of the play.

Most dramatists whose plays were performed in the English theatre during the first half of this century followed Ibsen rather than Shaw, attempting to conceal rhetorical conventions in order to suggest that action on the stage was spontaneous and autonomous. Ibsen's 'realistic' style became a cliché style in the hands of Galsworthy, Granville Barker and numerous writers of 'problem' plays in the first two decades of this century. The well-made play typical of Robertson and Pinero emerged again with a coating of Ibsenite seriousness and daring.

T-C

There were however some dramatists who recognised the freedom that direct exposition can give and the expressive value of undisguised rhetorical conventions. In *Strange Interlude* Eugene O'Neill extended the use of the soliloquy by allowing characters to speak their thoughts at length while others were within earshot. Again, in *Emperor Jones*, Jones played out most of the action alone through his spoken thoughts and fantasies. Use was also made of these devices by writers of poetic drama at the time of its revival in the 'thirties. Auden and Isherwood use soliloquy in the traditional manner in *The Ascent of F6* where Ransom sometimes reads, sometimes speaks to himself. They also introduce an interesting device, half Chorus, half soliloquy for Mr and Mrs A, who represent the 'small' or mediocre people, and act as foils to the heroic characters. (The only development of this device seems to have taken the form of slogans or meaningless noise in recent improvisations and antirealist plays of the avant-garde theatre.)

In the same period Eliot uses both the theme and some of the conventions of Greek tragedy in *The Family Reunion*. Yet the play operates on two levels. Agatha has both an oracular and a mundane voice. The former expresses, as the Choruses also express, the true meaning of the play, while the latter expresses her role in the ordinary world, where as an aunt and head of a woman's college she conforms to a popular image. The weakness of the play lies in the failure to integrate rhetorical and authenticating conventions which exist side by side. In his later plays Eliot reduces the rhetorical conventions to the minimum and even disguises his verse so that it is scarcely distinguishable from prose. Only the structural relationship of *The Cocktail Party* to the Alcestis legend reminds the audience that the rhetoric which should express meaning has been suppressed. The tenuousness of this relationship is such that few spectators would have grasped it without Eliot's own explanation.

In the contemporary theatre, although there have been few developments in poetic drama, modified forms of rhetorical devices have emerged, especially in the non-realist theatre. Speech is often used that seems to be directionless, neither addressed exclusively to the audience nor to other characters. In *Waiting for Godot* Vladimir speaks while Estragon appears to be partly asleep, partly a listener, certainly always present:

Was I sleeping while the others suffered? Am I sleeping now? Tomorrow when I wake or think I do, what shall I say of today? That with Estragon my friend at this place, until the fall of night I waited for Godot? That Pozzo passed, with his carrier, and that he spoke to us? Probably. But in all that what truth will there be? (*Estragon having struggled with his boots in vain is dozing off again. Vladimir stares at him.*) He'll know nothing. He'll tell me about the blows he received and I'll give him a carrot. (*Pause*) . . . We have time to grow old. The air is full of cries. (*He listens*) But habit is a great deadener. (*He looks again at Estragon*). At me too someone is looking, of me too someone is saying, He is sleeping, he knows nothing, let him sleep on. (*Pause*) . . .

Meaning in Beckett's plays is seldom obscure but usually ambiguous because the kind of rhetoric he uses is hard to define. It is difficult to tell whether people are presenting thoughts about themselves, their inner thoughts, or, as in *Play*, clichés that are substitutes for their thoughts. It is clear however that Beckett regards people as capable of expressing very little. Most speech is not far removed from Lucky's tirade. He does however rely on an elaborate stage rhetoric of precise gestures and signs, of silence and sound (the spotlight is the interlocuter in *Play*) and of movement.

These devices have been used by most non-realist playwrights, such as Ionesco, Arrabal and Adamov, though these dramatists have little else in common. Brecht, however, in an attempt to make the theatre less literary and more expressive has made explicit use of traditional rhetorical devices. Realism or antirealism are irrelevant to Brecht's intention, which is to express moral dilemmas in such a way that the audience will be stimulated to think about them and propose solutions. Brecht realised that for a dramatist aiming at epic theatre and attempting to rouse in the audience a desire for social and political action rhetoric must be used to draw the spectators closer to the action, to make them feel that the situations in which the actors were involved on the stage were relevant to their own lives outside the theatre. He believed that 'even to dramatise a newspaper report needs something more than the dramatic technique of a Hebbel or an Ibsen'.[14] His solution was to try to persuade spectators that the decisions and outcomes of action, the motives and intentions of the characters were in doubt, even if the situation he was representing was familiar from history or legend. In this, Brecht perhaps comes closest to the actualities of exposition which occur in social reality. He tried to make the spectator understand, not the whole character of Galileo, an acknowledged impossibility in real life, but the situation he was in, a situation which could have relevance to the spectator's own life. The actor was supposed to offer the character critically: 'Whatever he [the actor] doesn't do must be contained and conserved in what he does. In this way every sentence and every gesture signifies a decision; the character remains under observation and is tested. The technical term for this procedure is

14 *Brecht on Theatre*, trans. J. Willett (Methuen, 1964), p. 30.

'fixing the "not . . . but" '[15] The demand is for criticism rather than empathy from the spectators. They are present, therefore, at the enactment as if they too were 'walk-on' characters brought on for a single performance.

For Brecht, therefore, rhetorical conventions were very important. He wanted empathy not for the characters but for a point of view. It was situation and not character that he presented rhetorically. He tried 'not to inspect motives' and to show actions as 'pure phenomena', 'detached' from the personality of the character performing them. For instance, in *Mother Courage* she herself was supposed to represent not one of the 'little people' caught up in the great abstraction of the war but a petit bourgeois who through her small business contributed to the great business of war. In spite of its destruction of her family she never learned to reject it. It was her livelihood and she learned nothing from it. In order to suppress her individuality Brecht made her present herself as if she saw herself always in the third person. Her songs and grumbling soliloquies are not private thoughts but comments on her role and its identification with the wagon:

> 'Here's Mother Courage and her wagon!
> Hey Captain let them come and buy.'

The wagon is not a symbol of her servitude but the physical sign of her occupational role. At the end of the play it is all that remains of her and her family. Self-interest, rather than self, is what survives.

Verse is one of Brecht's most effective rhetorical devices. The interpolated verses narrate in a stylised form incidents that are not acted out, comment satirically on the action or suggest alternative moral points of view. Through verse he is able to address the audience directly without destroying the sense of authenticity.

Other dramatists who are not as totally committed to Brecht's political position have been influenced by his rhetorical methods of defining situation. Osborne in *Luther*, Arden in *Serjeant Musgrave's Dance* and Brendan Behan in *The Hostage* have adopted something from his style. Arden concentrates on the situation not the character of Black Jack; he also suggests alternative moral messages and conceals the pacifist intention of the play so successfully that it can be missed; as he himself admits: 'this play appears to advocate it [complete pacifism] with some timidity.' But as in Brecht's plays the moral stance of the play can be discovered from the songs alone. Brecht has brought back to the theatre an understanding that rhetorical conventions can emphasise the reality of events, which are complex or hard to grasp, in a way that extends beyond naturalism. Naturalism can only pretend that action on the stage has significance in the real world. If the rhetorical conventions are emphasised, actions in the

[15] *Ibid*, p. 137.

play can be believed in as theatrical events with a strong relationship
to real events that have happened or might happen. Powerful as
Brecht's influence has been in the postwar English theatre the apoliti-
cal, antirealist drama, most of which has been French, has shown a
parallel alternative development. Like Beckett, Ionesco and Genet
use rhetorical conventions, stylised speech and actions, which
convey a private imagery. The audience is given little help with its
interpretation.

Genet's symbolism appears at first to be explicit and heavily
underlined but its effect is to suggest questions rather than correspondences. In *Les Nègres* he uses masks to emphasise the symbolic relationship between black and white. The mask itself is the only
answer offered to his question: 'Qu'est ce que c'est donc un noir? Et
d'abord c'est de quelle couleur?' Similarly in *Les Bonnes* doubt lies in
the degree of reality that is assumed to inform the ceremonies played
out by Claire and Solange. When their last attempt to kill Madame
fails they agree to 'make a scene' so that the drama can be acted out
even if Claire has to take the place of the victim. Yet the play never
ends; whether Claire drinks the poison in the tea in earnest or in play
remains uncertain. The drama itself seems to be inescapable. It is
rehearsed, produced, acted and endlessly performed in imagination.
In this repetitive form it symbolises the complex nature of exploitation from which people are never free. *Les Bonnes*, the most
concentrated of Genet's plays, deals with a single situation, reflected
in multiple mirrors. Yet the same can be said of *Le Balcon* and *Les
Nègres*, more diffuse though less complex plays. In both, the central
situation (the consciousness of blackness and whiteness in *Les
Nègres* and the fantasies of domination in *Le Balcon*) is played out
in a series of theatrical performances in which identities are lost and
rediscovered. In all these plays the symbols and the things symbolised are inseparable so that the audience is constantly aware of
the interplay of play-world and social reality.

Ionesco defines situation through rhetorical conventions that at
first seem unfamiliar because there is apparently no exposition either
direct or indirect in his plays. All his situations are about states of
mind which he expresses not through action but through images. He
attempts 'to exteriorise by using the anguish of my characters
making the *set speak* and the action on the stage more visual, trans-
lating into concrete images terror, regret or remorse, and estrangement'.[16] Such images as the growing corpse in *Amedée*, the mud
of the past in *Victims of Duty*, or the ceaseless flow of furniture in
The New Tenant, are direct assaults on the consciousness of the audience, producing in spite of the uneasy laughter that they can arouse,
alarm, terror, even despair. They make direct statements to the audi-

[16] Ionesco, *Notes and Counter-notes* (Calder, 1964) p. 108.

ence which can be clearly understood in spite of the incoherent action that they instigate on stage.

It is from all these modes of expression, questions, symbols and images that most contemporary experimental dramatists have chosen their rhetoric. In addition the Living Theatre now claims to have introduced the theatre of 'answers'. Often, however, with the questions that cannot be answered and the symbols that cannot be interpreted, the images that cannot be accurately placed, plays like Ann Jellicoe's *The Sport of my Mad Mother*, Albee's *American Dream* and Rosalyn Drexler's *Line of Least Existence*, dwindle into private fantasy. The rhetoric of such plays seems to be divorced from the rhetoric to which people are accustomed to respond in ordinary life.

All the stage technical devices which I have reviewed under the general title of 'exposition' are concerned with the necessary purpose of conveying information to the audience which will enable them to formulate the appropriate definition of the situation which they need to grasp the composition of action deployed on the stage. All of them, clearly, are not peculiar to the theatrical occasion (they would hardly fulfil their purpose if they were) but are conventionalised renderings of rhetorical procedures familiar enough in real life. The difference lies in the need to make public to the whole audience what is ordinarily a matter of confidential conversational traffic or remains even unvoiced, and therefore mystifying, in the business of everyday life.

The Senecan set speeches, like the declamations of contemporary 'participant' performances, are no more than straightforward briefings—memoranda addressed by the playwright to the audience conveying the relevant context or an explanation providing the information necessary to keep interest alive in the inevitably abbreviated slices of action occurring between the actors. Almost, they can be regarded as minutes of previous events or other meetings necessary for getting through the agenda, or as footnotes. Ibsen's characters recapitulating the past fall clearly into the same category of prefatory notes, and the innovation of incorporating them as remarks in the text uttered by characters in the play relies heavily on the assumption that the audience at this time would be familiar with the standard explanatory opening of the nineteenth-century novel. Shaw's speechifying monologues sometimes serve the same purpose, but just as often seem to act as explanatory footnotes or commentaries. The same explanations feature also in plays by Brecht and Arden, but are incorporated in songs which are bracketed within the play action proper, and declare their separateness by the stylistic shift from ordinary speech into sung verses.

Soliloquy, on the other hand, is peculiar to the drama, and the

traditional problem which this sets the producer and actor underlines its distinctiveness. O'Neill's revival of it in *Strange Interlude*
seems to have been solved by the actor's adopting a trancelike pose, a
self-conscious breaking of the frame of conventions which served to
keep the action itself within the definition of the situation common
to the characters on stage. O'Neill's soliloquies are partly a
manoeuvred departure from the devices adopted by Ibsen to serve
part of the same purpose. He uses confidential utterances delivered
by friends or enemies to reveal attitudes or states of mind at variance
with the personae assumed during the rest of the interaction. But
they are also revelations which reset the frame of the ensuing action,
as are O'Neill's revelations of his characters' thoughts.

But soliloquy, at Shakespeare's hands and to some extent O'Neill's,
can go beyond personal disclosure. Ritual permeates tragedy and its
modes survive more distinctly. There is something both inspired and
prayerful in the soliloquies of Lear, Macbeth and Hamlet; they seem
driven beyond their parts in the play to utterances which are at times
universal judgments on the human condition, at times prayers for
deliverance from their own subjection to it.

This quasiliturgical element is more obviously present in the
chorus of classical drama, and in the rather diffident revival of it in
for example Jonson's *Catiline* and in the poetic drama of this century. Auden and Isherwood's chorus produces no more than a de-
based public opinion voice, Eliot's a transcendental inspired
commentary, whether from his characters in the *Family Reunion*
or from the impersonal grouped chorus (the 'choir') of the plays
meant for performance in ecclesiastical settings.

Moving further in the same direction, there is the implication of
'other worlds'—of alternative realities—which derives from myth.[17]
When Vladimir says 'At me too someone is looking, of me too
someone is saying "He is sleeping, he knows nothing, let him sleep
on",' Beckett is raising the same awkward question as Lewis Car-
roll:

> He shouted so loud that Alice couldn't help saying 'Hush! You'll
> be waking him, I'm afraid, if you make so much noise.'
>
> 'Well, it's no use *your* talking about waking him,' said Tweedle-
> dum, 'when you're only one of the things in his dream. You
> know very well you're not real.'
>
> 'I *am* real!' said Alice, and began to cry.
>
> 'You won't make yourself a bit realer by crying.' Tweedledee
> remarked: 'There's nothing to cry about.'
>
> 'If I wasn't real,' Alice said—half-laughing through her tears, it
> all seemed so ridiculous, 'I shouldn't be able to cry.'

17 See p. 2.

'I hope you don't suppose those are real tears?' Tweedledum
interrupted in a tone of great contempt.

Beckett's later plays, in fact, exist virtually entirely in the implication of mythical worlds other than those represented in the
almost extinguished vestiges of human life actually exhibited in
speech, action and stage equipment.

Genet, in contrast, invokes constantly a political and social reality
of non-alienated existence lying at the other side of the looking-glass
from the scenes and actions of *Les Nègres*, *Les Bonnes*, and *Les
Écrans*. Brecht actually invites his audience to see his action from the
other, *real*, side of the looking-glass. Mother Courage's references to
herself in the third person, reducing her to the completely alienated
creature of a system dominated by false consciousness, is a direct
appeal to the spectator's critical awareness of another world—hence
the constant attempt to thrust the action *between* actors and audience, and constantly reiterated manifestos directed towards arousing
the audience into a positive, critical, participative role. The rhetoric
of both, despite the immensely more sophisticated techniques involved, has clear affinities with the elementary didacticism of contemporary *Agitprop* and the medieval Morality and Miracle plays.

Finally, at the opposite pole of expository conventions, there is the
need to provide inside information to the audience, which will give
them an understanding of the action which is appropriate to the
definition of the situation intended by the author but which needs to
be different from, deeper than, that which prevails on stage. The
archetypal form is the 'aside'—common enough in real life, and institutionalised in a multitude of ways—in legal procedure, in
confidential reports and testimonials, in prefatory information given
to people before a newcomer arrives, and, indeed, in whispered
asides in meetings, parties, and debates. The theatrical aside is, then
a straight takeover from commonplace practice, the difference lying
in the oddity of private communication taking place between two of
the participants on stage in such a way as to communicate the information to a large public audience too while implying that it is un-
heard by the other players on stage.

The breaking of the situational frame within which the action is
defined as taking place makes it peculiar to the double character of
theatrical occasion, and underlines it in a way which goes against the
grain of the authenticating conventions which are employed to conceal it—hence Ibsen's triumph in managing eventually to dispense
with asides altogether. Yet the aside, especially when addressed directly to the audience, as by Jonson, can actually enhance the 'sense
of theatre'. The contrived complicity between player and audience
brings into play the special pleasure derived from receiving

confidences, the inside information which makes for privileged understanding of what underlies the manifest relationships and interplay of social interaction, discussion and argument, into which concealed interests and motives enter. Music hall comics have always exploited the trick, and it survives (in Marx Brothers and Bob Hope films) even in the unlikely world of the cinema. Less ingenuous, but not necessarily more successful, is the display of eavesdropping by characters in the play on others, and the inside information provided for the audience by their eavesdropping on interchanges meant to be kept secret from other characters. All these variants of the form are ironic in intent—either directly[18] or by way of 'dramatic irony'. The trapping of characters in situations whose significant relationship to other parts of the action is unsuspected by them, but known to the audience,[19] is effected in this way.

[18] See: Tom Burns 'Friends, enemies and the polite fiction'.
[19] Jay Haley has developed the theme in terms of a rendering of psychoanalysis as one-upmanship: Jay Haley, *The art of psychoanalysis*, reprint from an article in *E.T.C.*, Spring 1958, pp. 3–11.

6

Rhetorical conventions: space, setting and time

Maps are very abstract things. The spaces and places we know are idiosyncratic networks of rooms, houses, buildings, streets, railways, airports, vehicles and so forth and stretches and patches of countryside, coast, sky and sea connected by our own uses, memories, interests and activities. The terrestrial world known to each individual resembles the psychologist's conception of the 'schema'—the awareness of our own body and senses—which is both 'good enough to be going on with' and the effective use we make of it, plus any present awareness or recollections (fortunately somewhat short of total recall) we may have of pleasurable or painful feelings. This is a very different conception from the anatomist's and physiologist's 'map' of the human body. As Tom Brennan and Michael Lee[1] have pointed out, the sense, indeed the knowledge of a neighbourhood as a defined area of relevant resources, interests and actions can vary in the most extraordinary way from person to person; and Lee uses the concept of 'schema' to denote the representation of the neighbouring world which is personal to each individual.

Places in this network define themselves in terms of settings for the activities we and others pursue in them. This sorting out of place into a network of settings is now a familiar aspect of lives, both at work and outside it. It has been dealt with at some length in an unpublished report by Tom Burns of his study of occupational milieux in the British Broadcasting Corporation, from which the following lengthy extract is taken:

Physical Setting
There is a various, shifting, but necessary relationship between our selves in their different aspects and locations, and the scenes,

---

[1] T. Brennan, *Midland City* (Dobson, 1948); M. Lee, 'Urban neighbourhood as a socio-spatial schema', *Human Relations*, xxi (1968), 241–68.

furnishings and costumes which equip the events through which they move. The relationship is usually regarded as emblematic. Just as accent and clothing are used to place a person socially, intellectually and culturally, so are furniture, house and even district used as map references for the present position and compass direction of a social career. We persuade ourselves that we can read in streets and frontages, and in the interiors deliberately, cunningly or rudely offered for view the incomes, the social standing and the pretensions of the dwellers within, attaching the correct social weighting to looped window curtains as against straight hanging ones, to flights of china ducks as against African masks, to an assortment of table lamps as against a central light.

It is therefore the easiest thing in the world to find the social exchange value of the buildings and furnishings which form the context of working activities in the Corporation. The departments which were the subject of this study are divided between Television Centre and Broadcasting House with its Portland Place annexes. The contrast between the architectural manner of Television Centre and Broadcasting House, between the heavy fortress shape and 'head office' treatment of Broadcasting House and the 'technological' design and exhibition styling of Television Centre is not confined to the difference in dates—the dating of sound broadcasting and the novelty of television. The sentiment expressed by the man who said that Reith lived on in Broadcasting House and not at Television Centre could be read, without being too fanciful, into the peculiarly appropriate siting of the two buildings: Broadcasting House forced into the most inconvenient of sites but standing guard at the south-eastern approaches—from Whitehall, Parliament, and the West End—to the solid upper professional crust of British society located in the district between Liberty's and Lord's; Television Centre finding a location which will above all allow it to grow, but in a district which derives its strongest flavour from exhibitions, dog racing, and the film industry. And the differing balance of emphasis between central authority and organisation structure on the one hand and programme-centred activities on the other is demonstrated by the reversal of basic design in the two buildings—the sound studios enclosed by the carapace of offices at Broadcasting House, and the irruption of studios, design shops and engineering sections outwards from the hollow, office-ringed drum in the middle of Television Centre.

The symbolic references, both intentional and unintended, are hackneyed enough, but none the less real, taking realism in this case to stand for a fairly wide consensus about them. But the references are not, of course, one-way. Television Services, and work on that side of the Corporation, differ from the sound broadcasting side partly because of the difference between Television Centre and Broadcasting House. So, because the two buildings have caught so much of the sense of their time and social function, because they represent so clearly the polarities of the Corporation's self-conception, the imprint of each contrast is made deeper and more distinct.

The contrast is rooted to some extent in the nature of each medium. There is size. Studio 3 in Television Centre is almost three times as big as the Concert Hall in Broadcasting House, and the ordinary sound studio has a cosy domesticity in comparison with the ordinary television studio. Television has its enormous and baffling array of lighting equipment, and scenery sets, cameras and microphones mounted on trucks and mobile cranes, all contributing to the sense of occasion and momentous technicality. And this sense is almost, as they used to say, palpable in the studio gallery, overlooking the studios, the loft from which producers direct programmes with the aid of a secretary (to check the script and to time action), a vision mixer (to switch the sequences of scenes fed into monitor screens from the half-dozen or so cameras and prepared film sequences into the single output channel), a technical operations manager, responsible for the functioning of the crew on the studio floor, and lighting and sound supervisors in the next-door rooms. It is here, in darkness which is punctuated by the monitor screens, illuminated control panels or desk lamps and which terminates in the window overlooking the studio, that the union occurs of large-scale technical and human resources, of the social, intellectual, political and cultural processes involved in television, and the awareness of an immediate but unknown audience of millions. It is too much to say that all this is caught in the design of the producer's gallery, but every physical appurtenance, from the noiseless floor covering to the arc of the control desk skewed across the room and facing not the studio window but the double rank of monitoring screens, realises and reinforces it. It is an intensely dramatic place, dramatic not only in the obvious sense of the felt presence of an unseen audience, or of the manipulation of unseen performers and technicians, but in the immediate experience of the excitement and desperations which are enacted in it day after day as the final studio rehearsals move towards performance in front of 'live' cameras. This highly charged mental and moral environment is caught, reflected and magnified in the whole design and styling of the room. Instead of being dominated by the technical apparatus it really belongs to, the management and design of the gallery smooths and fits the complexities of the control panels and communication links into harmonious or compliant relationship with the one task. One feels the 'cockpit' sense. This rendering in visual, sensitive terms of the television combination of technology, dramatic performance and mass communications, each carrying the highest and most 'contemporary' of esteem, makes the production gallery the most glamorous of work settings, where the term 'the coal face', used for the task of producing television programmes, becomes understandable in its entire metaphorical rightness and ludicrous inappropriateness.

The offices are offices. But even when their occupants are functionally remote from the studios, the circular form of the inner space of the Centre and of the corridor which runs around every floor, is a reminder of the singular purpose of the building, no less concrete and more constant than the traffic of dozens and sometimes hundreds of performers, studio crew, and production team members through the restaurant and cafeteria. One can almost forget the existence of the studios and the technical apparatus of broadcasting in the Langham Hotel and even in the offices of Broadcasting House, which overlook streets and overhear the traffic of the everyday world outside the Corporation. The distinctness of television, so far as the Corporation is concerned, lies as much in the totality of the occupational milieu created by it and for it as in its presentational range, its youth and its greater appeal.

The relationship between the members of the Corporation staff and the environment in which they work takes on ecological aspects which are rather more clearly apparent than in most occupational settings. Idiosyncrasy can be displayed more easily at Portland Place, and makes itself felt in the disposition of furniture, in prints and photographs on the walls. Television Centre offices are less domesticated than usual: the coloured holiday post-cards are on the wall behind the secretary, but they are fewer, and usually from remote or exotic places. There are the token bookcases in the more highly placed executive offices and occasional joke notices in others, but the main visual representation of the occupant of an office is the particular kind of paper cluttering his desk. The most significant observation on this relationship in Television Centre lies perhaps in the fact that many people, even those who had worked there from its opening, confessed to losing their way in the building, which is designed on the simplest of plans: a drum, with circular corridors on each floor providing the circulation space.

What we have so far considered is, of course, the crude data from which occupational settings are composed, rather than the settings themselves. If one envisages the physical surroundings within which a single person's working day is accomplished, buildings and their component rooms are resolved into a more or less diffuse network of working spaces connected by communicating passages, stairs, lifts, streets, telephones and vehicles. Working lives are in fact spent in one of the many networks built out of the total physical structure of all the buildings owned and operated by the Corporation and the interconnecting routes and recognised meeting places outside. This conception is again more familiar when it is applied to a whole urban society, which organises itself into social systems within

the fabric of the city. Such systems are either physically segregated, like the 'worlds' of Fleet Street, of the law, of medical
consultancy, of Wardour Street or of discount houses, or no-
tionally—but just as clearly—defined as milieux, like the worlds
of advertising, gambling, scientific research, music, trade union
affairs, and 'show business'. Within the Corporation, analogous
'worlds' are built out of the whole system of buildings and
traffic between them, worlds which may in large measure be
physically adjacent, even largely congruent (and organ-
isationally closely allied), but which are in actual—social—fact
quite distinct.

It is perhaps only initially surprising for a man in Schools
Broadcasting (Sound), to be able to say: '(Schools) people in Television Centre and here never meet on any occasion. It was once
suggested that we should get in a bus once a year and go down
there and have a tea-party!'

The fuller force of the distinctness of the individual networks
begins to come home when a manager in Technical Operations,
asked if he 'managed to get round the studios', where the crews
for whom he was managerially responsible worked, replied:
'Not as much as I would like. . . . I am, of course, very interested
in studio work, but I have to make a distinct change of gear. I've
got to say to myself, "Well I'm going down today to have a look
into studios". When I get into studios I don't want to come into
the office, and vice versa, you see.' The isolation of the producer
from his fellow producers, and his willing absorption in the
production 'team' has already been noticed. This is true of other
specialist members of the team.

'Being a floor manager, I can't really speak about floor managers in general. That's a thing you might note, that floor managers don't know other floor managers terribly well.'

T.B. 'This is true all through, it seems. People in the same
department on the programme side don't know their colleagues.'

X. 'Yes, we simply meet them socially—at odd times.'

But even here, the segmentation and, more important, the
feeling of separation, works itself out in the development of
even smaller systems.

'Different people—classes—in the studio, technical people, are
very inclined to stay as a group—in the canteen and between
rehearsals. They don't mix . . . The same is true of scenery staff.
You usually get five or six allocated, and they stay together. It's
something which is traditional. You know, they eat together,
and so on . . . It's one of the things I found a bit off-putting when
I came into television. At the lunch breaks, dinner breaks, unless
I had an assistant, I'd be entirely on my own, because the scene
shifters had gone off together, the technical crew would put two
or three tables together and eat together, the producer and sec-

retary—probably through sheer pressure—have a sandwich and beer somewhere—and one would find oneself on one's own. In the studio itself, there's not much of a barrier between sections ... As for producers being isolated from each other, they can after all see each other's shows. I should think there's less isolation between producers than there is between producers and the rest of the production staff'.

It was therefore not eventually surprising, though at first and at times thereafter disconcerting, to find that, moving as I did from department to department, and even from group to group within departments, I was also shifting from one social system to unconnected others, and that the people who worked in the same department, walked the same corridors, ate in the same restaurant, and followed each other occasionally in the same studio, existed in different worlds. Such worlds derived their own distinctness, necessarily, through the reduction of the other places and the other people inhabiting the same building to an anonymous background of Corporation activity.

While for the most part the networks coexist in the same physical milieu of studios outside rehearsal rooms, workshops, conference rooms, restaurants and BBC Club, there are certain junction points which serve to bind individuals and even groups together almost irrespective of their occupational network. Patronage of the 'George', a self-consciously preserved Edwardian pub and, at a rather more exalted level, membership of the Savile Club, provide for the exchange of shop and other forms of social insurance familiar in the life of the British professional classes. More important in the life of the Corporation are the links established at the outset of careers in training courses or, for migrants to the London area, in a period of work in a Region. But these links form part of the network of useful acquaintanceship. ...[2]

There is a fluctuating line separating public and private places of the social world. The street and open spaces of towns and village and countryside, once the common space in which much of ordinary life was carried on in public, are now, for the most part, merely thoroughfares or 'scenery'; much more of our lives is carried on in rooms, in buildings and premises reserved for special use by specified individuals. Consonant with this shift of threshold between public and private has developed a sizeable change in manners, the emergence of 'privatised' conventions of social intercourse as well as preoccupation with the private, secluded, sectors of our lives, and the development of specialised settings for different modes of

---

[2] T. Burns, Cultural Bureaucracy: A study of Occupational Milieux in the BBC undertaken in 1963/64, (unpublished), pp. 23–6.

action—from bedrooms to motorways, from private offices to factory farms, from telephone booths to cinemas.

Hans-Paul Bahrdt has discussed the development of urban life in the West from pre-industrial to contemporary generations as dominated by the shift of the setting of more and more of our life space from public to private places.[3] Indeed, in modern American cities almost the whole of life is played out in private places, transit between all of them being accomplished, so far as is humanly and technically possible, in private too, by automobile. The public space of large American cities has become, for most Americans, an unfamiliar and fearful environment, as haunted and as dangerous as the wildernesses which surrounded the settlements of medieval Europe.

At the same time the last three centuries have seen another displacement of the world beyond social reality, from a circumambient and superhuman heaven and hell and an utterly remote, fantastically reported foreignness, to a world of scientific rather than metaphysical mysteries and potencies, and of speedy and eventually immediate communication of action and events and places, with an assured reality of their own and an unbridgeable detachment from the social reality we inhabit.

The development of the conventional handling of space, time and setting in the theatre over the same period of historical time reflects, embodies and interprets, into something approaching meaningful *social* convention, these changes in the social dimensions and significances of the space and time we ordinarily inhabit. Drama, too, has moved from public to private action. It has replaced common space by settings connected by the network of the players' travellings just as it has translated the eschatological context of mundane existence into the representation of the utopian and catastrophic potentialities inherent in the world of reported events,[4] and the folk myth of fantastic alternative realities into dreamworlds of sophisticated luxury and nightmares of the crushing insignificance of human existence.

In the semidramatic tropes performed within the church, floor space, already differentiated by liturgical use, was more strictly defined within these limits by the action. The action itself focused the spectators' attention on the whole acting space, on one part at a time or on different parts, where two sets of action were occurring. In the *Quem quaeritis* the chancel represented an unlocated space

---

[3] H-P. Bahrdt, *Die Moderne Grosstadt* (Rohwolt, 1961).

[4] The contrast is expressed most neatly by the significance which attaches to Donne's original sermon and the use to which 'For whom the bell tolls' is put by Hemingway in his novel of the Spanish war written for an isolationist American public.

across which the disciples *travelled* to the sepulchre in a journey of unspecified length. Apart from the sepulchre which was not introduced into the earliest performances of the trope, there was no specific setting. But different localities were clearly specified by the action and were equally clearly appropriate to different parts of the church. In this way the principle of multiple staging was established.

When the fully dramatic plays emerged from the church, at first into the churchyard and later as part of the Corpus Christi procession out into the streets, these placing conventions were retained with slight modifications. The wagons were usually elaborately decorated to represent a specific location. Yet the actors could still descend into the street, which represented the same interstitial space as the church chancel, for parts of the action.[5]

When plays took place in inn yards or game-houses of the Cornish 'round' type, acting space seems to have been defined in much the same way. Richard Southern's reconstruction of performances in the round theatres suggests that spectators shared the *platea* with the actors. The actors had their places on scaffolds erected at different points on the perimeter, from which many of their speeches were made. But to encounter the other actors or to dominate the play actors descended into the *platea*. On these occasions the acting place was cleared of spectators by stytelers, whose job it seems to have been to shift and rearrange the audience so that lines of sight were kept clear.[6] Here the spectators must have become accustomed to constant forming and reforming of the boundaries of illusion through conventions shared with the actors.[7] The Theater, the first permanent theatre to be built for plays only, was designed on the same round plan and retained many of the same conventions.[8] 'Houses' or 'mansions' were used to represent a specific locality. But 'houses' not in use, even if they represented a distant place, remained on the stage, while the next episode proceeded without presumably disturbing the audience's concentration. In the same way actors who were no longer dramatically 'present' were not

[5] In the Coventry play of *Herod and the Slaying of the Innocents* the direction is given: 'Erode rages in the pagond and in the strete also.'
[6] R. Southern, *The Mediaeval Theatre in the Round* (Faber, 1957). This reconstruction of production in the 'rounds' is mainly based on the sketch and stage directions in the original script of *The Castle of Perseverance* with confirmatory evidence from The Fouquet Miniature which (c.1455) shows part of a circular theatre.
[7] The ease with which spectators can become accustomed to such a convention was demonstrated by the success of the performances by the Teatro Libero of *Orlando Furioso* in both Italy and Scotland in 1970. Once again the spectators filled the acting space and the actors performed amongst them.
[8] F. Yates, *Theatre of the World* (Routledge, 1969) pp. 91–5. Yates has suggested that the round plan may have been derived from the Vitruvian theatre rather than the medieval 'rounds'. It seems possible that both types of theatre may have been in the mind of Burbage and his associates.

obliged to leave the stage. They could remain visible but 'out of play'.

On the stage of the public theatre place was only indicated by the actors. M. C. Bradbrook[9] suggests that Shakespeare's imaginative setting of scene through the words of his characters has misled us into supposing that the audience was accustomed to this method of scene setting. Examination of other sixteenth and seventeenth century plays shows that the place or setting is seldom clearly defined and that it is often difficult to tell where an encounter is taking place. Shakespeare discovered the possibility of using physical description not only as a means of presenting the play but also of interacting with the theme. The symbolic relationship of setting to character and situation appears in progressively sophisticated forms in his middle and later plays. It seems clear, however, that with other dramatists of the time appreciation of characters and action did not depend on definition of place either realistically or imaginatively.

In the public theatres separate precincts, stage and auditorium, were allotted to actors and audience. This innovation led to endless difficulties. Spectators could buy stools on the stage but although this practice brought in more money it seems to have been regarded with some resentment by dramatists and players from the very beginning. There is no record of favourable comment on the close proximity of the audience and the intimacy which this proximity might engender.

This intrusion of the audience into the actors' precinct persisted until the middle of the eighteenth century, when Garrick finally drove the intruders off the stage of Drury Lane. Throughout it was an imposition inflicted by a privileged class on the actors and the poorer spectators whose view of the action was often obscured. It cannot be regarded as the same kind of deliberate obliteration of the distinction between actors and spectators that occurred in the court masque, which was a form of semidramatic 'play'. Drama rested firmly on the distinction between performers and spectators and between the spatial worlds of the stage and the auditorium. Jonson's and Beaumont and Fletcher's dramatisation of the relationship between the two which has already been discussed indicates a reliance on the spectators' grasp of conventional definition at the same time as acknowledging and exploiting the familiar juxtaposition.

Early in the seventeenth century architectural structure was employed as a device to resolve the problem. In 1605 the proscenium arch was first used in the court production of *The Masque of Blackness* and the stage was transformed into a 'picture'. Indigo Jones, who must have taken the idea from his knowledge of Palladio, arranged the

---

[9] M. C. Bradbrook, *Themes and Conventions in Elizabethan Tragedy* (Penguin, 1935), p. 8ff, discusses conventions of place and setting.

'mansions', free standing, as in the round traditional theatre, to accord with the optical principles of a landscape in receding perspective.[10] This, as Glynne Wickham says, marks the beginning of the process dominated by stage designers which led to the acceptance in the nineteenth and twentieth centuries of 'images of actuality which have for so long now invited audiences to accept things seen and heard on stage or screen at their face value'.[11] Yet until the closing of the theatres in 1642 the two kinds of staging existed side by side, mansion staging in the public theatres and scenic staging in lavish performances at court and sometimes in the private theatres. There was no rigid division between the audiences of the public and private theatres so that some of the same people must have become accustomed to the two sets of spatial conventions.

With the closing of the theatres the medieval tradition of the round theatre, mansion staging and unlocated space, for the time being, came to an end. The new Restoration theatres under the patronage of the court revived the staging traditions of the court masques and private theatres, enhanced by innovations introduced from France and Italy. The stage with elaborate setting and ingenious stage machinery became a living picture. The acting space was no longer 'framed' by the action but by the scenery and the physical boundaries of the stage and proscenium arch. For some time the apron stage outside the proscenium arch was quite extensive, but during the eighteenth century it dwindled until by the end of the nineteenth century it was usually only used for curtain calls. Theatres built in the first half of the twentieth century, have usually been designed without a forestage. The curtain is drawn to disclose a picture.[12]

This enclosure of the play by a new set of spatial conventions had two effects. It set limits to the theatrical world into which the audience was not supposed to stray. It also presented this world as a contrary or alternative reality. The illusion could be created, with the co-operation of the audience, that the events that occurred on the stage were temporarily as real as those that occurred outside the theatre. In fact the audience was now asked to make a greater imaginative effort to sustain the illusion that the stage itself represented the world of the play rather than the world of the actors. Place could no longer be evoked at one moment to be replaced at the next. Instead place could only be altered by change of scene, involving very often a complete change of scenery. The movement from common public space to private settings, already occurring in social life with

[10] An imitation of Palladio's last masterpiece, the *Teatro Olimpico* at Vicenza.
[11] Wickham, *Early English Stages* i, 316.
[12] Or sometimes dispensed with—a compromise between open and picture-staging.

the rapid development of domestic architecture, required a similar shift in theatrical presentation, with plays depending much more on action within private settings.[13] Change of scene and setting, with the characters moving from one private place to another, develops the conception of social space as a network although public common ground, often the forestage outside the proscenium arch, is still used in Restoration plays as the place for casual encounters, confrontations, and assignations.

Post-Restoration dramatists took advantage of the new elaborate settings to add a further dimension to their plays. Characters were not merely created but created in a visible context which could help to condition the audience's response. The introduction of period costume for historical plays at the end of the eighteenth century was accompanied by elaborate stage sets and machinery that could create sensational effects. This became fully effective in the nineteenth century. First gas lighting, and at the end of the century electric lighting and limelights, box-flats and elaborate furnishings provided the realistic settings (realistic in the sense of photographic representations) the plays of Ibsen, Strindberg and Chekhov required.

This was the period of the domestic play. Not all scenes took place indoors but the country house gardens of Chekhov and Turgenev are only extensions of the country houses, summer rooms rather than parts of an outside world. Ibsen's attempt to return to his early poetic style with the accentuated symbolism of *When We Dead Awaken* involved him in demanding difficult outdoor scenes and effects, completely unsuited to the realistic stage of which he had made so much use. The theme of this play suggests that it was intended as an act of expiation for his desertion of poetry and that he could only see it staged in his imagination. In his earlier realist plays he had succeeded in making use not only of space in full view of the audience but also of rooms and views that only the actors could see clearly. In *The Wild Duck* it is in the attic off-stage or partly visible to the audience that old Ekdal goes hunting, and there that, at the climax of the play, Hedwig shoots herself. The spectators are never allowed to forget the importance of this unseen space.

Ibsen was well aware that in seeking to make his plays 'real' he was creating an illusion. As early as 1874, before the tag 'social realist' had been attached to him, he wrote to Edmund Gosse of his aim in *The Emperor and Galilean:* 'The illusion I wished to produce

---

[13] This system of scene change is less suitable for pre-Restoration plays in which rapid change of location is integral to the complexity of the plots. Various compromises have been made, attempts to link together several scenes in one place or alter the sequence of the action. But recently a return has been made for most Shakespearian plays to the open 'placeless' stage without set or scenery even on stages such as that of the Stratford Memorial Theatre that were originally designed as picture stages.

was that of reality.' Later of *An Enemy of the People* he wrote to August Lindberg: 'The effect of the play depends a great deal on making the spectator feel as if he were actually sitting, listening and looking at events happening in real life.' He realised that this illusion depended in part on a distancing of the play from the spectators. When *Ghosts* was performed at the Møller in 1883 he complained that the distance between spectators and actors was too short. Realism of this kind does depend upon complete separation of and distance between actors and audience.

It also required complete dominance by the world of the lighted stage over the darkened auditorium (a practice introduced by Irving at the Lyceum in the 1880s[14]) through which each individual member of the audience 'loses touch' with his neighbours and is reduced to the role of a voyeur. The cinema, when it came, was a natural extension of the conventions of space, time and setting, and of this dominance of the stage over auditorium, established[15] by the realist theatre of the nineteenth century.

The development of the theatrical conventions of space and setting I have sketched is, as I remarked earlier, both a reflection and an interpretation—for better understanding in society—of the changes undergone by general life style over the centuries from Elizabethan to Victorian times. The rank, occupation, relative wealth, cultural pretensions and interests of an individual who, in sixteenth-century England, spent the greater part of his waking life outdoors in the presence of people of all conditions and in indoor places which, in daylight, were accessible to most, were expressed in the clothes, decorations and accoutrements he carried on his person, and in his manner of speech, gesture and demeanour. Nowadays expressive differences of this kind are conveyed largely by the private settings, domestic and other, in which he acts out his various roles. Social distance itself has been translated into spatial distance; the mixture of great houses, slums, stables, merchant households incorporating country houses and warehouses, market stalls and 'ordinaries' which were packed densely together in the cities of the sixteenth and seventeenth century[16] sorted itself out until we can read, in the physical layout of the city, the social structure of the community it houses:

[14] Earlier in the century in many gaslit theatres house lights had been dimmed but complete darkness in the auditorium was not appreciated until stage lighting became efficient in the last decades.

[15] Established, but in a curiously insecure way. Audience involvement was still present as much in the hurrahs which greeted the hero and the boos for the villain in melodrama as in the catcalls and derisive comments which the audience supplied when the dominance of stage over auditorium failed to come off (see Dickens, *Great Expectations*, ch. 31).

[16] 'The first noticeable thing about these towns would have been the stench. There was no sanitary system; an open cesspool in the court often served the richer inhabitants; the poor, as with Eastern peoples today, made a public convenience

We know, roughly but sufficiently, that there are slum areas and well-to-do areas, Whitechapels and Mayfairs, and that in between, there are gradations of respectability, wealth, and cultural pretensions which attach to different slices of the social pyramid and also to different localities, Paddington, Pimlico, Islington, Camberwell, Willesden, Fulham, Bayswater, Highbury, Lewisham, Golders Green, Twickenham, Highgate, South Kensington, Hampstead, Belgravia all have quite specific social earmarks for Londoners, each representing important expressive aspects of the income, occupations, social standing, culture and so forth of the people who live in them—or rather, of the *kind* of people who *are supposed* to live in them. In times past, the equipment and accessories which served as emblems of social, cultural and moral claims were matters of approval rather than architecture, deportment rather than home address, amount and design of jewelry rather than make of car or summer holiday location. The social maps we now carry inside our heads have become much more important navigational aids for our working and family lives than the socially discerning eye or ear.

All these social areas can be ranked crudely in order of the money value of property. But one dimension, even though it is not a continuous gradient, but a series of uneven steps, following the strata of society conceals more fundamental differences, even divergencies, between these strata. And the marks by which we distinguish one street from another, one household from another, on this gradient, have a significance beyond their use as indicators. It is the easiest thing in the world to 'place' the run-down Victorian terrace, with its front steps and area, as easy as it was to give the correct class reading of accents or of pigeon-fancying as against bird-watching.[17]

House interiors have become stage sets in which decoration, lighting, furniture, pictures and sometimes even books are chosen not so much for their comfort, convenience or instruction as for their appearance. The setting is seen as designed, consciously or by default, to reveal an image of the owners. The new owners' hasty disclaimers of responsibility for the decoration left by the previous occupants of a house reveal this conception of houses as extensions of the person.

---

of every nook and cranny. The unpaved streets were narrow, often only six feet wide; at Bristol they were too narrow for carts, and sledges had to be used for moving goods. The houses of the poor were one or two room hovels, frequently made only of weatherboard with a pitched roof, placed back to back; or they were the houses of the rich, deserted because their owners were seeking more salubrious suburbs—ramshackle warrens of filth, squalor, and disease. Most cellars were inhabited, not only by people but also by their pigs, fowls, sometimes even by their horses and cattle. All tradesmen and craftsmen used the street as their dustbin, including butchers who threw out the refuse of their shambles to decay and moulder in the streets': J. H. Plumb, *England in the Eighteenth Century* (Penguin, 1950), p. 12.
[17] Tom Burns, 'The city as looking glass', *Prospect*, Winter 1960.

The visitor to a house may be surprised by discrepancies but always gains information, supplied deliberately or accidentally by the occupants about their social status, artistic or intellectual pretensions and attitude to material objects (to be merely used, cherished or treated as sacred).

Throughout the process of creating a setting the individual is himself subjected to the conditioning of the material objects that surround him and to which he has given meaning. People choose a new house or neighbourhood, not only because it conforms to the tastes which they already have but often because it offers scope for a new way of life for the realisation of tastes and a style of life that they have not previously been able to enjoy.[18] They often expect to become a different kind of person and sometimes they do. Just as people can be imprisoned by a one-class neighbourhood so they can also be imprisoned by the furnishings and decor that proclaim them to be certain kinds of people. A specific setting makes its own demands for appropriate behaviour, and can provide embarrassments for intrusive behaviour much like the embarrassment which attaches to persons who find themselves or their behaviour being treated by others as 'out of place'. Power to change setting or to select for a particular meeting an appropriate background has become a matter of some consequence. In private life people take great pains to select the right background for major consequential acts, for love, quarrelling or parting; for we are all too conscious of the effect of congruities and incongruities. The 'pathetic fallacy' derives from the commonplace knowledge of the relationship between action and setting.

The selection and display of appropriate backgrounds is strictly institutionalised in professional and workplace settings. In any business firm offices with differing standards of space, design and furnishings are allocated according to status. Space is of primary importance but size of desk and provision of carpeting is also carefully considered.[19] From such signs a visitor can quickly assess the importance of the executive with whom he is confronted and the amount of power he is likely to wield. But the signs are, as much as anything, addressed to the occupant (in the same way advertising is known, in the trade, often to be addressed as much to the client as to the potential customers, and in many cases, even more directly to him than to them). The importance given to business deals prepared

---

[18] 'The most frequently reported changes that do take place are not caused by the move to the suburb, but are the reasons for moving there in the first place': Herbert Gans, 'The Effects of the move from City to Suburb' in L. J. Dahl, ed., *The Urban Condition* (Basic Books, 1963) p. 185.
[19] In one large firm the promotion from 'staff B' to 'staff A' cannot always be marked by a change of office. Instead the eight-foot partition is heightened to reach the ceiling.

over an expense-account lunch is usually correlated fairly carefully with the expensiveness of the restaurant or club.

Buildings that are devised to house permanent institutions, government buildings, schools, churches, law courts and hospitals are, like stage sets, prepared for certain kinds of scene, and announce their uses by much more than the equipment they contain, the allocation and layout of space, and the functional appropriateness of their furnishing. Expressiveness, particularly towards the end of the nineteenth century, and well into the twentieth, outweighed utility: design was in terms of the definition of social function rather than of instrumental function or utility.

Definition of social function in this way is (as in the theatre) a means of social control. This is not anything new. The cathedrals and churches of medieval and renaissance Europe displayed in architectural form the formidable power of the Church, as did palaces and castles that of kings and nobles. Our present heritage of nineteenth-century buildings preserves certain forms of behaviour which would be anomalous outside them. Members of Parliament inevitably derive a certain amount of dignity and importance from the fabric of the Palace of Westminster; and Asa Briggs has documented the expressive functions of civic buildings, railway stations and the other monuments to the supremacy of nineteenth-century industrial society. Architectural styles since the Second World War characterise vividly a society which no longer firmly believes in a hierarchical order, however hesitant it may be to make radical changes.

Changes of style express social norms rather than social practice. The open-plan for some new primary schools suggests an attitude to education that implies freedom and voluntary participation for the child. But apart from the fact that these schools are exceptions and the teachers capable of working in them a minority of the profession, the children are still likely to move from them into old authoritarian style secondary schools. They are hardly models of the society which the child is going to enter. Attendance at the new 'free' school is, moreover, still compulsory and sanctions on certain kinds of behaviour still exist. School, it seems, can be a nice place if the child is prepared to be a nice person, nice in the quite specific way that the décor suggests that he should be.

Social control was most obviously built into the nineteenth-century prison. Howard's belief in the possibilities of personal reform was the principle on which designs for the new prisons of the 1830s such as Pentonville and Barlinnie were conceived. Designed as total institutions they were intended to remake the prisoner. On entry he was ritually stripped of all the material and moral marks of his former identity, and thereafter could seek repentance and reformation.

The exhibition of social values through style is just as important at the domestic level. Georgian and Victorian houses were designed for an upper-class way of life dependent on the presence of servants. They can, with some difficulty, be divided up and converted for a less formal servantless way of life, but remain to some extent museum pieces, not expressive of the style of life of their inhabitants. The attempt to treat such houses as stage sets, perceptibly unrelated to the rest of the town, is often expressed through Preservation Societies which watch over their treatment by their owners. There is considerable middle-class enthusiasm for such discipline. A journalist, living in such a house, wrote recently demanding more control:

> We own our house and we paint it the colour we like—but I would not mind one bit if a decree went out that the whole street like those few 'protected' ones such as the Nash Terraces was to be painted in a uniform approved style or any edict which would indicate that someone was trying to regard the street as a décor for living and not just as the heterogeneous exteriors of separate properties.[20]

There seems to be inherent in the current civic preservation movement an appeal for a producer and stage-manager for the enactment of specific life styles, including perhaps the choice of people to play parts appropriate to the setting and thus subject to the kind of social control which is thought to attach to the past.

Places and settings are therefore not seen merely as neutral backcloths for social action. They are perceived in relation to the individual in such a way that action is at the same time contained by the setting and is the container of it. This is a point that Kenneth Burke makes about performance in the theatre: 'Stage-set contains the action ambiguously (as regards norms of action) and in the course of the play's development this ambiguity is converted into a corresponding articulacy ... a scene is to act as implicit is to explicit.'[21] This prescription is a little too flat. It does not predicate the dynamism of the relationship between action and setting of which we are aware both on and off the stage:

> The link between act and setting is so much part of ordinary experience that it is a familiar literary convention. In literature, scene is often used to symbolise action or provide metaphoric resonance; it may also become fused with the diplomatic device of appointing or contriving encounters in places where the total visible enclosure and furniture will 'accord with' the intention of the initiating actor. The decayed mansion of *Baby Doll* amplifies the basic tonalities in the conduct of its inhabitants;

[20] G. Tyndall, *The Guardian*, 16th April, 1969.
[21] K. Burke, *Grammar of Motives* (University of California Press, 1945), p. 7.

the elegant apartments of Noel Coward's comedies activate a
precise array of sophisticated responses. What we are concerned
with here is the more fundamental compatibility of act and
scene.[22]

In the novel this relationship has been effectively articulated by
Henry James. Kate Croy waits for her father in the 'vulgar little
room' where he lodges: 'To feel the street, to feel the room, to feel
the table cloth and the centre-piece and the lamp, gave her a small
salutary sense, at least, of neither shirking nor lying. This whole
vision was the worst thing yet—as including in particular the interview for which she had prepared herself; and for what had she come
but the worst?'[23]

Conversely, contrast between action and setting can be as emotive
as compatibility. Those who find themselves obliged to conduct a
scene in an unsuitable setting may be sensitive to the discrepancies
but can also manipulate them for effect. The visit of the Queen to a
council house where she takes a cup of tea in the small sitting-room
does not detract from but seems to enhance her status. Similarly
Menuhin's concert during the Edinburgh Festival in 1965 at a cinema
in a large and somewhat neglected housing-estate, was a dramatic
confrontation between an artist and a normally uninterested audience. In both cases participants are aware of the dramatic tension set
up by the contrast between the expected and the unexpected setting.

On the stage it is not possible to present such relationships so
directly. The substitution of one real object for another real object
means that setting in the theatre is only experienced at one remove.
The chair is real but it represents a more real chair in the real world.
Its juxtaposition with a canvas set emphasises this. The weakness of
the realist theatre has always lain in its imposition of a fixed setting
observed objectively by the audience, uncoloured by the dramatist's
intentions. The rhetorical conventions become inflexible. Glynne
Wickham saw the origins in this attitude to staging appearing as
early as 1520 with the conflict between 'the typically medieval con-
tentment with emblematic comment on the significance of the visual
world versus a new, scientific questing for the photographic image
. . . a search for the technical means to reproduce actuality as opposed to an almost exclusive concern with extracting the
significance behind outward appearances'.[24]

At about the same time Vitruvius's treatise on architecture had
been translated into Italian. This treatise contains a section on

[22] Tom Burns, 'The forms of conduct', *American Journal of Sociology*, lxiv (1958),
140-1.
[23] Henry James, *The Wings of the Dove*, p. 1.
[24] Wickham, *Early English Stages*, ii, pt 1, p. 209.

theatre construction which became very influential in Italy. It expresses a view of setting that is programmatic rather than symbolic or realistic:

> There are three kinds of scenes, one called the tragic, second the comic, third the satiric. Their decorations are different and unlike each other in scheme. Tragic scenes are delineated with columns, pediments, statues and other objects suited to kings; comic scenes exhibit private dwellings with balconies and views representing rows of windows after the manner of ordinary dwellings; satiric scenes are decorated with trees, caverns, mountains and other rustic objects delineated in landscape style.[25]

Although this view of scenery was not adopted by designers of the sixteenth century public theatre Inigo Jones learnt much from the Italian style and presented court masques in settings such as Vitruvius had described.

As a form of subdrama (or dramatisation of episodes) the masques required scenery that could evoke a certain mood (tragic, comic or satiric) rather than a type of action. As both actors and courtiers participated in the masque they were concerned with style rather than representation of events.

The pursuit of the means of reproducing realistic scenes on the stage continued until the end of the nineteenth century. Throughout this time the stages of the old sixteenth-century theatres were regarded as primitive. Lack of scenery and stage machinery was considered one of the disadvantages suffered by the actors of the period. It was not until 1895 that William Poel produced Shakespeare with a minimum of scenery in an attempt to stress the advantages of this method. But the 'modern' dramatists, such as Ibsen, Strindberg and Shaw were interested in developing realist techniques of staging and acting as skilfully as possible. Ibsen was, as we have seen, concerned to reproduce actuality, and tried to counteract the loss of a metaphoric dimension by using the whole scene symbolically and extending its resonance to scenes off-stage. Settings in his plays represent first, the social status and style of life of the characters, and secondly, their emotional relationships, the conditioning of their moods and actions. Significantly it is place as often as person that gives the name and implies the theme of the play. Thus The Doll's House is the overstuffed prison which cages Nora and from which she makes a physical and emotional escape. Rosmersholm is a place which produces, as Mrs Helseth says, children who 'have never been used to cry as long as folk can remember' and 'When they grow up they never laugh. Never laugh as long as they live.'

[25] P. Vitruvius, De Architectura, trans. M. Morgan (Cambridge University Press, 1914), p. 150.

In trying to make his plays realistic Ibsen was consciously concerned to emphasise authenticating conventions. He wanted his characters to seem to be leading real lives in the real world. He wished his function as presenter and the use of rhetorical conventions to be suppressed.

Strindberg consciously aimed at displaying his own subtle understanding of the technical ways in which the illusion of reality might be produced. In the Preface to *Miss Julie* (issued to the spectators when the play was performed in Paris at the Théâtre-Libre, in 1893) he wrote: 'As far as the scenery is concerned, I have borrowed from impressionistic painting its asymmetry, its quality of abruptness, and have thereby, in my opinion, strengthened the illusion. Because the whole room and all its contents are not shown, there is a chance to guess at things—that is, our imagination is stirred into complementing our vision.'[26] The modern anti-realist theatre has not abolished this development of convention so much as extended it. Beckett's later plays require a 'stirring of the imagination' to create an 'anti-world' beyond the merely visible and audible which is comparable only to the feats required of the viewers of Mondrian and his followers, who have reached their level of abstraction by a comparable route.

The appearance of producers as independent professionals towards the end of the nineteenth century also helped dramatists and actors to define the play-world in realistic terms, to fake reality with conviction. Watching the stage from the front and designing the movements and spatial relations of the actors, the producer was able to appreciate the spectator's view of the play in a way that the actor-manager as member of the cast could not. In many cases producers such as Meyerhold and Reinhardt took a choreographic or spectacular view of the scene and exploited the play for visual effects. But those like Antoine, Stanislavski and Vakhtangov, who wanted the play to approximate to real life, paid conscientious attention to every physical detail of scene and setting. The scene as a whole was always given an audience reference rather than an actor's reference. Tyrone Guthrie, in a lecture whose title nicely renders this conception, describes Reinhardt 'performing the one really creative function of the producer which is to be at rehearsal a highly receptive, highly concentrated, highly critical sounding-board for the performance, an audience of one'.[27] The stage is becoming virtually equated with the field vision of a fixed cinematograph camera, with stage action devised by a manager standing at the focal point.

[26] A. Strindberg, Preface to *Miss Julie* 1888, trans. E. Björkman in *Plays*, 1913, ii, p. 109.
[27] Tyrone Guthrie, 'An audience of one', transcript of talk delivered before the Royal Society of Arts, London, 1952, in *Directing the Play*, ed. T. Cole and H. K. Chinoy (Bobbs-Merrill, 1964), pp. 245–56.

By this time the audience had become fixed in front of a 'moving' stage. Theatres were actually built which physically allowed for this, but ordinarily the stage world was composed of a succession of sets and scenes, separated in time and space by blackouts, swift mechanical changes or small-scale 'movement' scenes, acted on a strip of forestage, in front of a 'drop'.

Realism in relation to stage production is, of course, an elusive term. It can retain its nineteenth-century meaning of apparent realism or naturalism, i.e. scenery looking as much like the natural and man made surroundings of the real world as possible.[28] Or it can come to mean that the set either sketchily or symbolically represents the setting while its difference from the real world is always kept in mind. This was the aim of Brecht's anti-illusionist technique.

In this century the drive towards greater dramatic realism of the first kind caused some dramatists to reject Ibsen's complex and articulated symbolism and to create an artificial distance between people and their surroundings. Shaw remained an exception. Although he avoided Ibsen's symbolism he composed settings in a sign language familiar to the spectators. His stage directions described the scene in detail and emphasised its reflective quality. The stage directions for *Candida* 'place' the characters definitively. They are excessively informative:

> Altogether the room is the room of a good housekeeper, vanquished as far as the table is concerned by an untidy man, but elsewhere mistress of the situation. The furniture in its ornamental aspect, betrays the style of the advertised 'drawing-room suite' of the pushing suburban furniture dealer; but there is nothing useless or pretentious in the room, money being too scarce in the house of an east-end parson to be wasted on snobbish trimmings.[29]

Such explicitness about detail has been taken over by the cinema where simulation of reality can be much more convincing. Realist dramatists have during this century concentrated more on the reproduction of authentic speech, manners and behaviour in different class milieux than on the verisimilitude of setting. They have often adopted the second method of representationalism.

It is still possible to attach a great deal of importance to the definition of location, even when realism is treated in this way, by distributing a few objects about the stage. Brecht, as producer-drama-

---

[28] Vakhtangov used real grass to cover the stage when he brought the Moscow Arts Theatre to perform in London. In such ways 'naturalistic' producers hoped to make the audience forget that they were really inside a theatre and that there was no real sky above the real grass.

[29] Bernard Shaw, *Candida*: stage directions for Scene 1.

tist, was determined to revive the imaginative possibilities of the
theatre by replacing the illusionist technique to which people had
become accustomed by a *partial* illusion that merely indicated the
relationship of the theatrical to the real world: 'The illusion created
by the theatre must be a partial one in order that it may always be
recognised as illusion. Reality, however complete, has to be altered
by being turned into art, so that it can be seen to be alterable and be
treated as such.'[30] With this aim he preferred to use bare stages on
which movable pieces of scenery, screens, encampments or houses
could be erected in full view of the audience—suggestions of place
which could stir the spectator's imagination to complete it and realise its associations. Thus, for his Berlin production of *Mother Courage*, three-dimensional structures like the parsonage and the
peasant's cottage were introduced. For them Brecht required properly built walls, but the structures remained incomplete, indicating
only as much substance as the action called for. Movable screens
were used to distinguish camp scenes from scenes on the road, and a
revolving stage to indicate travel. Finally the names of the various
countries were suspended above the stage in large black letters. In
this way Brecht expanded the repertoire of rhetorical conventions
concerned with space and time, recreating the improvised symbolic
style of the sixteenth-century theatre, making use of some of the
mechanical aids of the realist theatre such as the revolving stage and
sometimes indicating changes of time or of space by colour pro-
jections and lighting effects. In fact he used all means that came
to hand to evoke the historical occasion or social milieu associated
with the place represented, the battlefields of the Thirty Years'
War, in *Mother Courage*, the Chicago/Berlin of Arturo Ui's rise to
power, and the oppressive Florence of *Galileo*.

Non-realist and anti-realist dramatists who affront the conventional expectations of cause and effect as a framework for events
have also to divest their plays of any conventional social definitions
by invoking specifically theatrical conventions of space, setting and
time. In fact the origins of this type of drama lie in the hallucinatory
experiments of the 1890s—in the Ubu Roi plays, Alfred Jarry's experiments which were taken up later by Artaud and linked with the
surrealism of the 1920s.

The most extreme form of the 'placeless' theatre was that conceived by Artaud who founded the Théâtre Alfred Jarry, 'créé en
réaction contre le théâtre et pour rendre au théâtre cette liberté
totale qui existe dans la musique, la poésie ou la peinture et dont il a
été jusqu'ici curieusement sevré'.[31] This idea of completely abstract
drama, placeless, timeless and plotless, first reached England in the

---

[30] *Brecht on Theatre*, Willett, p. 219.
[31] A. Artaud, *Oeuvres Complètes* (Paris, Gallinard, 1961) ii, 33.

plays of Ionesco and Beckett, which were followed not only by imitations but also by plays of other European dramatists working in the same idiom. Ionesco is explicit about the abstract form of his plays. He is in fact trying to restore reality to the stage, this time the kind of inward reality that maintains us in a world of social unrealities. His dramatised self declares: 'For me the theatre is the projection on to the stage of the world within: it is in my dreams, my anguish, my dark desires, my inner contradictions that I reserve the right to find the stuff of my plays . . . It is these hidden desires, these dreams, these secret conflicts which are the source of all our actions and of the reality of history.'[32] In such drama the audience is expected to accept the convention that space and time are divorced from geography and chronology and can be handled by the dramatist with complete freedom.

Other contemporary dramatists, less explicit about their intentions, have avoided defining space or have deliberately suggested 'placelessness'. Beckett in *Waiting for Godot* uses a single tree to indicate a focus in limbo. Even Estragon and Vladimir in the second Act are uncertain whether they are in the same place that they were in in the first. At the same time the tree is an ambiguous symbol (possibly of the crucifixion) and also a convenient object on which to hang oneself. In either case it is an object around which their thoughts revolve. In all Beckett's plays place suggests a condition of the spirit rather than a physical area (and in this way is close to the three dimensions—heaven, world and hell—that provided the setting for the Miracle plays). The characters in *Play* speak in disembodied voices from beyond the grave; in *Happy Days* the sand-pile into which Winnie sinks suggests the state, not the location, of live burial. Place is irrelevant to Beckett's apparently existential view of the human condition. His characters do not belong to any recognisable milieu but are, as in Heidegger's phrase, 'thrown into being'.

Specific place is also rejected by Genet who is primarily concerned with the identities and relationships imposed by society. He constructs social milieux that belong to certain kinds of social order but not to any recognisable place—the brothel in *Le Balcon*, the house-prison of the servants in *Les Bonnes*, the theatrical courtroom in *Les Nègres*. Through the language of the characters fantasy worlds are created which are superimposed on the world represented on the stage. The networks of the world of social reality are replaced by contrived networks, with the artificiality of the connections of time, place, setting and characters emphasised at their expense.

The idea of 'placelessness' has been extended in the most recent experimental drama, in happenings, improvisations, the 'theatre of reality' and the 'theatre of environment', to the auditorium and the

[32] Ionesco, *Improvisation, Works* trans. Donald Watson (Calder, 1958-70) iii, 150.

theatre as a whole. The acting space in most avant-garde theatre is conventionally defined by the actors themselves who include members of the audience and any part of the theatre in the performance. Happenings usually have no coherent theme but many improvisions and semi-improvisations based on a script use the same technique of 'framing' the whole or parts of the theatre and 'putting on' members of the audience.[33] In such a theatre everyone is liable to be 'on-stage' so that there is no possibility of escape to a position from which the theatrical world can be viewed objectively as separate from, contrasting with, or even, complementary to the 'real' world, outside the theatre. Reality invades the theatre as theatricality invades the real world. There is in fact a blurring of the distinction between reality and illusion, a distinction on which the drama of the theatre has traditionally depended.

In ordinary life experience of environment (of what becomes setting in the theatre) is closely related to experience of other people. It is as Alfred Schutz has said 'knowledge of an intersubjective world'. 'It is not my environment nor your environment nor even the two added; it is an intersubjective world within reach of our common experience.'[34] It is this intersubjective world which is defined by those who are involved in a social situation and it is through their actions and understanding of each others' actions that this definition is made. An extra strain is put on their capacity to maintain a definition if a familiar setting with its accustomed physical props is removed. A Quaker meeting can be held anywhere, but if it is held in a member's sitting-room instead of the Meeting House everyone is aware of the effort required to maintain corporate meditation without being distracted by the domestic references of the furnishings of the room. It is however possible to do this so successfully that an outsider entering the silent room will know at once that he is in the presence of some kind of religious ceremony.

Definition of the situation has been described by W. I. Thomas as 'an interpretation or point of view, and eventually a policy or behaviour pattern'.[35] This concept is only valid in terms of interaction between people. It is the prerequisite of all social behaviour: 'When an individual appears before others his action will influence the definition of the situation which they come to have ... the others however passive their role may seem to be will themselves

[33] The similarity of this technique to that of the medieval 'Rounds' immediately comes to mind. But we have no record of the medieval audience's response. It seems probable that the modern spectator, in such a situation, is both more aware of his role and more anxious about what may be expected of him.
[34] Schutz, 'The dimensions of the social world', in Collected Papers ii, 31.
[35] W. I. Thomas, Primitive Behavior (McGraw-Hill, 1937), p. 8.

passively project a definition of the situation by virtue of their response to the individual and by virtue of any lines they initiate to him.'[36]

One of the most elaborate literary presentations of definition of situation is found in *Don Quixote*. In the first part of the book the knight by his complete faith in his own interpretation of the world creates a world of chivalry in which not only is he a knight but the inn is a castle, the innkeeper a castellan and the whores at the inn door beautiful ladies of the castle. Not even the most contrary or cussed behaviour of those who seem to act the parts he has given them, can disabuse him of his rightness. In the second part of the book, however, the history of his early adventures has already been recounted in a book, which most of those whom the knight encounters have read. They are therefore prepared to enter into his pretences and to help him to maintain the world of illusion. It is at this stage that Don Quixote himself implies a lack of true faith in his own experience of reality and a realisation of the collusion that is needed to maintain it. After the journey in Clavileño, contrived by the Duke and Duchess, Sancho presumes to overreach his master in the description of his adventure. Don Quixote restores the balance by whispering to him: 'Sancho, if you want me to believe what you saw in the sky, I wish you to accept my account of what I saw in the cave of Montesinos. I say no more.'[37]

On formal occasions the importance of a person or of the occasion was often defined simply by a moment's preparatory silence or by a physical movement such as standing up or to attention. As behaviour becomes less formal such usages are often regarded as meaningless and allowed to lapse. People then find themselves faced with problems of definition both of themselves and of others which they cannot always easily resolve. In informal circles people often find it difficult to effect introductions. In the theatre a similar process from formality to informality has taken place. The theatre now dispenses with the medieval presenter and prologue and epilogue which defined for the audience the boundaries of illusion. This makes heavy demands on the actors' expressiveness and on the audience's understanding of the conventions that are being used. At a performance of Genet's *Les Bonnes* some spectators apparently failed to understand the nature of the double impersonation that was taking place at the beginning of the play in the scene between Solange and Claire. When they realised that the maids were acting out their relationship with their mistress they felt that the dramatist had deliberately deceived them. Yet the failure of definition must have been the responsibility just as much of themselves and of the actors, otherwise the whole

[36] Goffman, *Presentation of Self*, pp. 6, 9.
[37] Cervantes, *Don Quixote* trans. Cohen, p. 726.

audience would have missed the point. In modern plays obscurity often derives from a refusal to define, and a misapprehension of the audience's sophistication.

On this obscurity is founded the kind of bewilderment which has so often been the first response to twentieth-century innovations in the theatre, but also, more deeply, the fear of estrangement from the common definition of the world and of one's place in it, and the onset of awareness of the complete artificiality of the phenomenal world of social life we take as real life, which is variously interpreted as *anomie* and *angst*. The anxiety of the individual confronted with a situation from which the props of accepted convention have been removed, and which remains obstinately undefinable according to the rules he knows can, of course, be subdued. The audience can extend the dimension of the interaction between itself and the stage by framing it—i.e. invoking a wider frame of reference and detaching itself from involvement by treating the stage action as pretentious, nonsensical, a confidence trick. The alternative is acceptance —the anxiety can attach to the possibility of oneself living in a solipsist world—a possibility to which modern audiences have to some extent been exposed for some decades by Kafka and the varieties of Kafka-like literature. *The Trial* and *The Castle* concern the fruitless search of K, the central figure, for some common ground he can share with other characters, or with his own recollected past about his situation or with the meaning for others of the actions in which he is himself involved.

Theatrical convention, until recently, has operated in terms of recognisable definitions of situations which are constantly redefined as new information is revealed in action and speech. The frame is constantly broken and re-established in more comprehensive terms, which bring new comprehension to what went before and renew interest in the coming sequence of action. But both the frames and the particular breakings of frame into new definitions are composed so as to control the audience's response (and to forestall counteraction). The purpose of dramatist and actors is to control the audience's interpretation and judgment. This is implemented through sequential selection not only of incident and characters but also of setting. The action is framed by relevances of setting which have to suggest the intersubjective world of the characters involved in the action. These relevances are not necessarily visible or audible but are constantly 'brought to mind'. Thus Macbeth himself is framed by a battlefield setting. Administration of his household, and later of his kingdom is a remote aspect of his life. It is as a warrior that he is presented and motivated. It is of course possible to impose a different frame. A production, incorporating Gordon Craig's suggested interpretation stressed, rather than the man of action, the man under a spell moving in a world of supernatural rather than natural forces.[38]

Contrivance of frame implies contrivance of relationships to this frame and within the frame. Relevances and conditions taken for granted in ordinary life must be emphasised or subdued.

Thus in the theatre the intersubjective world has to be faked. What the audience sees is a generalised sketch of a particular environment in which all objects seem at first sight to have the same weight and value for each of the actors involved in the scene. In fact the components of the setting are inevitably adjusted to give significance to the main characters and to emphasise the relevance of action to plot. Although the film camera can suggest the larger setting, the indifferent irrelevant world, in which context the action of the story takes place, this is difficult in the theatre. In the theatre the only alternative to relevant setting is ambiguously defined setting or absence of setting. Both are used in the contemporary theatre. In happenings, and varieties of improvisation, random objects are often strewn about the stage. These cannot be regarded as irrelevant as they seem to have a symbolic relationship to the action. They suggest, as the action does, absurdity, accident and an assault on the accepted ordering of the world. Complete absence of scenery (without the few emblems or signs used in the Elizabethan theatre and now often used at Stratford Memorial Theatre for plays of the same period) also suggests the isolation of the individual or the non-physical level on which a drama such as *Waiting for Godot* or *Huis Clos* is to be perceived.

In the modern theatre there are in fact three main modes of setting: (1) the representational, for realistic or spectacular plays, e.g. *The Royal Hunt of the Sun* at the National Theatre; (2) the semiological, where the audience is expected to make much of little, to develop an imaginative picture from a few signs, e.g. productions of Brecht by the Berliner Ensemble; and (3) the symbolic, e.g. Seneca's *Oedipus* at the National Theatre. Sometimes a play can use something from all three with a certain ambiguity. As I suggested earlier, the tree in *Waiting for Godot* can be at the same time an indication of an outdoor place, a suitable realistic setting for the tramps, a sign of desolation as a spiritual condition, and a symbol of the crucifixion, suggesting to Estragon a place to hang himself.

Most plays can be treated by the producer in any of these three ways. *Hamlet* has been set realistically, semiologically in the Stratford style (with bare stage and emblematic setting) and even by Charles Marowitz, 'absurdly' with the inevitable ambiguous sym-

[38] Performance of *Macbeth* by Keele University Theatre, Edinburgh 1968, based on G. H. Craig's ideas for a production of *Macbeth* in *On the Art of the Theatre* (London, 1911) pp. 269–76.

bolism of the genre. But performances, of the most recent avant-garde movement, which have developed from happenings to plays such as *Paradise Now* and *Frankenstein* can only be produced in the symbolic mode. Improvisation contrives action, setting and theme in the same mode and creates the setting as much as the characters. This form of drama makes a statement which can hardly be analysed in terms of form and content.

This development seems to be related to the present emphasis on theatricality in ordinary life. The planned demonstration is something very different from the riot even if riot should emerge from it. The demonstration itself (the word seems to have become current in this sense in the nineteenth century; 'a public manifestation of feeling; often taking the form of a procession or mass-meeting'[39]) is not a performance of a fictional action but a presentation of real feelings and opinions. Assembling supporters *en masse* to demonstrate the weight of public opinion in visible, numerical form, both to the participants themselves, to the non-participating public, and to the relevant 'powers that be' is a well-defined, traditional convention of political action. Certain theatrical forms—burning effigies, shouted slogans and songs—were always present. But in recent years the demonstration has come to develop new styles. In September 1970 more than 600 members of the electricians' and plumbers' unions marched through Glasgow in protest against the 'disciplining' of five of their fellows. But they wore masks and carried two black coffins which they placed on the doorsteps of the offices of the Company. Earlier the CND committee had decided to replace the Aldermaston march by an outdoor theatrical performance which they felt would make a bigger public impact. Later in the same year council workers on strike at Newham borrowed costumes from the theatre at Stratford East for a protest march led by the theatre's producer, Joan Littlewood.

A demonstration is what it says it is—a show, a gesture. Gestures may be threatening, but threats may also be empty, or treated as such. The containment of demonstrations by the police is one way in which the 'powers that be' can empty the gesture of real meaning. Before there were any police the demonstration had taken the rather more formidable character of riot. The riot was traditionally the one means of political action open to the politically impotent; it has reappeared as a way of restoring meaning to demonstrations. Alternatives are assassination, secret acts of violence, sit-ins, hi-jacking, kidnapping and the like, all of which have also been increasingly used in recent years. Action, that is, has been brought back into public places which have been emptied of ordinary everyday life. And it is public action which can also capture the attention of enor-

[39] *Shorter Oxford English Dictionary.*

mous television audiences. It is this which gives them the peculiar theatrical quality which has been attached to them, a quality which is heightened by television and newspaper reporters' interest in the 'production' of dramatic news.[40] Demonstrators and political activists in Northern Ireland, Uruguay, the United States and the Middle East, and in universities everywhere during the past few years, have in a peculiar form of collusion with the controllers and producers of news and information, developed a whole repertoire of theatrical public gestures as a form of political action. There seems to be a sense in which, in society at large, theatrical modes of behaviour are always displacing direct instrumental action within the settled power structure. Political action in contemporary society, where any reality which attached to democratic pluralism is fading, or where it has never been contemplated, has otherwise become polarised between the general election and international or civil war.

The one occasion on which real action and theatricality were combined seems to have occurred in the 1968 May events in Paris. Paul Béaud analysing the relationship between art and life in this critical period described 'a new theatre' that has 'scarcely any points in common with the old: it need be no more, for example, than miming a scene in the street (a demonstrator chased by the police, etc.) parodying a sequence from the television news, or feigning a political argument" in order to get the passers-by to join in, and then moving on to another place.[41] He sees this not as a freak development but as 'the most spectacular expression of the juncture between the cultural and the political, of the merging of art and action',[42] that has been characteristic of trends in France, and some other Western countries, in the last forty years.

This theatricalisation of public life entails a heightened awareness and manipulation of frames and settings in which action is staged. Demonstrations that take the form of marches derive a symbolic power from the setting of long roads and city streets through which they pass.[43] The diversion or control of traffic is an instance of

[40] See J. D. Halloran, *Demonstrations and Communication* (Penguin Books, 1970), for a detailed account of the way in which the Grosvenor Square demonstration of 1968 was precomposed for presentation in newspapers and television by reporters and broadcasters who had apparently decided beforehand on the news angle appropriate to the occasion, and selected the events which were eventually reported in terms of a previously agreed definition of the situation.

[41] P. Béaud in A. Willener, *The Action-Image of Society*, trans. A. M. S. Smith (Tavistock, 1970), p. 273.

[42] *Ibid*, p. 276.

[43] G. Steiner refers to this as a common perception: 'Scene and structural environment, experienced as dramatic setting, are drawing close. Politics (notably violence) as agreed ritual, action in the streets modulating into acting, the concrete or the derelict landscape as deliberate back-drop—these are notions that occur readily as one thinks about the failure of mimetic and participatory forms': 'The future of the book', *The Times Literary Supplement*, 2nd October, 1970.

dramatic production. The decoration of the walls of buildings with slogans and the use of the street as a place to sit are other ways of converting a place into a setting for a specific occasion. Innumerable books of photographs of the May events in Paris taking place against slogan-marked walls have been produced, illustrating the visual importance of the setting.

The theatrical metaphor was most widely used in literature during the sixteenth century and early seventeenth, at a time of intense public living when royal and civic ceremonial was constantly visible in the towns. The withdrawal into private life, characteristic of bourgeois capitalist society, now seems to be challenged by a rediscovery of theatricality as a mode of acting out ordinary life. The manipulation of settings and frames is an aspect of this conscious use of rhetoric

Conventions of time are of course inseparable from conventions of space in the theatre as in the real world. Travelling in limitless space the conception of time also has to be adjusted. Even in painting, the temporal dimension is important and has to be relevant to the spatial dimension. As Gombrich says, we 'scan' a picture and could not do so without retinal persistence; one remembers what has passed and has expectations about what is to come.[44] In looking at the paintings in the Sistine Chapel one has a sense of events occurring in time although it is the extended time, of which we are not 'sensibly' aware, from the creation to Judgment Day. It is God's time and differs from the human time of which one is aware in Breughel's Seasons. This again differs from the caught and fleeting moments of Impressionist painting—the feeling is projected that Degas's dancers and even Cézanne's apples only look as they do in the pictures for a moment and will never look like that again.

In literature, especially in the novel, the sense of time is a more essential part of the structure. Frank Kermode calls books 'fictive models of the temporal world'.[45] Yet the book can be read quickly and the discriminations of time depend on considerable concentration by the reader. In the theatre time as part of the structure of the play becomes much more prominent. The audience knows that the play is going to last two to three hours, or in the Japanese or Indian theatre many more. Within these confines the dramatist has first to project the time-rules that will govern the events and make them coherent, secondly to use time to create suspense, emphasise certain events and produce the climax or climaxes that are essential to even the least eventful drama.

[44] E. H. Gombrich, quoted in F. Kermode, *The Sense of an Ending* (Oxford University Press, 1967), pp. 53–4.
[45] Kermode, *The Sense of an Ending*, p. 54.

The first task, creating a conventional temporal framework to support the play, has never caused much difficulty. Rules established in the seventeenth-century French theatre on the basis of an arbitrary interpretation of Aristotle erected a twenty-four hour boundary which in spite of its restriction relieved the dramatist of the necessity of working out his own time scheme, although these rules were not always strictly followed. The disregard of this rule in the English theatre, though criticised by those critics and writers who upheld the classical tradition, does not seem to have worried audiences, who, in the sixteenth century, knew little of the conventions of classical drama. Medieval religious drama had prepared the ground by its simultaneous presentation of cosmic space and time and temporal earthly events. In the later secular theatre, this freedom was exploited to the utmost in the translation of characters and action from one space to another, and to traverse time between scenes. Time, indeed, is a pretty elastic commodity in Elizabethan drama. Such matters as the 'double time' in Othello and the speed of Hamlet's return to Denmark seem to have passed the notice of all but critics of the last generation or two. Equally, the presentation of simultaneous action in successive scenes by such devices as the dumb show or conjuring (in *The White Devil*[46]) seems as far as we know to have troubled nobody at the time. Shakespeare used the freer time conventions to speed up or slow down stage action in terms of the development of the play or, indeed, the ageing of characters. The 'real' time of *Macbeth*—the interval between the murder of Duncan and of Macduff's family, for instance, is of little importance beside Macbeth's own time scale—the headlong plunge into deeper and deeper guilt. When he speaks of his age: 'My way of life / Is fall'n into the sere, the yellow leaf', the words carry the sense of moral degeneration into that of time actually passing.

This symbolic use of time is in keeping with the symbolic use of space—the 'houses' representing distant places on different sides of the stage. Both space and time gained expressiveness from their flexibility and inconsistency.

In the same way the movement towards realism in theatre construction, styles of acting and dramatic construction, affected the conventions of time. Although it was not considered necessary to return to Aristotle's rule, the passage of time in the plays of Ibsen, Chekhov and Strindberg was made to seem as plausible as possible. Ibsen avoided the time span required for a long series of events by concentrating the fateful events of most of his plays in the past. The

---

[46] In *The White Devil* a conjuror exhibits to Brachiano the murders of Isabella and Camillo which are later reported. These dumb-shows, unlike earlier ones which were either prophetic or allegorical, have here become necessary parts of the action. At the same time they retain an air of unreality.

revelations, deliberate or accidental, of this past then serve to activate the events of the play in the present. Beate's death in *Rosmersholm*, Mr Aveling's dissipations in *Ghosts* and John Gabriel Borkman's crime and imprisonment, dragging many other events in their train, dominate the action of the plays. Strindberg, less obtrusively, also uses recall and memory of the past in this temporal network sense, not so much for its events as for the mould in which it has already cast the characters. Edgar and Alice in *The Dance of Death* are locked in a battle that began long ago, a battle whose development is dictated by that past. Time in the plays of both these dramatists simulates time in real life but depends on a convention that action in the present has less freedom and power of development than we normally assume that it has.

In contrast to Ibsen and Strindberg, Chekhov lingered over the present. His emphasis is on duration and its accompanying boredom in the long discursive days. The past is very important, but not as a separate era, rather as a part of the present and of a future which can hardly be very different. In his plays space and time belong noticeably to the same dimension. The cherry orchard which once bore fruit and is now barren, the theatre in the garden (in *The Seagull*) left to rot, these are symbolic in a way that we all recognise as familiar. They are symbols of nostalgia and represent time passing just as our childhood homes, long forgotten, do in the real world.

The twentieth-century rejection of realism affected time conventions along with place conventions. Placelessness is accompanied by timelessness in both the earlier anti-realist plays of Ionesco and Beckett and the later, contemporary avant-garde theatre. Ionesco and Beckett made this more explicit. Beckett's repetitiveness—in *Play* and in *Godot* where Estragon and Vladimir are in doubt about events of the immediate past (the first half of the play) was a way of demonstrating the artificiality of all time conventions. Ionesco is equally drastic though more fantastic in his handling of the past which in *Victims of Duty* can be dredged up with all its mud into the present.

The new theatre of improvisation and semi-improvisation rests not so much on timelessness as on the convention that action is being created instant by instant, and hence that traditional dramatic conventions of time can be disregarded. This means that the actors must be sensitive to 'timing' but not necessarily to any structural concept of the time within which the action takes place. An improvisation is ideally open-ended. It should be able to start and end at any moment, when the actors feel that they have either accomplished something or run out of ideas. In practice, of course, the duration of the action is usually controlled by the audience. In the absence of controlled, composed, definitions and breaking of frames by playwright and stage performers, interaction between players and audience has, as yet, no framework of convention which can sustain the occasion, except in the very prescribed circumstances of certain milieux, in which mutual understanding has been built up over a period.

'Timing' is, however, a rhetorical convention exploited in all drama in such ways that the audience will be able to assess the relative significance of events and characters according to the drama-tist's and actors' intentions. Although timing in Shakespeare's plays has to be interpreted, guessed at or invented to a large extent by the producer, later dramatists from Shaw to Beckett and Pinter have been careful to specify occurrence and often duration of pauses. Pinter's pauses have been rightly recognised as being as important as speech. The last scene of *The Caretaker* is structured by the pauses which represent both the negative attitude of Aston and the isolation of Davies, and finally fill the ending with a 'long silence'.

In improvisations 'timing' is even more essential as a means not only of ensuring that the audience, deprived of the traditional dra-matic logic of developmental action, understands situations and events as they occur, but also of relating action to the lives of spec-tators and actors. For the most part improvised theatre rejects the-atrical time and accepts the time which is real for the audience. The 'La Mama' group and the Living Theatre are often concerned with the political events in the extra-theatrical world, and must pretend to adopt the same time scale as the audience. The fabricated nature of this time scale is thus exposed and 'timing' revealed as a significant feature of communication both inside and outside the theatre.[47]

[47] When, however, the audiences cannot play their part and respond to the actors' directions they are often subdued or silenced. Dialogues do not always 'come off' in the theatre any more than they do in the outside world. The main problem for the improvised, non-literary theatre lies in its complete freedom. In *The Theater of Mixed Means* Richard Kostelanetz suggests that in such drama 'the theatrical situation reverts to its barest essentials, time and space; and the creator's primary problem becomes animating the space and time he allots himself'. But without 'plot, development, characterisation and dramatic explicitness' what measure or meaning can be given to space and time? If they are not to become meaningless they must be equated with the conventional realities of the ordinary world so that we are constantly reminded that we are in a theatre or hall (not in Athens) for a space of time between other appointments (not for a passage of years), occupied only in 'filling the space' and 'passing the time'—in the last resort, in action which defines itself only too clearly as inconsequential, and a matter of indifference for both players and audience.

7

Authenticating conventions

We can begin with the problem posed by Georg Simmel in his incomplete and posthumously published essay on theatre as an artistic form:

> While every other form of art transcends real life and creates an object which is beyond life, the actor has to do the opposite. The material basis is already fashioned into a work of art, and it becomes the actor's task to turn this purely idealised, mental, drama back into some realistic statement. The text of the play already exists as a complete work of art. Does the actor now elevate this to a higher level of art? Or, if this does not make sense, does he, by manifesting it as a living embodiment, reconvert it into convincing reality? [But if so, why do we ask from his acting an impression of the work of art itself rather than of material reality?] It is out of this paradox that the philosophical problem of theatrical acting must be resolved.
>
> The character as it is in the text is never, so to speak, a complete person as perceived by the senses, but a complex of those qualities of a man that can be captured by words. The playwright cannot render voice, tone, quickening or slowing of speech, nor the gestures, nor the unique character of the living, breathing totality of a person. Instead, he has delineated the mentality, the apparent behaviour and the destiny of this personal totality in the single dimension of the bare words of the text. And this text of the drama is itself perceived as a creation in its own right; so far as the total action of a performance is concerned, it stands as a symbol, from which that action cannot be worked out by some logical routine. Similarly, the actor translates this one-dimensional end product into visible, three-dimensional reality.'[1]

Simmel, in this passage, is concerned with the individual

[1] G. Simmel, 'Zur Philosophie des Schauspielers' in *Das Individuelle Gesetz* (Suhrkamp, 1968), pp. 75–6 (by translation, Tom Burns).

actor—inevitably, perhaps, in the circumstances of nineteenth-century theatre, when performances had been dominated, indeed directed, by the leading actor. But for us the reference is more clearly applicable to the whole performance of a play as a translation of the 'one-dimensional end product' (the text) into the 'visible, three-dimensional reality' of actual performance.

This, again, is a matter of composition, of a conscious assembling of objects, modes of conduct, styles of speech and demeanour which are both recognisable and apt for action, the character parts, the relationships, and the rhetorical conventions established for the mode of interaction between stage and audience. Aptness—'convincingness'—is always specific to the rhetorical definition of the situation. A recently published interview with a producer of the National Theatre gives some indications of the way in which this quality of convincingness is generated (and of how it relates to the rhetoric of the presentation):

> *One does think back on National Theatre productions as more tatty-wigged and scruffy-trousered than the usually immaculately dressed Restoration set.*
>
> You remember Brecht was a big influence, and we hadn't ever really seen that sort of thing. The idea of what is called 'breaking down' of costumes to make them look worn and used became very commonly accepted. At the time I did *The Recruiting Officer* the thought of having mud on Plume's clothes was considered really revolutionary. I'm not sure now that it doesn't look a little phoney—it's something to do with defining the theatricality of these plays that is very important ...
>
> *What were you looking for in the design for* The Recruiting Officer?
>
> Oh I just took Allio to Amersham, which was the nearest Queen Anne main street that I knew, and said, that's what I think an eighteenth-century main street would look like. And he drew Amersham and put the main street on the stage ...
>
> *At the same time as you're plotting loosely, are you beginning to give the actors some sense of the period—of its social relationships particularly?*
>
> I don't think anyone cares a fuck about whether they bow in the right manner or any of those 'quaint' period things. But there are two problems to solve. One is class attitudes, which have changed, and which actors often find difficult to identify: they use over-simplifications of working-class attitudes—and of attitudes to the working class. For example, take the way the

servants are treated: they are called 'fellow' whereas one's equal
would be a 'gentleman'. Actors *always* get that wrong, saying
'fellow' in the modern colloquial sense, to describe an equal
rather than an inferior. The other thing is that there are certain
things which women do now which they couldn't do
then—though curiously enough this wasn't such a difficulty in
The Recruiting Officer because Silvia is such an outspoken and
free person. But even in that play there are certain things which
are just horrific to us now, like when Balance hears that his son
has died and says 'I was pleased with the death of my father,
because he left me an estate, and now I'm punished with the loss
of an heir to inherit mine'. In all the writings of that period until
the family became a cult, there were no sentimental relationships between sons and fathers. All that a father meant to a son
was that he inherited his property, and the sooner he died the
better.[2]

This Humpty-Dumpty authoritativeness of the ascription of meanings to social class and to personal relationships (and the total neglect
of the connotations of satire in Farquhar and his contemporaries)
indicates clearly enough the element of composition in the provisions
for authenticity in the behaviour of the character players towards
each other. What is also clear is that the producer's skill lies in
negotiating his way towards a coherent subset of understandings.
The audience is forced towards a categorisation of objects, utterances and actions in a seemingly definitive way—a way which is
definitive (authentic) for the purpose in hand. Beginning with the
preliminary definition of a mock-up of Queen Anne architectural
styles (the main street of Amersham!), intonations in the mode of
address adopted towards servants as against equals, clothes that look
used, and a multitude of other visual and verbal cues, the audience is
drawn into acceptance of a reciprocally shared experience, unique in
time and place.

In ordinary life the particular code of communication established
for a specific occasion will be 'negotiated' by the adoption of a
specific ordering of language ('parole' in Saussure's term) drawn from
a body of language ('langue') assumed as common to the participants.[3] But this specific ordering is identified by a contextual set

---

[2] Interview with William Gaskill 'Finding a style for Farquhar', *Theatre Quarterly*, i
(1971), 16, 18.
[3] 'Langue' (language) and 'parole' (speech). The distinction which Saussure insisted upon relates to the notion of *language* as a totality of grammatical rules and
vocabulary as 'the norm of all other manifestations of speech', whereas speech is
the 'executive side' concerned with actual utterances by individual speakers.
Speaking does, of course, follow rules of grammar, but these make up the 'grammatical system that has a potential existence in each mind, or, more specifically, in
the minds of a group of individuals': F. de Saussure, *Course in General Linguistics*
(posthumously composed from lecture notes of courses given 1906–11), trans. by
W. Baskin (McGraw-Hill paperback edn. 1966), pp. 9 and 13.

of coded meanings, also assumed to be common knowledge, which attach to setting, intonation and gestures. Further, the specificity of understandings is something developed in the sequence of interaction itself, so that previous remarks can be 'filled in' as to their appropriate significance by later, consequential, interchanges.

As Cicourel puts it, this principle of 'reciprocity of perspectives' in ordinary life

> means assuming (i) that each would have the same experience if they were to change places, and (ii) that until further notice they can disregard any differences that might arise from their respective personal ways of assigning meanings to objects and events. Thus the participants assume they employ a standardised native orientation to the immediate scene; they are both receiving the same kinds of information, recognising the same kind of features that are presumed to carry the same 'obvious' and subtle meanings for both ... A consequence of the reciprocity of perspectives principle is that members will assume, and assume others will assume it of them, that their descriptive accounts of utterances will be intelligible and recognisable features of an environment they know in common and take for granted as 'the same' for all practical purposes ...
>
> The reciprocity principle instructs [sic] the actor [i.e. person involved in social interaction] to impose an idealised interchangeability of standpoints during interaction and follow a similar procedure for assigning meaning or relevance, but when discrepancies or ambiguities appear, speakers and hearers will attempt to normalise the presumed discrepancies (similar to the reduction of dissonance or incongruity as in Festinger[4]; Brown[5]). This sociological cognitive principle differs from psychological notions in the 'known in common and taken for granted assumption' members assume about appearances: that everyday appearances are essentially the 'same' for 'everyone'. The sociological conception presumes that this common sense principle provides each member with instructions for unwittingly (and sometimes deliberately) evaluating and striving for a reciprocally assumed normal firm judgment of his utterances and perception. The member's unwitting acquisition and use of these principles provide a common and standardized system of implicit signals and coding rules. Without such principles everyday interaction would be impossible, for nothing could pass as 'known' or 'obvious' and all dialogue would become an infinite regress of doubts'[6] (see above, pp. 28–30).

[4] L. Festinger, *A Theory of Cognitive Dissonance* (Row, Peterson, 1957).
[5] R. Brown, *Social Psychology* (Free Press, 1965).
[6] A. V. Cicourel, 'Generative semantics and the structure of social interaction' in *Proceedings of the Conference on Sociolinguistics*, 1969 (Luigi Sturzo Institute, Rome, 1970).

Doubting does occur, of course, and in the theatre, no less than in ordinary social activity, the reciprocity principle enunciated by Cicourel presumes that ambiguities or half-understood meanings will be clarified later, as well as current utterances clarified by previous remarks or actions.[7] The theatre provides a playground in which these processes can be demonstrated, illustrated, and extended beyond the common boundaries of our everyday social reality.

Obviously, all this goes on in the context, or on the basis, of widely diffused typified experience and knowledge of typical situations:

> Only a small fraction of man's stock of knowledge at hand originates in his own individual experience. The greater part of his knowledge is *socially derived*, handed down to him by his parents and teachers as his social heritage. It consists of a set of systems of relevant typifications, of typical solutions for typical practical and theoretical problems, of typical precepts for typical behaviour.[8]

This we can take as elementary and common knowledge, as we can also the consequent 'structuring' of this stock of knowledge, at any given moment, into what William James called 'knowledge about', meaning firsthand, clear, competent knowledge and understanding, and the much larger stock of 'knowledge of acquaintance' which is known about, or believed in, as matter of fact and left unquestioned—like the technological 'how' of television, or the rules governing educational or occupational success and failure, or the layman's knowledge of economic policies, medical practice, or 'the news'.

But the structure of knowledge has spatial and temporal dimensions: the actual here and now present which I perceive and can act on in this room, in this building, directly and immediately and to which, if I leave it (by telephoning somebody, walking away from it, switching on the television set, or 'losing myself' in thought), I can return. But this physically and mentally actual world, and the business of absenting myself in the ways I have mentioned, are what they are, and constitute a presently relevant system, because of the nature of the world itself on the one hand and on the other of my own biography to this moment, a biography which, however susceptible to chance and circumstance I know it to be, yet displays a discernible causal path which possesses its own consistency of motive, design and plan which I have in some cases framed myself, in some cases submitted to. Thus, in so far as I can consider myself an ordinary and normal person, both the actually present world, my movements away from it, my ability to return to it, and my stocks of 'knowledge about' and 'knowledge of acquaint-

[7] *Ibid.*
[8] Schütz, 'Symbol, reality and society' in *Collected Papers*, i, 348.

ance' all have a composite quality of relevance to me and to my future. What is more, relevance can be extended or amended in accordance with what I see as my interests and needs; beyond the horizon of what is the already possessed relevant world, there are experiences, information and problems for solution or jobs to be done which will extend that world in what Gurwitsch and Schütz[9] call a 'relevant' or 'theoretically relevant' way. But this extension is anything but a random exploration; since what is being added to is not a hoard of individual bits of knowledge but typifications, of which acts and percepts are instances. An act of recognition, of placing in context, of, in short, interpretation, has to occur which will make the novelty 'more or less' akin to what we knew before. So it is that the business of living involves what Grathoff calls an 'iterative procedure' of constituting types. 'Every construction of type and every typification goes before the background of and in intimate relation to already acquired types and presedimented typical knowledge of typical situations. But iteration implies still more. One has to avoid the misleading conception that a stock of typified experiences is something like the "memory" of a computer. Every sedimented experience refers to a typical solution of a typified problem lived through by the individual. This lived experience is still "living" in the sense of its potentially being "reactivated" in the process of further advancement of knowledge. But this implies an ongoing reconstruction (often in terms of language) of typical contexts encompassing typified social objects.

'The iterative constitution of types and social objects implies that every type carries', as Schütz has called it, 'an *index* referring the type to its constitutive context.'[10] The indicativeness of typical social forms and by which they are built into the structure of our personal social world, therefore, is a function of the circumstances in which the need arose to interpret novelty by typifying it, and so extend our existing horizon in a relevant way.

There is nothing particularly difficult or unfamiliar about all this; it is, professedly, an extension or an exploration of ordinary commonsense knowledge of the world, though many of the writers who have involved themselves in the exploration have made pretty heavy weather of the odd cross-currents of philosophy from Peirce and James, from Brentano and Husserl, and from Wittgenstein and Austin. The first, and minor point of this brief excursus is to establish that the 'rules of the game' which we follow in orienting ourselves to situations, in informing ourselves of what is going on, are, of course,

[9] A. Gurwitsch, *The Field of Consciousness* (Duquesne University Press, 1964); Schütz, 'Some structure of the life world', in *Collected Papers*, iii, 116–32.
[10] R. H. Grathoff, *The Structure of Social Inconsistencies* (The Hague, Nijhoff, 1970), p. 54.

acknowledged and followed by playwright, producer and actors in an 'as if' manner on the stage, but in such a way as to make what is made to happen by them clear to a third party. The audience has to be drawn along into the same extensions of their assumed typifications as have been composed for the players of the play.

But the major point is that there is a clear inconsistency between the purview of the audience, the complex of 'relevant typifications' assumed available to it, and the proffered extension of its assumed thematic field by the action and utterances occurring on stage. There is, at first sight (when the curtain rises) an unbridgeable gap between the 'beyond the horizon', non-indicative action going on up there and the structured typifications of our world as members of an audience.

We are frequently beset by inconsistencies in real life, from childhood on. No parent can deal adequately with his children's first encounter with hostility from the social world or with damage from the natural world, with their first personal experience of the actuality of death, or with their first acquaintanceship with their own inadequacies. Indeed, the process of dying, and clearly perceptible physical or mental deformity, present ordinary people in everyday life with impossible gaps of relevancy. What Grathoff calls 'permanent gaps' occur in 'dramatic situations which resist strongly any typification in lived-through experience.[11]

This is not merely a matter of 'shutting our eyes' to reality (though one does find youngsters, and older people, literally doing this on occasion, even in the theatre or cinema). Grathoff ingeniously explains the customary procedure by drawing on Peirce's account of 'abductive' or 'retroductive' reasoning 'i.e. reasoning from consequent to antecedent', the logical structure of which Peirce illustrates by this kind of instance: 'A certain man had the Asiatic cholera. He was in a state of collapse, livid, quite cold, and without perceptible pulse. He was bled copiously. During the process he came out of collapse, and the next morning he was well enough to be about. Therefore, bleeding tends to cure the cholera.'[12]

Peirce argues that this is an act of insight which, although we know now in this particular case it is fallacious, is common to all kinds of reasoning processes. Explanation follows a backward path from consequence to event. In the case of unimportant happenings or for the uninformed man in the street, explanation may stop here; it is adequate. For the expert, the medical scientist, living before the causal sequence which may lead to cholera was known, this phase of abductive reasoning would form a first step, leading in turn to the

---

[11] Grathoff, *op. cit.* p. 57, see also p. 131
[12] C. S. Peirce, *Collected Papers* (Harvard University Press, 1965), v, 272, quoted by Grathoff.

framing of a hypothesis, which could be tested in other cases, and according to the ordinary rules of scientific procedure. The process has been described dozens of times, although Peirce's emphasis on the leading place occupied by abductive reasoning, which formed the central feature of his pragmatism, has not been followed up until recently.[13]

The ordinary processes of abductive reasoning, of 'commonsense' explanation, tie the novel experience or novel social action into the proximate set of typifications. When unbridgeable gaps or inconsistencies arise, as they frequently do, then there intervenes a painful interruption or embarrassed silence, tears, shocked laughter, or anomic terror—a sense of the precariousness of the order of life and our construction of social reality.[14]

The *social* function of drama, as of children's play[15] (and films, fiction, and, formerly, poetry) is to supply the means whereby social inconsistencies and unbridgeable gaps with which the world constantly confronts us can be tied into the pre-existing thematically relevant world of social reality which has been constructed for us and by us as a total set of typifications. From Greek drama on, the dramatist and the theatre have provided audiences, i.e. representatives or sections of contemporary society, with the means whereby the anomic can be rendered nomic: comprehensible within the structure of relevance within which we can work out our lives. By presenting the possibility of some form of abductive reasoning explanation at some level of adequacy can be found. But to do this at all, the mock social reality of the stage must 'carry conviction'— must present, as Simmel says, its own 'visible, three-dimensional reality' in social, as well as physical terms.

Authenticity on the stage, therefore, is founded on the same principles by which a particular code of understandings is generated in everyday life. But though founded on everyday principles of reciprocity, there is a difference in that the audience's acceptance of the generative grammar which governs interaction (which is quite distinct, as Cicourel underlines, from the generative grammar by which single utterances are created and comprehended between people with the same native language) is a mute 'third party' understanding. It depends on their acceptance of the authenticity of the representation of the generative grammar governing reciprocal

[13] Except by A. N. Whitehead, cf. the passage on imaginative reasoning in *Process and Reality* (Cambridge University Press, 1929), pp. 5–6.
[14] P. L. Berger and T. Luckmann, *The Social Construction of Reality* (Allen Lane, 1967), p. 119.
[15] A. T. M. Wilson has commented on the initiation and spread of children's street games which enacted 'flying bomb' incidents in London during the VI offensive of 1944. cf. 'The Dance of Death', 'Who's Afraid of the Black man?' and 'Dead Man Dark Scenery', p. 26 above.

speech and behaviour. This is where the audience's recognition of the 'double occasion' of theatrical performance becomes a necessary precondition. Authenticity becomes 'authenticity'—a good enough make-believe of the principles of reciprocity and of ways of tying inconsistencies and unbridgeable gaps which are constituted in the performance. The double occasion of theatrical performance pre-supposes a readiness to accept, for the time being, the code (the sub-set of generative rules) and the world of social relevance established for the duration of the performance. The point is that even here, there has to be the same intrinsic coherence that would obtain in everyday life, even though the code is preselected by the performers (or producer) and though the conventions established by the tradi-tion of theatrical performance may be added to those which obtain for social reality. Thus, the particular set of authenticating conven-tions adopted by Gaskill for *The Recruiting Officer* is not necessarily of itself more theatrically appropriate or convincing than the set of authenticating conventions employed by Trevor Nunn in his equally successful production of *The Relapse* to which Gaskill refers:

> *The Royal Shakespeare Company's recent production of* The Relapse *perhaps illustrated the kind of 'deeply romantic' ap-proach to Restoration comedy one could describe as the op-posite of your own ...*

> 'They all wore black and silver and huge wigs up to here, didn't they? I thought it was appalling: like a nightmare. It was a new kind of fantastication of production—to do everything in that colour scheme of black and silver and pink and silver. I don't think they had any feeling that social context was import-ant, and I don't think that they would ever say it was. I think they are interested in theoretical, abstract concepts of what a play is.'

> *This could never be of any value in approaching Farquhar?*

> 'Nor any Restoration comedy. All of them are plays about people at a certain time in society, about people's social be-haviour.'[16]

I suppose it could be said that, for the code of authenticating conventions adopted for *The Relapse*, the producer did not 'think anyone cares a fuck' about 'social context'. The rhetorical con-ventions adopted by Trevor Nunn were entirely different. In com-posing a production, producer and actors and designers, in combination, are engaged in a *bricolage* of the whole range of con-ventions of social interaction existing off-stage and within the tra-dition of stage conventions, which will induce a consistent semantic

16 *Theatre Quarterly*, i (1971), 20.

code for the interaction between the theatrical goings-on and the audience.

'Bricolage' is Lévi-Strauss's metaphorical term for the analogous process of myth-making. 'The bricoleur', Lévi-Strauss's translator says, 'has no precise equivalent in English. He is a man who undertakes odd jobs and is a Jack of all trades or a professional do-it-yourself man.'[17] He is

> adept at performing a large number of diverse tasks; but, unlike the engineer, he does not subordinate [sic] each of them to the availability of new materials and tools conceived and procured for the purpose of the project. His universe of instruments is closed and the rules of his game are always to make do with 'whatever is at hand' that is to say with a set of tools and materials which is always finite and is also heterogeneous because what it contains bears no relation to the current project, or indeed to any particular project, but is the contingent result of all the occasions there have been to renew or enrich the stock or to maintain it with the remains of previous constructions or destructions.

Lévi-Strauss develops the analogy between bricolage and myth-making at some length, helping himself out by bringing in at several points engineering or science by way of contrast: 'The engineer is always trying to make his way out of and go beyond the constraints imposed by a particular state of civilisation while the "bricoleur" by inclination or necessity always remains within them.'[18]

The imagery fits to some extent the distinction I have tried to establish between rhetorical and authenticating conventions, for the engineer, as Lévi-Strauss also points out, works within a 'previously determined set consisting of theoretical and practical knowledge of technical means, which restrict the possible solution'.[19] One could also pursue the analogy to the point of identifying the playwright with Lévi-Strauss's engineer, and the producer and designer and performers with his *bricoleur*, but the distinction is hardly as clear as that which Lévi-Strauss is trying to establish, except when one is considering truly innovating playwrights. Most plays, in fact, are *bricolages* of rhetorical conventions; some productions, such as Brecht's of Shakespeare, go beyond *bricolage* to invention.

In the theatre, the set of tools and materials which is 'always finite and heterogeneous' and which 'bears no necessary relationship to the current project, or indeed to any particular project' because it is 'the contingent result' of all previous occasions is the stock of recognis-

[17] C. Lévi-Strauss, *The Savage Mind* (Weidenfeld & Nicolson, 1966), p. 17 (translator's footnote).
[18] *Ibid*, pp. 19–20.
[19] *Ibid*, p. 19.

able social conventions and social indentities lying to hand of the audience. Authenticating conventions are those same conventions selected and sorted into a coherent *bricolage* of dramatic spectacle, to convey the speech, manners and styles of life thought to prevail at the time of the play and appropriate to the rhetoric of the production itself. Through them an effort is made, in Simmel's words, 'to turn the purely mental thing of the drama back again into a representation reality'.[20] Their function is to authenticate the world of the play, to act as authenticating conventions. They are, in fact, not, like rhetorical conventions, expressions and agreements between actor and audience but representations of the agreements that exist between people in ordinary life. As such they imitate the conventions that enable people to interact in the real world. Their function is to give authenticity to the world of the play. Yet the presence of the audience ensures that it can only be a quasi-authenticity in an ineluctably make-believe world. The most intimate, the most secret scene has to be acted in public. To make this possible the audience must accept the obvious overriding convention that it must be at the same time present and absent. Authentication of the play world can only take place with the audience's connivance, and thus with their acceptance of the overriding convention attaching to the theatrical occasion. Spectators must be able to recognise language, gestures and behaviour belonging to familiar social milieux, familiar either from their own world of social reality, or from their assumed knowledge of history, literature and previous experience of theatrical occasions.

It is only through these conventions that it is possible to achieve a definition of what is happening on the stage. When the spectator enters the theatre the rhetorical conventions of staging define the performance, implying that the actors will represent other people and that the situations will be fictitious situations that occur in a fictitious world. But when the curtain rises or the play starts the action must be defined in another way. The people in the play must be seen to be as E. Souriau has put it: 'Pas un collection d'êtres choisis au hasard, mais un microcosme en travail livré au jeu de ses propres forces intérieures.'[21] They must be seen to be engaged with each other in relationships and interactions, sustained by a common language of conventions.

Since the rhetorical conventions are used to stress, accentuate or subdue certain actions, words, gestures or relationships they are bound to be more prominent than the authenticating conventions. As we have seen, indirect exposition can do as much to falsify the intended impression of 'life-really-happening' as direct exposition; both

---

[20] Simmel, *The Philosophy of the Actor*, p. 77.
[21] E. Souriau, *Les Grands problèmes de l'Esthétique Théâtrale* (Paris, Centre de Documentation Universitaire, 1960), p. 8.

may involve devices that are undisguisedly artificial. It is, however, significant that these artificial devices were used most expressively at a time when the real, the authentic, had a much wider meaning than it does now. The medieval acceptance of the reality of the spiritual world and the relative unreality of the physical world means that we can assume that spectators did not judge authenticity only by the direct imitation of ordinary life,[22] or by the boundaries imposed by a social construction of reality in secular 'disenchanted' terms.[23] The conception of the ordered universe which the Elizabethans inherited from the Middle Ages implied that the physical world could be regarded either as a shadow analogy of the spiritual world, or as merely that part of the cosmos revealed to us on earth. Although intellectual criticism of this concept of a theocentric universe increased throughout the sixteenth and seventeenth centuries Marlowe and Shakespeare made full use of it as a dramatic framework.

In the Miracle plays the authenticity of the events concerning the miraculous birth of Christ was not disturbed by events from ordinary life, realistically and comically presented. In the *Secunda Pastorum* the sheep-stealing scene is not merely comic relief. It is a recognised part of life in a universe which also contains the Nativity. After tossing Mak, the sheep stealer, the shepherds lie down still brooding on the trick that has been played on them:

1ST PASTOR:
    'On these thefys yit I mene. . . .'

and are woken by the angel:

    'Ryse hyrd-men heynd, for now is he borne
    That shall take fro the feynd that Adam had lorne
    That warloo to sheynd this nyght is he borne.
    God is made youre freynd now at this morne,
    He behestys.
    At Bedlem go se
    Ther lygys that fre
    In a cryb full poorely
    Betwyx two bestys.
    This was a qwant stevyn that ever yit I hard.
    It is a meruell to neuyn thus to be skard.'[24]

[22] J. Huizinga, *Waning of the Middle Ages:* 'Individual and social life in all their manifestations are imbued with the conceptions of faith. There is not an action however trivial, that is not correlated with Christ or salvation' (p. 153).

[23] M. Weber, *Economy and Society* (New York, Bedminster Press, 1968), p. 506: 'As intellectualism suppresses belief in magic, the world's processes become disenchanted, lose their magical significance, and henceforth simply "are" and "happen" but no longer signify anything. As a consequence, there is a growing demand that the world and the total pattern of life be subject to an order that is significant and meaningful.'

[24] *Secunda Pastorum*, in *Wakefield Pageants in the Townley Cycle*, ed. A. C. Cawley (Manchester University Press, 1958), p. 60.

The speech of the angel is no different in style and idiom from that of the shepherds or even of Mak and his wife. Yet there was no suggestion of incongruity.[25] Normal familiar behaviour was contained within the pattern of spiritual events.

In the secular drama of the sixteenth and seventeenth centuries plots and themes no longer relied on religious consensus. Plots were drawn from classical legends, European and English history and fables, and occasionally from contemporary life. The themes of re-venge, sexual passion, the struggle for political power and military glory were also primarily secular. Most themes and plots were familiar only to the better educated sector of the audience. Their appeal to the illiterate, who made up a large portion of the public theatre audience, depended to some extent on the authenticity of the conventions of speech and behaviour in which the action was embodied. No longer were the characters all children of God sharing the same style and mode of expression. They used speech and manners considered appropriate to their status or occupation. Inevitably, however, the writer's stand-point is that of the educated person and a scaling of cultural values becomes apparent—a scaling which results eventually in some degree of stereotyping or reification of persons.

Shakespeare, however, by casting uneducated characters in roles whose importance was dramatically crucial, avoided the creation of reified types. Such characters hardly ever appear to provide 'comic relief' but to authenticate the action of the main characters and the domain in which they act. He, like the writer of the *Secunda Pastorum*, juxtaposed the ordinary with the extraordinary. But he made conscious dramatic play with the contrast. He could rely on the educated spectators' ability to appreciate the irony of Hamlet joking with the men digging Ophelia's grave, men whose speech is a foil to his, and the irony of the drunken porter in *Macbeth* delaying the discovery of Duncan's murder, a murder regarded by Macduff, and presumably by James I's subjects, as sacrilegious.

[25] There is now. The recapture of the essential, underlying congruity requires a special act of aesthetic creation:

> About suffering they were never wrong,
> The Old Masters: how well they understood
> Its human position; how it takes place
> While someone else is eating or opening a window or just walking along;
> How, when the aged are reverently passionately waiting
> For the miraculous birth there always must be
> Children, who did not specially want it to happen, skating
> On a pond at the edge of the wood:
> They never forgot
> That even the dreadful martyrdom must run its course
> Anyhow in a corner, some untidy spot
> Where the dogs go on with their doggy life, and the torturer's horse
> Scratches its innocent behind on a tree.
>
> W. H. Auden

Authenticating conventions are of course distinguishable at this period in the stage behaviour of all classes of people. There is no sense in which the scenes of low life are more realistic than those that take place among the courtiers. The behaviour of Hamlet with the grave-diggers is no more natural than his conversations with Horatio or even with Rosencrantz and Guildenstern. What passes for natural behaviour on the theatrical occasion can be underlined by the contrast with the caricatured behaviour of the fantastic Don Adriano de Armado in *Love's Labours Lost* or of the gull, Osric, in *Hamlet*. Such contrasts demonstrate the range of conventions of behaviour which the audience might be assumed to know.

In a period of public living when royal progresses, civic ceremonies and court revels familiarised most town dwellers with courtly manners these distinctions between true and false demeanour could presumably be understood. It is not perhaps too much to suggest that in the hierarchical society of the sixteenth and seventeenth centuries the courtier and peasant or journeyman could communicate more easily than those who are today still conscious of the disparity of their educational levels in spite of their share in a common culture. Because of the emphasis on appropriate dress and behaviour conventions of gesture, language and action were easily comprehended. The Queen herself riding through the city conversed with her people with a freedom that no monarch has adopted since then.[26] Shakespeare was able to draw on this public language so that the conversation of kings and courtiers and of uneducated people became a part of popular theatre.

Shakespeare however never surrendered the main action, even of comedy, to the lowborn. He presented society from the reference point of its highest ranks. It was in other seventeenth century comedy, that of Jonson, Massinger, Marston and Middleton in particular, that representatives of different estates, even those of the lowest, were often allowed to dominate the action, although, for comic or dramatic purposes, the representatives of the lowest were usually in or on the fringe of criminal society. The respectable poor were not considered interesting or articulate enough to provide the main dramatic action. They were seen always from the reference point of those above them in the social scale. Thus the conventional view of behaviour was still that of the dominant class.

Although with the growth of the bourgeoisie in the seventeenth century social groups were becoming more segregated it was still

[26] It is not merely a political change in the power of the monarchy that has turned the sovereign into a silent doll-figure waving from a car. Queen Elizabeth II makes speeches, and sometimes utters an appropriate comment on a public occasion. But she no longer converses with 'her people'. She has at command no public language such as Elizabeth I had in which to express at the same time dignity and intimacy.

possible for Jonson to use the occasion of Bartholomew Fair as a meeting place for the different strata of society: 'a strutting *Horse-courser*, with a leere-drunkard, two or three to attend him, in as good *Equipage* as you would wish. And then for *Kind-heart*, the Tooth-drawer, a fine oyly *Pig-woman* with her *Tapster* to bid you welcome, and a consort of *Roarers* for musique. A wise *Justice* of *Peace meditant* . . .'[27] Authentic portrayal of the language, manners and demeanour of people from different social backgrounds relied to a large extent on the audience's knowledge and recognition of this behaviour. In the late seventeenth century when the theatre had become the preserve of the upper classes the most successful drama-tists wrote comedy which dealt almost exclusively with this section of society, allowing for their relationships with servants, shop-keepers and those in service relationships with whom they would have daily contact. These people, like Jeremy in *Love for Love* and Foible in *The Way of the World*, played the traditional parts of the *zanni* of the *Commedia dell'arte*, shrewd and skilful at manoeuvring their masters' affairs in the interests of their own welfare and pros-perity, but always subordinated to their masters or mistresses whose affairs remained at the centre of the action.

With the emergence of modern drama at the end of the nineteenth century, an effort was made to reconstruct an authentic model of society on the stage when Shaw and Archer helped to bring Ibsen's plays into the English theatre. The 'shocking' nature of many of his themes, which dealt with taboo subjects in what was regarded as an immoral way, at first caused people to equate realism with represen-tation of the sordid, a reaction which was parodied by Shaw when he chose to advertise some of his own plays, dealing with what he con-sidered important subjects, as 'unpleasant'.

But Shaw was more interested in the rhetorical presentation of ideas, of the principles on which actions depend, than on the auth-enticity of action itself; hence the common contemporary criticism of his plays for their intellectualising, their failure to present 'real characters' or 'real life' although the comparison was usually with the stereotyped characters and situations of 'drawing-room' comedy, or what Shaw called the 'cup and saucer' play. A more just comment would be that Shaw's characters usually talk and act as people would if their values, motives and intentions were clearly and con-stantly articulated and related to their actions. Shaw, in fact, used rhetoric in order to expose authentic thought processes. He had less interest in the authenticity of mere action, and seems to have under-estimated the power of authentic action to reveal the political work-ing of the social structure.

[27] Ben Jonson, The Induction, *Bartholomew Fair*, ed. C. H. Herford, P. and E. Simpson, Oxford University Press, 1938.

The same sort of intentions lay behind the so-called realism of Ibsen. He too selected and slanted situations so that the rhetoric of his themes would be effective. He did however, as we have seen, pay much more attention to authenticating conventions. He was concerned to make his scenes appear to belong to real life, and he managed to suggest a wider social context for the central situations performed on stage. The Ekdals and Werles in *The Wild Duck* are clearly part of a working community in which many other people are involved although the part they play in the drama may be insignificant. The dinner party which opens the play establishes this as well as exposing Ekdal's humiliating position in the community. The link in Ibsen's plays between rhetorical and authenticating conventions lies very often in the symbols which enable him to express meanings on more than one level, through objects which, like Lövborg's manuscript, Sölness's tower or the unseaworthy vessel in *Pillars of Society* also have an instrumental function. The weight of rhetoric in Ibsen's plays is more noticeable now that spectators have become accustomed to a more commonplace mode of expression in any play that attempts to represent the social world realistically.

While Ibsen was writing Strindberg had already taken a step in the direction of making authenticating conventions more expressive. In *Miss Julie* the situation between Jean and Miss Julie grows out of their painful awareness of the distortions caused by the master–servant relationship. Given the distance between mistress and servant at this time Jean's awareness of the significance of class differences sounds practical rather than academic. Their expression of social distance is authenticated by reference to the actions in which they are involved. Jean (to Miss Julie): 'We never carry on like this; we don't hate each other. With us love's just a game—something to do in our time off; we haven't got all day and all night for it like you.' Later the significance of the servant's uniform (not a symbol but a *sign* of servitude) is emphasised. Jean can no longer find the power to command his mistress when he has put on his livery. It becomes clear that personal relations are distorted by the conventions that one social class imposes upon another. Kristina is less distressed by Jean's faithlessness than by Miss Julie's degradation: 'You wouldn't go working for people who don't know how to behave. It'd be degrading if you ask me.'[28]

It is inevitable that social conventions represented as authentically as possible on the stage should reveal the way in which the social structure was perceived at the time when the play was written. Family relationships, relationships between men and women, rich

---

[28] Discussion of class differences in a master/servant relationship such as that of Tanner and Straker in *Man and Superman* remains a discussion. The relationship is not expressed authentically in action.

and poor, and master and servant are all expressed in language (verbal and gestural) which define these perceptions and their implications. Conventions used on the stage only approximate, however, to the social conventions which they are supposed to reproduce. There is a transformation that takes place when familiar conventions are presented in drama. The simplest actions or exchanges of the ordinary social world—forms of language, and gesture used for greetings, partings, declarations of love or announcements of death—seem to acquire quotation marks. Remarks and action imported for authenticating purposes from social life and governed by its conventions are, in fact, composed into the rhetorical framework of the play.

It is the absence of a clearly defined rhetorical framework, a 'construction' to be put on speech and action, which gives Pinter's plays (as against his film scripts) their peculiarly 'theatrical' quality. The quotation marks, so to speak, *are* the construction. And this provides the ground for Nigel Dennis's scathing criticism of the attempts to 'explain' Pinter's plays:

> The question, What are Harold Pinter's plays really about? has been a constant puzzle to Harold Pinter. Again and again he has done his best to explain himself to himself, but it has never come to much and there is little hope that it ever will. 'I only formulate conclusions after I've written the plays,' he has said. 'I've no idea what I'm obsessed with—just so pleased to see the words on paper.'

After dismissing the critical assistance proffered by Martin Esslin[29] and James R. Hollis,[30] Nigel Dennis offers his own explanation:

> Does this mean that Mr Pinter must remain as enigmatic as before? It would be a pity if this were so, because there is no doubt at all that his plays *work*—that the puzzles they represent in no way prevent them from being extremely theatrical. But how is this to be explained—and explained in words that really have some meaning?
>
> I would like to suggest that the proof of the pudding is in the acting. Actors are not very intellectual people as a rule, though they are always pleased to hear that the play they are appearing in has intellectual value. But they are hypnotically attracted by Pinter's plays and dearly love to appear in them. One of Pinter's first supporters was Noel Coward—the last actor in the world, one would have thought, to appreciate those grimy dens and grimier denizens.
>
> This appeal to actors is due, I think, to the fact that Pinter

[29] Martin Esslin, *The Peopled Wound: the work of Harold Pinter* (Methuen, 1970).
[30] James R. Hollis, *Harold Pinter: the poetics of silence* (Southern Illinois University, 1970).

himself was a professional actor before he took to play-writing—and is still acting when he supposes himself to be writing: this is the nature of the 'intuition' of which Mr Esslin speaks so warmly. Mr Esslin and Mr Hollis are convinced that this intuition is guided by some deep understanding of human nature; in fact, the understanding is of nothing but of what an actor can do. Any ideas that are present in a Pinter play are merely second-hand oddments inherited from more thoughtful playwrights: the originality of all the plays lies in the very peculiar scope they offer to the actors in them. All Pinter plays are like elaborations of the drama school exercise, when the student is told (say), 'You are alone in a room. Suddenly, the door opens. You see a man standing there ... O.K. Now, you improvise the rest.'

The test for the student is to conduct the make-believe that follows with sincerity and conviction. Any text that he or she may improvise is negligible—any *words* will do provided they supply a motive for moving, or sitting transfixed, for pausing or blustering, for registering emotion, for building an atmosphere. Mr Hollis has not called his book *The Poetics of Silence* for nothing, and both he and Mr Esslin attach huge importance to the famous Pinter pauses, the long stretches of inexplicable silence. They are quite right to do so. Their mistake is to suppose that these have some profound relation to the human condition, when in fact they are related only to the art of acting—'exfoliations of *histrionic* givens' as Mr Hollis would, or should, say. All playwrights must 'think themselves into' their characters in order to put life into them, but Mr Pinter is perhaps the first playwright to think himself exclusively into the actor: it is this that he is 'obsessed with'. A dialogue such as the following:

ELLEN: It's very dark outside.
RUMSEY: It's high up.
ELLEN: Does it get darker the higher you get?
RUMSEY: No. (*Silence*)

is virtually meaningless in thought or intellect, but put two good actors on the stage and see how it will hum—what deep significance, what frightening overtones, what enigmatic images it will produce. It is perfectly legitimate theatre, of a childish sort, and it is God's gift to the acting profession. An actor is not concerned with what something is about; he is only interested in how he can act. In Mr Pinter he has found a playwright who is equally uninterested in what the work is about: the work is simply the acting thereof.[31]

'What the work is about' is always, of course, implicit. Each

[31] Nigel Dennis, 'Pintermania', *New York Review of Books*, xv, no. 11 (December 1970), 21, 22.

member of each audience for each performance construes his own version of what the play is about. But, as I have tried to make clear, everybody present, or involved in it as playwright or producer, at a theatrical performance is presumed to be possessed of a 'common and standardised system of signals and coding rules' (Cicourel) by which the stage action, no less than everyday life, is presumed to be governed and interpreted. In presenting only those utterances, gestures, demeanours, actions and events which are relevant to his theme and intentions, the playwright (and producer) assume responsibility for the quotation marks which enhance the consequentiality of everyday behaviour and modes of social action represented on the stage, because he selects and determines the thematic relevance of characters, utterances, events and action. On its side, the audience, simply by its presence, distorts the thematic relevance of the social order presented on stage, and there is a tacit undertaking by the presenters of the play that even the most ordinary of actions and conversations will have enhanced consequentiality, will be framed in quotation marks which will give additional significance,[32] and will present a model for the tying-in of specific social inconsistencies to the audience's construction of typified reality.

Rhetorical convention attaches to all social action. It is impossible to perform any action with others present (and often even when alone) without making it thematically expressive. The 'aesthetic communicative aspect' is always present even when a person is silently listening to someone, asking the way or buying a ticket. In performing such actions he demonstrates something about himself, about the other person or persons present and about the meaning or significance of the transaction.

When such scenes are staged and performed before spectators the expressive qualities must be stressed, so that impressions and meanings are conveyed to non-participants as well as to participants. It is this requirement that results in many simple actions seeming, on the stage, false, insincere or overacted. It is a measure of the actor's skill if he can give this expressiveness an intended non-accidental quality. (This can apply even more strongly to the behaviour or gestures of a politician being interviewed in public or on television.)

Brecht made a virtue of this inevitable 'framing' of the smallest act or gesture on the stage. He regarded the stressing of the frame or the quotation marks as intrinsic to 'epic theatre'. Walter Benjamin claimed Brecht's power to make 'gestures quotable' as 'one of the substantial achievements of epic theatre'.[33] But Brecht's technique

---

[32] 'Overacting' and 'underacting' are imprecise terms for an actor's failure to achieve the correct level of enhancement which a particular audience will expect of modes of behaviour selected for relevance and framed for stage performance.
[33] W. Benjamin, *Illuminations*, trans. H. Zohn (Cape, 1970), p. 153.

rested not on a new discovery but on a conscious effort to make the spectator understand something that happens in all drama and all acting. He did not invent the 'quotable gesture' but taught his actors to emphasise it rather than disguise it.

Thus the contrasting attempt to present behaviour on the stage with complete authenticity has great difficulty in eliminating the quotation marks. K. H. Brown in *The Brig* and a recent Greenwich Village production in which a real family simply lived on stage offered slices of real life[34] with all its inconsequences and inconsistencies. But even on such occasions the simplest gestures and intonations are over-expressive because the spectators' attention is directed to this expressiveness rather than to the outcome of the action in wich they cannot be directly involved. If people spit or swear on the stage they seem to do it less to further the action than to demonstrate that they are the *sort of people* who spit and swear.

Jack Gelber in *The Connection* tried to overcome this difficulty by playing with the idea of authenticity. *The Connection* is more than a play-within-a-play. Using Pirandello's 'mirror' technique to manipulate levels of reality, Gelber presents the play as a film in the making. Author, producer and the two cameramen stand between the audience and the characters, sometimes identifying with the audience, sometimes caught up with the characters to the extent of accepting their drugs. Even the actors are fictionalised—presented as real junkies improvising their parts. At the beginning of the play the 'author' and 'producer' define this situation for the spectators:

> JIM: This word magician here has invented me for the sole purpose of explaining that I and this entire evening on the stage are merely a fiction. And don't be fooled by anything anyone else tells you. Except the jazz. As I've said we do stand by the authenticity of that improvised art. But as for the rest it has no basis in naturalism ...

The jazz of course is authentic and is contrasted with the junk:

> 'What I mean to say is that we are not actually using real heroin. You don't think we'd use the real stuff? After all, narcotics are illegal.'

In the course of the play the insistence on the improvisation is less explicit and the authenticating conventions are more effective although less prominence is given to them. But Gelber's preoccupation

---

[34] The unfamiliarity of the situations represented in *The Brig* gave them a dramatic interest which the 'ordinary family' could not offer. This suggests that any totally unfamiliar milieu, such as a military prison is for most people, carries even in ordinary life its own quotation marks.

with authentication does draw attention to a problem of the theatrical technique that has become more acute as spectators have, through exposure to television and films as well as plays, become more aware of and sensitive to shifting levels of reality and illusion and more suspicious of the authenticity of presentation.

The success of this play when it was performed by the Living Theatre in 1959 seems to have depended in part upon the novelty of its theme and techniques but more upon the creation of this spectator-awareness. The 'quotation marks' are deliberately emphasised so that the distinction between the world of real junkies and the world of theatrical junkies is always apparent. Yet when the play is read as a text the idea of pretending that the actors are real junkies and that the whole play is improvised is ineffective. One realises how much the authenticating and rhetorical conventions that render the action convincing and acceptable arise from the physical confrontation of actors and spectators and the creation of a common world of imagination.[35]

In plays in which the dramatist intends to convey more than photographic realism, more than the authenticity of the action, the communicative aspects of action are still more prominent. The expressiveness of ordinary patterns of behaviour is heightened to convey information about theme, situation or characters. The framing of certain sequences of action, and the limitation of context inevitable in drama produces constraints which bracket the action or actions in such a way that the presence of quotation marks is felt.[36]

Deliberate framing of actions is obtrusive in plays where interest lies mainly in the plot. The maid who opened the play in so many first scenes of comedies or thrillers of the 1920s and '30s demonstrated with her every action the status and expectations of the family she served. Arranging the room before her employers appeared was as significant as her mode of address when they were present. But in this kind of drama the range of authenticating expressiveness could be reduced to concentration on the mechanics of the plot rather than on the dramatic presentation of characters, plot and theme in their interrelated complexity.

In plays which try to represent reality on other levels, the plays categorised as 'absurd' and more recent plays where coherent mean-

---

[35] Spectator-awareness in the modern theatre is not of course an advance. The modern theatre is trying (with many abortive experiments) to recover the creative relationship that existed between actors and spectators in the medieval and sixteenth-century theatres and made these imaginative worlds possible (see chapter 6, p. 73).
[36] An exercise in shifting the frame from the major to the minor action can be observed in Tom Stoppard's *Rosencrantz and Guildenstern are Dead* (New York, Grove, 1968). He deliberately frames and extends action which goes on in the margin of *Hamlet* and therefore throws into relief the dramatist's usual arbitrary exercise of selectivity.

ing seems to be absent or masked (for example, plays of Stanley Eveling, Megan Terry, Rosalyn Drexler, David Mowat and others) the rhetorical elements in action are emphasised. This is particularly noticeable when hitherto banned actions are introduced into the performance. Nudity and obscene language are often used not for the sake of their relevance to the action but as demonstrations of liberation or rebellion against the established rules of behaviour. They are not aspects of ordinary behaviour (the ordinariness of nudity on public occasions is still a long way from being accepted) but symbolic gestures.[37] In these anti-realist plays rhetoric seems more important than authentication. No clues are given for placing the eccentric or abnormal characters in the ordinary world, to which they are often not intended to belong.

The revival of rhetorical emphasis in the theatre has occurred at a time when the elements of theatricality in everyday life have been recognised by psychologists and sociologists and brought to the attention of the layman by popular journalists. The well-disciplined representational play of Maugham or Galsworthy now seems to many spectators much more of a distortion of reality, of life as we know it than the 'unrealistic' plays of Pinter or Genet. Such dramatists seem to be returning to the Elizabethan view of a multidimensional reality of which only a little at a time can be perceived. But, unlike the dramatists of the sixteenth century we have more clues to the reality we can observe and test, fewer to the untestable spiritual reality which we take for granted, according to our beliefs, as there or not there. In its place the ordinary world can be made to suggest that its only value is symbolic although its reference is uncertain. The ambiguities in Beckett's plays are caused by a symbolism that cannot be resolved except in dramatic terms. Winnie sinking in to the sand heap, Nell and Nagg in their dustbins do symbolise fears that we recognise even if we do not accept a religious or psychological interpretation. Doubt about reality and identity is made into a dramatic joke:

> HAMM: We're not beginning to mean something?
> CLOV: Mean something! You and I, mean something? (*Brief laugh*)
> Ah that's a good one![38]

[37] Symbolism here is used as the expressive aspect of meaning which, as Suzanne Langer has said in *Philosophy in a New Key* (Harvard University Press, 1957) has itself three functions: signification, denotation and connotation. Thus, Macbeth's vision of 'a dagger' signifies the possibility of violence, denotes an hallucination and connotes the idea of murder in Macbeth's mind. All these functions are appreciated though not necessarily distinguished by the audience.
[38] *Endgame*, Faber and Faber, 1958.

This kind of self-consciousness has now become a prominent feature of avant-garde plays. Authenticity is no longer expressed through the direct reproduction of social conventions, modes of speech and gestures of friendship, love, anger or fear. Instead these are offered in a language that seems strange to the speaker and the quotation marks which 'bracket out' stage action from social reality are emphasised, as in this passage between Estragon and Vladimir:

> Vladimir: It's the start that's difficult.
> Estragon: You can start from anything.
> V: Yes but you have to decide.
> E: True.
>
> *Silence*
>
> V: Help me.
> E: I'm trying.
>
> *Silence*
>
> V: When you seek you hear.
> E: You do.
> V: That prevents you from finding.
> E: It does.
> V: That prevents you from thinking.
> E: You think all the same.
> V: No, no, impossible.
> E: That's the idea, let's contradict each other.[39]

Conversation as a game, upon the stage, by being bracketed out from social reality is a heightened version of the same game played in ordinary life, and thus 'frames' ordinary life itself.

In this way rhetorical conventions are used to present authentic behaviour not only at the level of action but also of speech and even thought. They have once more become, as they were in the sixteenth-century theatre, inseparable from authenticating conventions.

The return of the contemporary theatre to a more stressed rhetoric and its emphasis on the symbolism of action appropriate to the theatre implies that there is an audience capable of responding to this rhetoric and interpreting symbolism in some way that has relevance or 'makes sense'. However small and unrepresentative of the population as a whole it may be, the audience that attends the theatre lives the rest of its life outside the theatre and communicates on a 'sensible' level with those who never set foot inside a theatre. In looking for equivalences between theatrical behaviour and behaviour in ordinary life, one can find clues in the social conventions

[39] *Waiting for Godot*, Faber and Faber, 1956.

that are used and the elements of rhetoric and authenticity, commonly seen as insincerity or sincerity, that constitute them. These elements are crystallised in the concept of role through which action takes place in the real world and on the stage.

8

Roles, symbolic types and characters

'Person: L. *persona*, a mask used by a player, a character acted; in later use, a human being' (*Shorter Oxford English Dictionary*)

Marcel Mauss, in his analysis of *l'ideé due moi*, contrasted the Christian concept of '*personne morale*' and hence *l'être sacré* with the notion, which he suggested obtains in primitive societies, of *personnage*. The presentation of a total role by an individual in the sacred dramas on ritual occasions establishes him as a person, just as his position in the kinship system defines the totality of his roles in the society.[1] The stress in Mauss's lecture was on the way in which, in primitive society, a complete character is made explicit and given a fixed 'sanctified' social reality through ritual, and particularly through ritual dance and drama. '*Personnage*' serves as a complete, schematised, typification—a total role. In complex, urbanised, advanced industrial societies the social self—Mauss's *personne morale*—is realised in a multiplicity of roles in distinct situations and milieux, each with its own ritual processes attached to it, and each, therefore, achieving social reality through the mechanism of the shared typifications available to the participants and understood by them as giving a common meaning (i.e. understandable to the others) to events, actions, demeanour, utterances, gestures, and expressions.

Both Clyde Mitchell and V. W. Turner have, seemingly quite independently of Mauss, extended his basic *aperçu*. Mitchell's *The Kalela Dance*[2] is an elaborate and precise account of the adaptation of dance forms by young urban industrial workers in East Africa

[1] M. Mauss, 'Une catégorie de l'esprit humaine', Huxley Memorial Lecture, *Journal of the Royal Anthropological Institution*, lxvii (1938), 265ff.
[2] Clyde Mitchell, *The Kalela Dance*, Rhodes Livingstone Paper 27 (Manchester University Press, 1956).

to carry off the western style dress and deportment with which they have become familiar and which is materially accessible, and yet unachievable in terms of shared typifications. The dancers and the social activities accessory to them provide circumstances which enable them to realise *personnages* in accordance with the kind of transformations[3] valid for tribal societies. Turner, in his studies of Ndembu, has discerned a cyclical process of the development, crisis, and resolution of conflict in tribal societies which accords with the matrix of behaviour available to the range of *personnages* available, and which, over time, approximates to repeated performances of a 'social drama';[4] and this enables a tribal society to contain personal hostilities, factional disputes and political schism within a range compatible with the survival of the social order of the tribe.

Definition of character, in these instances, is visible to the outside observer as amounting to a sanctified system of ultimate social controls—a symbolic universe bounded and maintained by relationships and social norms which have become alienated (in Feuerbach's, not Marx's, sense) and so reified, objectified, compelling. They represent the most concrete instances of what Berger and Luckmann refer to when they write: '*All* social reality is precarious. *All* societies are constructions in the face of chaos.'[5] What Mauss, Mitchell and Turner (and there are innumerable other instances in the literature, though these accounts are closest to the matter in hand) are discussing are the most clearly visible instances of the construction of specific social realities, their encapsulation in ritual (and ceremony) and the corresponding construction of social identities which, severally and jointly, maintain the symbolic universe representing the particular total reality (the cosmic system of typifications prevailing in a society) through action.

In Western society, something of the notion of *personnage* is preserved in familiar 'symbolic types, like strangers, playboys, fools, villains, heroes'[6] which are comparable to the *personnages* we have mentioned as the typical social identities arrived at in primitive societies, although rarely realised in actual social life—except, significantly, in play forms, including, of course, simplistic drama (from *commedia dell'arte* to nineteenth century melodrama) as well as children's games. What does happen in actual social life is ascription of this completely reified personnage to others as a 'purging device': 'Chiefly, the social type of the fool functions as a device of

---

[3] J. Piaget, *Structuralism*, trans. Chaninah Maschler (Routledge, 1971).

[4] V. W. Turner, *Schism and Continuity in an African Society: a study of Ndembu village life*, Rhodes Livingstone Institute (Manchester University Press, 1957).

[5] P. L. Berger and T. Luckmann, *The Social Construction of Reality* (Allen Lane, 1967), p. 121.

[6] R. H. Grathoff, *The Structure of Social Inconsistencies* (The Hague, Nijhoff, 1970), p. 122.

status reduction and social control. Reduction of persons through the fool's role is a continuous and collective process ... Fool ascription acts as a purging device eliminating upstarts, pretenders, and incompetents from positions of influence.'[7]

But people can also 'play the fool' in order to 'reduce' others. The episode in Evelyn Waugh's *Decline and Fall* in which, on Paul Pennyfeather's first encounter with his form, one boy after another claims the same name, has the effect of completely wrecking any of the typified social relationships between teacher and class by exposing the symbolic apparatus of adult dominance as an artifice to be maintained, if at all, by 'shared typifications'. Similar wrecking devices of self-caricature as well as lampooning and stereotyping the other as tyrant, boss, or Quisling of 'the system' have been exploited in recent years by militant students in confrontations with presidents, rectors, and vice-chancellors of universities in all Western countries as well as with police and judges in the United States.

Social action in ordered interaction in contemporary complex urbanised society is kept within bounds by the observance of the conventions of behaviour—which, as Goffman has pointed out, requires a preliminary *commitment* to the social occasion in which any individual finds himself, or enters, a commitment which requires that he maintain the shared typifications relevant to that occasion, and which will enable others, as well as himself, to sustain a 'role'. In such societies, the concept of role has been developed as forming the essential link between the patterned social realities of the various and changing institutional worlds into which the individual enters, on the one hand, and the human reality of individual consciousness, identity and uniquely patterned behaviour on the other.[8]

The understanding of the nature of social roles has been regarded as crucial to any elucidation of the relationship of the individual to society. If society is not, as every sociologist is driven to insist, to be endowed with an existence and validity independent of the people who compose it and who in fact create it, roles have to be assumed as the means whereby the individual maintains the norms of any social occasion, or shifts in conformity with a change of occasion, or a new emergent form of occasion.[9] Generalised, reified, roles such as these,

---

[7] O. E. Klapp, 'The fool as a social type', *A.J.S.*, lv (1949), p. 162.

[8] There remains some mystification about the commonsense reality of individual uniqueness, despite some work on pattern recognition in recent years by psychologists, linguists and 'machine intelligence' students. Despite the semantic and phonetic constraints imposed on speech by the socially prescribed processes of language acquisition, each of us can recognise scores of disembodied voices on the telephone immediately, and can identify equally instantly some hundreds of compatriots by their faces, despite the fractional differences of shape, size and colour of physiognomic features.

[9] Garfinkel has explored, in deliberately bizarre fashion, the strength of this commitment to preserve the rationale of normative behaviour even in the face of planned

which can be taken up and discarded, contribute to the image of society which each member of it perceives. Thus conformists, pro-testers, retreatists are all clearly discernible parts of this image. None are outside society.

Role theory has become a major preoccupation of sociologists. It is through the analysis of roles that the norms and constraints which seem to govern individual social action can be interpreted. Yet, even at this level, distinctions have emerged between the formulation of the theory by older, pre-1940 sociologists and social psychologists such as Linton, Park and Mead and earlier writers who used terms such as role, mask or 'part', as terms of common and literary usage and also between pre-1940 writings and more recent developments of 'role theory'. Among the earliest writers is Marx who, in the analysis of social epiphenomena refers to the 'character mask' of the bourgeois employer. In *The Eighteenth Brumaire* of Louis Bonaparte he uses the metaphoric language of the theatre to describe the events taking place on the stage of history. In fact he introduces this book with the comment that, as Hegel has remarked 'all facts and per-sonages of great importance in world history occur twice. He forgot to add: the first time as tragedy, the second time as farce.'[10] Marx employs this language in a way that has much significance for pre-sent day sociology, but without the intention that is sometimes read into it of equating social life with the theatre. Urbanék[11] suggests that Marx's attitude to role is part of his theory of alienation and that it is the reification of persons and personification of things that traps the individual in the rigid framework of roles. But alienation, as used by Marx, comprehends a complex of attitudes and ways of behaviour that transcend the concept of role as it is now used. In connection with alienation, 'role' or 'mask' implies that the indi-vidual's actions and self-expression are reduced to the performance of prescribed acts and that these prescriptions are derived from the power (partly acquired from the alienated power of others) that sus-tains the role. In general, Marx used the terms, 'reification' and 'per-sonification' much more effectively than 'role'.

During the period (roughly that between the wars) when sociology

---

'fooling' or an experimental situation designed to confront actors with completely random responses. See H. Garfinkel, *Studies in Ethnomethodology* (Prentice-Hall, 1967), esp. ch. 2, 'Studies of the routine grounds of everyday activities'.

[10] K. Marx, *The Eighteenth Brumaire*, trans. D. de Leon (Chicago University Press, 1914).

[11] E. Urbanék, 'Roles, masks and characters—a contribution to Marx's idea of the social role', in *Marxism and Sociology*, ed. P. Berger (Appleton-Century, 1969), p. 194ff.

became established, following the work of Durkheim, Simmel and Weber, the concept of role became crucial to the elucidation of the relationship between the one and the many, between the individual, as a unique personal identity, and society. In this sociological tradition 'role' has been used not in the Marxist sense as a metaphor (usually with critical implications) but as an analytic term. It is assumed that all societies, in all historical periods, generate roles which each member of that society learns to perform or at least to recognise. The analogy of social with theatrical performance is as we have seen already so familiar that its extension can be easily handled.

The theatrical metaphor suggests that in ordinary life, as on the stage, we take parts and fit into situations and scenes that are part of a larger scheme of action. In fact, although this approximates to the truth, most people do not really believe in predetermined action. We do believe that we can choose between courses of action and can ourselves affect both our own and the actions of others. In the first place we regard the roles that we adopt as means of imposing ourselves on society. It is only gradually that we come to realise the extent to which the role can impose itself upon the 'self' which plays it. Even after this has happened choices which are not wholly determined by the role can face us. For instance the role of the servant has changed so much that it is often difficult for both employer and employee to know what demands can legitimately be made and what privileges should be expected.

Secondly, nearly everyone experiences some changes of role which present him with new situations in company with different actors. Even the basic roles, mother, father, child, husband or wife can be rejected for purposes of action. Although a mother may not be able to forget the child she has abandoned or the husband the wife he has left, either can behave and be treated by others as though wife or child had never existed.

The ability to change from one role to another and yet remain recognisably the same person (recognisable in more than physical characteristics) is observable in all social interaction. However much a person may try to emphasise or reduce the discrepancies between performance in different roles, a personal style of action and response is usually distinguishable. The mythical double character (Dr Jekyll and Mr Hyde) is regarded as a pathological monster. The idea of such a character is both attractive and repellent, offering opportunities of power and at the same time negating the self and its conscious enjoyment of these opportunities. Normally, the different roles played by one person are regarded as linked by a retaining memory with the power of organising perceptions. David Hume formulated this concept of identity which has now become a commonplace: 'Memory not only discovers the identity but also contributes to its production, by producing the relation of resemblance among the perceptions.'[12]

Experience and memory of experience in different roles do affect the self as a whole so that the school teacher who has previously worked in a factory knows more about his own capacity for different kinds of behaviour, and more about his response to the expectations of others than the school teacher who has been trained through school and university for this one occupational role. The relationship of the self to a role is therefore much closer than that of the actor to his part in the theatre. The actor is less affected by the experience of being or being regarded as one of these characters.[13] The actor in fact simulates the process of role change by emphasising the expressive elements of role behaviour. But in both ordinary life and on the stage these modes of expression have to be learned and practised.

Human beings are taught not only the basic animal skills such as eating, drinking, and walking, which will keep them alive, but also a range of social skills through which they can communicate with others. They have to learn to convey and interpret meanings through language, gestures, facial expressions and actions. This process of socialisation begins as soon as a child becomes aware of those who surround him. Although he receives a certain amount of direct instruction at a very early age—he is told to say 'thank you' and is told 'not to touch'—most of his social learning during his preschool years is informal and expressive. Brecht has rightly discerned the theatrical quality of this kind of learning:

> One easily forgets that human education proceeds along highly theatrical lines. In a quite theatrical manner the child is taught how to behave, logical arguments only come later. When such and such occurs it is told (or sees) one must laugh. It joins in when there is laughter, without knowing why; if asked why it is laughing it is wholly confused. In the same way it joins in shedding tears, not only weeping because the grown-ups do so but also feeling genuine sorrow. This can be seen at funerals whose meaning escapes children entirely. These are theatrical events which form the character. The human being copies gestures, miming, tones of voice. And weeping arises from sorrow

[12] 'Identity depends on the relation of ideas and these relations produce identity by means of that easy transition they occasion': David Hume, *Philosophical Works* (Edinburgh, 1854), p. 323. Hume used the term 'identity' to convey the idea of the 'known' or self-conscious 'self' which assumes the many roles that are played. But today it is often used as a substitute term for role, as the 'situated self', announced by certain signs. It will I think be less confusing to use it as much as possible in Hume's sense.

[13] An actor who played Othello in 1970 in South Africa had the uncommon experience of feeling what it was like to be black when he left the theatre without removing his make-up. But such an experience affected him as a person, not as an actor.

but sorrow also arises from weeping. It is no different with grown-ups. Their education never finishes. Only the dead are beyond being altered by their fellow men.[14]

There is, however, inherent in the process of socialisation a progressive movement towards the organisation of mimetic behaviour into role-playing. This has a subjective and an objective aspect. Not only does society provide the individual with positions and the techniques for performing the roles attached to them, the individual is also made to realise that he can only become a part of society through performing such roles.

The social system is in fact a system of roles which are defined by the negative and positive sanctions of law, custom and norms of behaviour. Individual members of society have to learn a succession of roles, usually by the informal educational process of socialisation. A father in this country is bound by law to provide for his children and is prevented from causing them physical harm. He is expected to show them a certain amount of attention and afford them a degree of affection. But the degree of attention or affection that is expected of him and the way in which it is displayed varies according to the norms of the social milieu and historical period in which he lives. The Victorian paternal tyrant, accepted in both middle and working-class families, may still exist but no longer conforms to the requirements and expectations, held by society, of a 'father'. Social change is thus manifested in the structuring of roles. Obligations and expectations change but the outline of the role persists so that the word 'father' at any period, in any milieu, conjures up a recognisable image, however much it may have to be modified in practice.

Roles, therefore, have to be first perceived and then learnt. But before they can be learnt they must be perceived not merely as opportunities but also as inescapable mechanisms for coping with the business of living in the world: 'For society and sociology socialisation invariably means depersonalisation, the yielding of man's absolute individuality and liberty to the constraint and generality of social worlds.' Dahrendorf, following, in this regard, the orthodox sociological treatment of the subject, sees this as a process of 'internalisation': 'human beings . . . take something that exists outside them into themselves, internalise it, and make it a part of their personality. By learning to play social roles then, we not only lose ourselves to the alien otherness of a world we never made, but regain ourselves as personalities given unique shape by that world's vexations.'[15]

[14] *Brecht on Theatre*, trans. Willett, p. 152.
[15] R. Dahrendorf, *Essays in the Theory of Society* (California University Press, 1968), p. 57.

At the same time that roles are perceived as a means of placing ourselves in society they are also perceived as a means of consolidation of the self. The fact that roles are not lightly chosen but sought, and that anxiety attaches to the attainment of competent performance, is apparent not only from sociological evidence but also from Freudian analysis of individual development, especially those analyses that stress the psychosocial implications of behaviour. Role choice is a part of 'identity formation' which, as Erikson says, reaches an overt crisis at the end of adolescence, but continues 'as a lifelong development largely unconscious to the individual and his society'.[16] He also emphasises the relationship between 'the organised values and institutional efforts of societies on the one hand, and the mechanisms of ego-synthesis on the other', so that 'basic social and cultural processes can only be viewed as the joint endeavour of adult egos to develop and maintain through joint organisation a maximum of conflict-free energy in a mutually supportive psychosocial equilibrium'. This can be interpreted in sociological terms as the effort of society to create roles which individuals will recognize as offering patterns of behaviour through which they can make themselves effective in society.

In the sociological study of society 'role' has, therefore, been adopted not merely as a descriptive term but as a term expressive of the relationship between man and society. Before this term was adopted William James introduced the concept of the 'social self'. James used the term 'social self' to represent the image that the self projects to others:

> A man has as many social selves as there are individuals who recognise him and carry an image of him in their mind ... But as the individuals who carry the images fall naturally into classes, we may practically say that he has as many different social selves as there are distinct groups of persons about whose opinion he cares. *He generally shows a different side of himself to each of these different groups* ... We do not show ourselves to our children as to our Club companions, to our customers as to the labourers we employ, to our own masters and employers as to our intimate friends.[17]

These distinctive 'selves' can be equated with the roles which are now more commonly used to express the different kinds of behaviour adopted by an individual with different people or groups of people. The substitution of role for social self suggests a more dramatic view of the self as the player of parts. It also suggests that the self which takes up roles although hypothesised cannot be perceived

---

[16] E. Erikson, 'Problems of ego-identity', *Psychological Issues* (New York, 1959) no. 1, p. 113.

[17] W. James, *Principles of Psychology* (London, 1901) i, 294.

or defined, except through its actions. Actions, gestures and speech provide the evidence from which motives, intentions and a central core of selfhood can only be inferred. Thus a performed self is created with which the performer himself may be uneasy. A reified character, something apart from the 'self', is created.

Simmel speaks of the role becoming a man's 'reality', 'not only in being such and such a person but in having such and such qualities. In large things and small, enduring and ephemeral there are discoverable ideal forms in which our being must clothe itself'.[18] But he emphasises the organisation that must go into the creative process of filling this form with individual character. This is the same kind of organisation that an actor must employ in managing his role. Everyone knows, however, that he is not only a performer and a performed character but also an audience, both for performances in which he is a participant and those in which he has no part.

As a performer he is concerned not only with the performance of a task but also with the style of the performance, by which he tries to convey only those motives, intentions and ultimate aims which conform to his self-image. In this way he is engaged in contributing to the definition of the situation in which he is involved and by involving himself, commits himself to those shared typifications which will constitute the thematic field, and so define the possible strategies and tactics of future action. The establishment of definition depends upon exchange of information by all those present, information which is exchanged through movements, gestures, facial expressions, costume as well as language. A person who arrives at a formal party wearing informal clothes may be expressing contempt for formal occasions or for his host, ignorance of the nature of the party, or ignorance of the correct form. But the rest of his behaviour, defiant, apologetic or embarrassed will define the category to which it belongs. Goffman suggests that on occasions impression-management rather than the conveying of a correct impression may become a major concern:

> Instead of allowing an impression of their activity to arise as an incidental by-product of their activity they can reorientate their frame of reference and devote their efforts to the creation of desired impressions. Instead of attempting to achieve certain ends by acceptable means they can attempt to achieve the impression that they are achieving certain ends by acceptable means.[19]

Grathoff supplements and amplifies Goffman's notion of impression-management by insisting that all social action has to be pre-

[18] G. Simmel 'Zur Philosophies des Schauspielors', in *Das Individuelle Gesetz* (Suhrkamp, 1968), p. 80.
[19] Goffman, *Presentation of Self in Everyday Life*, p. 250.

ceded by some 'at least rudimentary "strategy" ' which anticipates
potential inconsistencies that are to be avoided, or to be overcome by
avoidance.[20] There are, he suggests, 'permanent' or fixed 'gaps' or
inconsistencies which are almost always avoided, which arise in dramatic situations which resist strongly any typification in lived-
through experience: 'These are situations of danger, of birth and
death, of suicide and homicide, which are indicated by ritual, taboo
and forbidden language' and he goes on to cite Glaser and Strauss's
Awareness of Dying as 'a page by page illustration of the phenomenon of "permanent gap": the immediate presentation of context
(the patient's awareness of his disease) and the mediate presentation
through the nurse, the physician, the family, *et al.*'[21]

Goffman, in fact, in an earlier essay, dealt with the manner in
which permanent gaps which are in danger of being closed (to the
embarrassment of some of the participants, or the threat of dissolution of a particular public order which is of concern to everybody except the victim—the 'mark' of the confidence trickster,
whom he takes as the archetype—to be sacrificed to its maintenance)
are kept in being as inconsistencies and cloaked with social in-
visibility.[22]

There are, in fact, very many occasions in which one becomes
aware of one's self, or visible to others, as distinct from one's role,
and recognisable as a dramatic performer, or rather a member of the
cast of a dramatic performance, and not as 'a person'. Worsley, along
with Dahrendorf, and many others, treats this as a common conscious experience, and prescribes an analytical distinction between
the self and his roles.

> Since the individual is not identical with his role but is the occu-
> pant or better the actor or player of it he is able to stand outside
> it. The Me is distinguishable from the I. He has an *attitude*
> towards his role and his attitude towards it may also be multi-
> valent . . . Because they constrain him, as Durkheim would have
> put it, he has interests, positive or negative, in his roles.[23]

Moreover those who are involved with him feel that willingly or
unwillingly they are being manoeuvred into the role of audience.

Eventually, from such a performance, another self emerges, the
self as character. The performed character is the character that is
seen by others and to some extent by the performer himself, although his knowledge of this performed self is derived mainly from

[20] Grathoff, *The Structure of Social Inconsistencies*, p. 147.
[21] *Ibid*, p. 57.
[22] E. Goffman, 'On cooling the mark out: some aspects of adaptation to failure',
Psychiatry, xv, (1952).
[23] P. Worsley in P. Halmos, ed., *The Distribution of Power in Industrial Society*,
Sociological Review, Monograph 8 (1964), p. 16.

the reactions of others. The performer gains, therefore, an impression that is different from that of those with whom he interacts.

Thus the performed self, distinguishable and yet not separate from the performer, is comparable to the character presented by the actor in a play. Yet the way in which this character is formed is significantly different. The script is replaced in ordinary life by an ongoing process. This process is set in motion by the objective demands of the role, and the subjective motives and goals of the actor. The first comprises role specifications, expectations and restraints. The subjective motives and goals are made manifest in a personal style and discernible attitudes. Both pressures, objective and subjective, are at work in the process of secondary socialisation. This process which begins as soon as a child moves away from his family to school or to take part in group activities with other children or adults entails a more self-conscious form of learning which increases in complexity as the child grows older and has access to more institutions. The boy who is learning to be a lawyer, a chef or a farm-labourer does not learn only the necessary skills. He learns at the same time a specific attitude both to his work and, to some extent, to that part of his life which takes place outside work. He also learns a language which he shares with those with whom he works and which always differs to some extent from the language of common discourse. It may include specialised words or turns of phrase (called by outsiders 'jargon') or it may merely limit or stress certain forms of expression: 'Since the roles of an institutional order involve specific modes of conduct and social integration of these modes it is only natural that special vocabularies should arise.'[24]

For a person who plays a number of roles, as most people in modern society are obliged to, strain and conflict arise from the irreconcilable nature of some of these modes of conduct and expression. This is partly because people feel constrained to play their roles in accordance with what they believe to be the expectation of others. These expectations create models of behaviour ranging from that which seems appropriate (i.e. according to the terminology used earlier, within the connotations of a thematic field), or not inappropriate, to rigid stereotypes, or reified *personnage*.

G. H. Mead's description of the way in which individuals become conscious of these expectations and attitudes involves typification of modes of appropriate behaviour to which the individual learns to accommodate. In so doing, he is made aware of a specifically social identity which he imputes to himself. Living through a variety of such experiences, the 'self' develops in terms of a generalised social

[24] Hans Gerth and C. Wright Mills, *Character and Social Structure* (Routledge, 1954), p. 278.

entity to which he has learned to respond in a 'typical'—i.e. personally identifiable—way.

> The organised community or social group which gives to the individual his unity of self may be called the 'generalised other'. The attitude of the generalized other is the attitude of the whole community. For example, in the case of such a social group activity as the Ball-game the team is the 'generalised other' in so far as it enters—as an organised process or social activity—into the experience of any of the individual members of it.[25]

For Mead, this process occurs in childhood largely through participation in play (which he sometimes equates, rather confusingly, with games). In a game the individual player knows what is expected of him in his particular position. He understands the aim of the game—winning, and the responses which are expected by the other players. Mead treats play (the game) as more than an analogy, as in fact a paradigm of the social situation. In the socialisation of the child he sees 'role-playing' as a 'play' pursuit, the make-believe in which most children indulge being converted by adults into the more serious 'game' pursuit with which society is concerned:

> He (the child) is continually taking the attitudes of those about him, especially the roles of those who in some sense control him and on whom he depends. He gets the function in an abstract sort of way at first. It goes over from the play into the game in a real sense ... The child passes into the game and the game expresses a social situation into which he can completely enter.

The process is achieved through language, 'a vocal gesture' which 'mediates the social activities that give rise to the process of taking the role of the other'.[26]

In the contrast between play and game is implicit the learning which is necessary for the performance of social roles. A person who dresses up and plays at being a policeman need only imitate the expressive movements, gestures and tones of voice by which the public can recognise him. But the person who takes the role as his occupational role needs the knowledge as well as the performing ability before he can exercise the rights and fulfil the obligations which the role entails.

There is also a difference in the intention of the performance given. While the occupant of a child's 'play role' gives a performance which is exclusively affective, and can be switched to performance in some other realm of social reality, or turned off, the performance of an occupational role is intended to be at the same time *affective* and *effective*. But the occupational or social role

[25] G. H. Mead, *Mind Self and Society* (Chicago University Press, 1934), p. 154.
[26] *Ibid*, p. 160.

preserves 'play' elements of expressiveness and it is through perception of this aspect of role-playing that people become aware of
one aspect of 'theatricality' in ordinary life.

Sartre stresses the way in which society renders 'play', in this sense
obligatory. The waiter plays at being a waiter in a café:

> There is nothing there to surprise us. The game is a kind of
> marking out and investigation . . . the waiter in the café plays
> with his condition in order to realise it. This obligation is not
> different from that which is imposed on all tradesmen. Their
> condition is wholly one of ceremony. The public demands of
> them that they realise it as ceremony . . . There are indeed many
> precautions to imprison a man in what he is, as if we lived in
> perpetual fear that he might escape from it, that he might break
> away and suddenly elude his condition.[27]

Play in this sense is a serious matter. A value attaches to the
waiter's performance for it is through his performance that he vali-
dates himself as a social being. Criticism or devaluation of his performance can be more wounding than criticism or devaluation of his
unprofessional self. His 'act' is therefore qualitatively different from
the 'act' of the actor in the theatre. Versatility, not good faith, is
demanded of the actor who can present Macbeth one night, and
Captain Shotover the next. In such changes he demonstrates not only
technical skill but feeling and empathy for different kinds of parts. In
ordinary life the change from one role to another, although un-
avoidable, can be painful. The same person can be at one time father,
son, friend, electrician, supporter of a political party and footballer.
The number of roles that he can assume is large (though not, of
course, infinite) and in many cases they overlap. Each role demands
'behaviour' and 'attributes' which may have to be modified if he finds
himself called upon to play more than one role at the same time. The
teacher whose own child is in his class usually makes an effort to
suppress the role of father while the other children are present, even
instructing his child to address him formally as Mr X. It is on such
occasions of role conflict that the individual becomes most conscious
of the techniques of role playing and of the contrivance needed for a
sustained performance. As Goffman has said 'the very obligation and
profitability of appearing always in a steady moral light, of being a
socialised character, forces one to be the sort of person who is practised in the ways of the stage,'[28] and again 'an honest sincere performance is less firmly connected with the solid world than one
might at first assume'.

But, if sincerity is impossible, degrees of insincerity are con-
trollable. Hypocrisy is recognised for what it is when roles in real life

[27] J.-P. Sartre, *Being and Nothingness*, trans. H. E. Barnes (Methuen, 1957), p. 59.
[28] Goffman, *Presentation of Self in Everyday Life*, p. 251.

are overplayed, especially on occasions that are set and produced as if they were theatrical. Conor Cruise O'Brien has described the United Nations building in New York as such a setting. People ask why the United Nations does not act, to which he replies: 'It seldom does anything else.' This catch answer is seriously meant: 'The dramatisation and moralisation of the interplay on the stage of the United Nations speeds up the process in the real world. The playing out of roles before the gallery evokes a need to sustain them into real life; the actor's reputation in his off-stage life will affect his reception on his next public appearance . . .'[29] O'Brien stresses the peculiarity of the theatricality of this institution not because theatrical behaviour is out of place in serious discussion but because the performance in the building on the East River seems to be intentionally self-sustaining. It is so far removed from the real events with which it is concerned that its affective aspect is stressed at the expense of its effective or instrumental aspects. Action in the U.N. Chamber, like action in a theatre, is contained by the walls of the building.[30] O'Brien does, perhaps, exaggerate the purely theatrical nature of the U.N. performance but he has perceived the dangerous opportunity that it provides for the over-theatricalisation or fictionalisation of life. When it becomes more important to sustain a role than to examine the kinds of action that it produces and stimulates in others the actors find themselves inventing their own scripts without reference to action in the ordinary world.

Yet, however suspect, the idea of the 'self' is rooted in common usage and is in fact 'given' in the making of social life. Uncertainty arises in discussion of the relation of the 'self' to the multiplicity of roles that it assumes. Is there a distinguishable 'self' which like the actor takes the part of father, husband, doctor, golfer or friend? All these roles can overlap but one can usually distinguish the one that the actor wishes to emphasise for the occasion. If a doctor's wife has to speak to her husband in his surgery while a patient is there, both husband and wife will usually 'play down' the marital role in order to avoid disturbing the professional role. Even if the 'self' is affected by the parts it plays the question still arises: can there be an autonomous self that is entirely his and is administered by him alone? That there can seems to be the view of role playing that most laymen prefer to take; yet the contemporary preoccupation in drama and the novel with the search for identity suggests that the existence of a

[29] Conor Cruise O'Brien, *The United Nations as Sacred Drama* (Hutchinson, 1968), p. 59.
[30] Brecht believed that society could be changed through theatrical performance but only by changing the minds of the spectators gradually. Lee Strasberg who believed that the spectators should be capable of rushing out of the theatre to make a revolution was suggesting a new function for the theatre which has not yet been realised.

knowable and constant 'self' is something about which there is a great deal of anxiety.

The relationship between the individual and his role depends on an attitude to the self or personal identity that is always under attack. Hume's view of personal identity as a 'fictitious' construct of the reflective imagination[31] is accepted by those who believe that the 'self' can only be made manifest through its actions. The idea of 'the presentation of self' can transcend the concept of 'role playing'. The 'self' emerges, as Goffman has said, as some kind of image 'which the individual on stage and in character effectively attempts to induce others to hold in regard to him'. Because of this conception of the 'self' Goffman does not consider the unperforming self to be observable or deducible; 'The self then as a performed character is not an organic thing that has a specific location, whose fundamental fate is to be born, to mature, to die, it is a dramatic effect arising diffusely from a scene that is presented and the characteristic issue, the critical concern is whether it will be credited or discredited.'[32] In this view of action the performer is, *if he can be under observation at all*, always 'on stage', always aware of other actors, and of the 'frame' which bounds the relevant actors and action. In ordinary life this kind of frame is recognised. Waiters or waitresses serving drinks at a large sherry party are aware that they are not really 'present' to the guests and should not be included in their conversation. Similarly a priest reading the Mass in a Roman Catholic cathedral completely disregards the visitors who are moving about to admire the architecture. They are outside the frame of his particular performance. Conversely the visitors probably include the service in their frame of reference as an aesthetic rather than a religious experience.

One component of the theatrical structure, the audience, is not constant in this concept of performance. Other 'acting' people or non-participating individuals can be manoeuvred into the position of acting as audience, as guests at a dinner party act the part of audience for the teller of anecdotes or as crowds play the part of spectators at a street fight or police chase. It is just as common, of course, for people to go out of their way to avoid an audience for scenes in which they may not appear to advantage. Most people try to avoid quarrelling or scolding their children before friends or even strangers.

There is, however, another way of identifying an audience. The 'self' in ordinary life can also be regarded as playing the part of audience. William James discussed the 'self' in terms of the 'I' and the

---

[31] D. Hume, *Philosophical Works* (Edinburgh, 1825), i, 323–33.
[32] Goffman, *Presentation of Self in Everyday Life*, p. 252.

'Me', the former being the active agent of the personality and the latter those aspects of the personality that the 'I' cares and knows about, the image of the self that the 'I' cherishes. Mead, as we have seen, interpreted the relationship in more dramaturgical terms. He described the 'Me' as an inner audience, observing, encouraging, or restraining the actions of the 'I'. This is also a way of describing conscience or inner criticism (the part played in Freudian analysis by the super-ego). Everyone has experienced occasions on which he has been disgusted, at the time, by his own behaviour. This disgust alienates him from his role. It is in this sense that the 'Me' can be said to provide an audience capable of criticising and restraining the 'I'. This audience can of course, like any audience, be deceived so that one is at times taken in by one's own act, by a display of moral fervour or of grief.

We have now reached the point at which Mauss's total *personnage*, realised in ritual and in the coherent structure of functional roles attached to an ascribed status in primitive society, has been transformed into a much more complicated and variable entity. Neither, it should be emphasised, is any more or less a construct of the social relationships and social occasions through which the individual lives out his life than the other, nor more or less a substruct of the social realities which he, in turn, is led to build out of the shared typifications prevailing in the social milieux and social occasions to which he finds himself committed through membership of the society at large and of the social sectors of it which he actually experiences. But in contemporary western societies, the experience of variability of occasions, of role-switching, of the novel and unexpected, connotes an awareness of the fracture of social identity, of *personnage*, into *personae*, into roles, into different social persons. We are commonly aware of a difference between 'self' and 'role', and, indeed, of a multiplicity of selves, of a distinction between the self-as-performer and the self-as-audience, observer, and critic of the self-as-performer.

It is on this reconstruction of the self and of social reality that the whole conception of drama and the theatre is founded. Plays are conventionally and recognisably the creation of a single individual, the playwright. The commonplace acceptance of the imaginative fabrication of a multiplicity of 'persons' engaged in actions and interactions which can be acted out by an assemblage of different individual actors reflects not only the commonplace acceptance of our capacity to occupy and act out a variety of roles but the universal recognition of this capacity in ordinary conversation, which comprehends the representation of thoughts, feelings and attitudes and quoted remarks, mimicry and other quasi-histrionic performances (most clearly exhibited in jokes, gossip, and anecdotes). Theatre serves as a ritual guarantee and an innovative laboratory for the exercise of this capacity to transcend the *personnage*—the reified typification into which we may be trapped by the normal symbolic universe of shared typifications, and to which we are constrained to commit ourselves in sustaining a role, or merely 'joining in' a social occasion. Theatre serves as a constant renewal of the claim to escape from the ritualised *personnage* into other moods, different representations of oneself, into new roles and different milieux, and gives access to entirely different conventional modes prevailing in other societies, other sectors of our own society, or other periods of historical time.

To take a slightly different approach, it is those features of the total self which are not 'on'—the potential selves and the self as audience to our own performance—which calls theatre into being. It is a means of fulfilling the complete self in the present, rather than in unrealisable situations or *in posse*. Again, in ordinary life,

> we can state what is going to happen and take over the responsibility for the thing we are going to do, and yet the real self that appears in that act awaits the completion of the act itself. Now it is this living act which never gets directly into reflective experience. It is only after the act has taken place that we can catch it in our memory and place it in terms of that which we have done. It is that 'I' which we may be said to be continually trying to realise through the actual conduct itself.[33]

In drama completed actions can be represented and their effects on those involved and on future action displayed. Although these actions are necessarily abstracted from real life they are as Simmel says: 'cooked up out of the (ideal) content of all existence',[34] for all appearance presupposes some kind of reality either as its own deeper foundation (of which it is the superstructure) or as its own antithesis (which it wishes to represent in a deceitful way).

It is through this 'cooking up', or reconstitution of his experience of life that the dramatist is able to display in the theatre the complexities of role playing. He demonstrates not only the intentions and motives of one particular character but also the way in which these intentions and motives are modified by the actions of those characters with whom he interacts in ways which we can in reality only suspect or infer. He demonstrates both the limitations and consequences of action, so that the spectator is able to see not only what does happen but what might have happened in specific situations. Because drama is composed (predetermined) action, the spectator observes choices, decisions and reversals from a vantage point which he can never occupy in ordinary life.

[33] G. H. Mead, *Mind, Self and Society* (Chicago University Press, 1934), p. 203.
[34] Simmel, 'Zur Philosophie des Schauspielers', p. 82.

Ordinary social conduct at its most routine or informal, the kind of conduct that takes place in families or amongst friends, is composed and contrived. Each person tries to produce himself in his own drama, to hand out parts to others and to make sure that some of them act the parts of spectators. But because there is no artistic control there is a certain amount of unpredictability, clumsiness and recalcitrance, among actors and audience. Climaxes do not always occur; scenes do not 'come off'; appropriate lines are not spoken; relationships often disintegrate, because, as in an improvisation, the actors dry up. Moreover there is no way, short of dying, in which a person can end his performance. He can discard his friends or move to a different place but he can never bow himself out of all human interaction. Action in the theatre is contrived for an occasion, for the play's duration. Social action is perpetually contrived.

It is this which accounts for the splitting off, in current microsociological analysis of social behaviour from the traditional preoccupation in sociology with the ways in which social roles are defined and graded, and with the contradictions and conflicts to which their incumbents are exposed—a preoccupation which derives from the initial acceptance of analogous relationships between drama and social life. More recent studies concentrate on the forms of 'symbolic' interaction and the fundamentals of situational definition ('ethnomethodology'). So-called 'dramaturgical analysis', an intermediate category between each of these kinds of approach, stresses the 'compositional' aspects of behaviour, particularly the strategies involved in claiming a particular status and the expressive behaviour which more or less successfully maintains the claim. It derives in the first place from Kenneth Burke and, not surprisingly, from Stephen Potter's 'Lifemanship' writings, and owes a good deal to the novels of Ivy Compton-Burnett, which are much concerned with the concealment and the revelation of 'true' identities and relationships and with the presentation of false ones (as well as with the foolishness of bothering about which is which).

Definition of character is a means of putting on show those personal traits and aspects of personal history that are relevant to the dramatist's purpose, and ignoring all others. Again, there is a specifically rhetorical convention involved. No real person can be defined as Hamlet is defined, his motives, his thoughts, his actions all displayed and all relevant to the pattern of dramatic action, but no further. Conversely, no real character can be as little known as Vladimir and Estragon in Beckett's *Waiting for Godot*. These two exist in a static situation and are incapable of making any of the responses which result in action and therefore make a person known. Of course the disclosure of information, the method of disclosure and its extent, if different in degree, is not different in kind from the disclosures about people that occur in ordinary life. The knowledge that this disclosure is a controlled, deliberate (if not always conscious) affair, the analysis of the ways in which disclosure control is exercised, and the purposes for which the information about one's identity is managed is now an established area of sociological study. The specifically theatrical quality of the convention lies in the fact that the management of the information supplied is related to the intentions of the dramatist and not the actor. Once again, the dramatic convention consists of the extension and exploitation of established social conventions. This enables us to see these conventions for what they are and allows us to transfer the perceptions so gained back into our observation of social convention proper.

A social act is defined in two ways: by its purpose and by its mode. In the most general terms, purpose is an attempt to control others, and 'mode' a way of defining the situation (or specifying the convention) which others will accept. A social act

> in formal terms, is a change affected by a person in a part of his total situation which is also part of the total situation of one or more others. The purpose of the act is to transform a relevant sector of the situation of a person in such a way that the same sector becomes the relevant part of the situation in which the other acts, or becomes involved. Social action means the attempt to control others' actions (and perceptions) by interpreting for them the situation and norms according to which they understand, decide, and act.[35]

In other words, social acts aim at conformity by others to one's own definitions or choice of convention, and thus to one's purposes. But, of course, the 'others' are social actors too, with their own purposes and modes. The consensus on what is thematically relevant which obtains in ordinary social intercourse, in the maintenance of ordered public life, and in the transaction of daily affairs and business is therefore not merely a mutual underwriting of a particular definition of the situation but a calculus of the bounds within which action and response (interaction) may progress. The conventions which obtain in bargaining and market transactions, in political controversy, a large assortment of conduct commonly directed towards outmanoeuvring others in sport, in winning social respect or prestige, 'keeping one's end up' socially, and in all forms of conflict and rivalry, enable each party in turn to enlarge upon the frame of reference established by the other, to invoke a definition of the situation or a specific conventional form which will make it more difficult for the other to replace by one larger still, which will lead to the achievement of *his* purpose of control.

These generalities have to be realised in concrete effective terms in

[35] Tom Burns, 'The forms of conduct', *American Journal of Sociology*, lxiv (1958), 138.

the interaction between players and audience. The success of a play depends on the continual expansion of the initially defined situation at a pace and by means which will induce acceptance by the audience. This development is effected by constant expansions of the situation through unanticipated action and by revelations of motives and interests at work among the characters beyond what the audience has hitherto grasped and taken as adequate. New light breaks in, revealing more than they suspected was at work hitherto.[36] This evolutionary, sometimes revolutionary, development of situation and character towards some ultimate, complete resolution at the end is what distinguishes dramatic action and roles from those of ordinary life. The distinction lies not merely in the total explication but in the dominance of the theatrical occasion (in which stage and auditorium are separately peopled) by the precomposed development of situation and role by the players without any comparable counteracting interpretation or breaking of frame by the audience.

The ambiguities, doubts and falsities of presentation which sometimes concern us in social life are also, of course, exploited on the stage. Early drama focused on this elucidatory function in quite specific ways.

Direct address to the audience, *soliloquy* and *asides* which were discussed in chapter 5 define at the same time not only the situation and the meaning of action but also the particular distinction between acted role and revealed *personnage*. The definition of *personnage* became quickly less precise (or interpreted less precisely) than definition of situation.

Iago's intentions can be accepted. He is believed to mean what he says when he speaks to the audience and his subsequent actions confirm that he does. But the spectator is less ready to accept his own version of his motives or of the kind of person that he is. Interpretations of Iago range from a view of him as the devil in disguise or as a personification of Vice to a view of him as a bluff soldier, *moyen sensuel*, spurred on by normal emotions of jealousy and envy.

In the case of a 'good' character or one who, like Hamlet or Macbeth, plays the hero, unambiguous definition of character is even more difficult. Few people accept Hamlet's self-descriptions at his own valuation even when they are in accord with his actions. Even if he is speaking his thoughts aloud, with apparent honesty, self-deception or posturing cannot be overlooked, and if he fains madness does he fain it also to himself? His actions and speech to others may

[36] The archetypal form of this transaction between stage and audience is the mystery or detective play—appropriately and familiarly regarded as depending on 'suspense'—the continued expectation of revelation of further, different, wider meanings to be attached to action already accomplished and characters already presented.

carry as much weight in defining his character as his direct speech to the audience. This at any rate is the view of the modern producer, actor and spectator; hence the many conflicting interpretations of Hamlet himself, ranging from Gielgud's sensitive intellectual to Warner's 'angry' youth and Tom Courteney's laconic tight-lipped marionette (1968), and the differing degrees of conviction given to their 'assumed' or 'real' madness.

Definition of character in realist plays in which rhetorical conventions are more deeply entrenched and implicit is more straightforward, as the information given by other characters is supposed to be relied on. The characters can only reveal themselves through interaction and there is much less scope for different interpretations. In fact the large-scale character, the heroic character, hardly exists in modern drama. The hero has made way for the ordinary or eccentric man such as Joe Orton's Mr Sloane, Osborne's Maitland in *Inadmissible Evidence*, or Pinter's Caretaker, Davies, who is only of interest because of his situation. Such characters as these are defined primarily through authenticating conventions which enable the spectators to recognise their behaviour and relate it to its context. Jimmie Porter in *Look Back in Anger* is defined in terms of his working-class origins, his middle-class university education, the upper-working-class job (keeping a sweet stall in the market) which he has chosen and his upper-middle-class marriage, all this within the context of the drab Midlands city where he lives. All this could be revealed by the actor's speech, gestures and demeanour. Yet it is through rhetorical conventions that Jimmie makes the nature of his situation understood. Instead of speaking directly to the audience he speaks to Alison and Cliff, recapitulating all the details of his biography under cover of bad-tempered outbursts. His eloquence is at odds with the kind of withdrawal that might be expected after four years of unsatisfactory marriage. It is in fact a device. He speaks through the other characters to the audience.

Since a film is a finished product before it is seen by the spectator it might seem that such techniques would be completely ineffective in this medium. They have in fact been little used by directors before Jean-Luc Godard whose aim, like that of Brecht, is audience participation. He likes to give the impression that his films are in the making as they are being watched, that the actors (as in *La Chinoise*) 'are sometimes in the film, and sometimes outside it, sometimes they speak directly to the spectator (which may give one the impression that one is the director with whom the actor is speaking)'.[37] Audiences respond both favourably and unfavourably to these experiments as they do to experimental theatre. But the fact that 'frame-breaking' is considered both feasible and valuable where there is no

[37] Programme note for *La Chinoise* (presented by Edinburgh Film Theatre).

face-to-face contact between actors and audience, indicates that it is a phenomenon that is believed to make art more 'like life' or make it 'come to life'.

Similarly the absence of recognisable social contexts in the non-realist plays of Genet, Beckett and the so-called 'absurd' dramatists means that rhetorical conventions are used, not to define character, but to define the spectators' common attitudes. Soliloquies, direct address to the audience, speech that takes place between characters but lacks the definition of conversation and patterned speech, are all used by Beckett and Ionesco to suggest the isolation, the inexpressibility of individual human experience. *Waiting for Godot* is a rhetorical expression of the human condition as it can be glimpsed in the tramp, the halfwit, the bully. Beckett does not seem to be concerned with the individual characters. In the same way Ionesco in *Rhinocéros* is concerned with the essential human being threatened by pressure to conform to some arbitrary social norm. Bérenger shows no identifiable individuality. He is merely the man who for no very clear reason says 'No'. In the course of the play his character dwindles and he becomes a symbol of resistance.

The use of particular rhetorical conventions is however firmly related to different conceptions of self, role and character (*personnage*). The way in which characters are presented on the stage by the dramatist and through the actors must always reflect the conventional view of the self and its relationship to its roles at different periods and in particular social milieux.

The *theatrum mundi* metaphor was derived from the idea that God was the sole spectator of man's actions on the stage of life. In the early religious theatre the spectator was given a God's eye view of human destiny, acted out in the Miracle and Morality plays. But in the secular theatre man became the spectator of man, however slight his identification with the dramatic characters might be. The drama became a potential means of exploring and experimenting with the whole range of human conduct. It is only constrained by the restricted and specialised experience of most dramatists and spectators, and by the conventions which underlie the actors' means of communication.

Each role both in the social world and on the stage has its own ritual attached to it, a ritual which expresses the role's rights and expectations. The secular drama is not therefore, like sacred drama, a means of creating an *idée du moi*, but rather of displaying the potential activities and relationships of a self, already developed, but perceived in different forms in different contexts.

9

Acting

In the previous chapter I have tried to work through the conception, the very idea of theatre, in terms which correspond to the conception of the self and the correspondence between the changes which both have undergone. This development reveals the social function it performs as a composed public image of the conventions to which the members of a society have to subscribe in order to sustain the shared typifications of relevant realities essential to ordered social life. The actor, in turn, can be regarded as the actual embodiment of these transformations and, beyond these, the living container of the states through which the idea of the self has passed. For he is still a performer of ritual, and thus a *personnage*, a player of socially determined roles, and thus a repository of the reifications of symbolic types into which we thrust ourselves and others in order to dispose of unwanted social realities, a public performer and utterer of acts to which different private meanings may be attached, and thus a model of self images and a revealer of possible reactions to them, an interpreter of archetypal cultural representatives, and thus an audience-critic of the identity we seek to establish. Latterly, at the hands of Pinter, Ionesco, and Stoppard, among many, he has also undergone further transformation into an ambiguous figure demonstrating the fragility of the constructions of social reality by which we conduct our lives; and, most recently, in the institutionalised Living Theatre and its more inchoate counterparts, an experimenter in the interchangeability of actual and potential relevant realities and thus an exponent of possible new moral and political states of being.

The actor, then, stands as the living embodiment of shared social typifications at a number of different levels. But these typifications exist independently of the theatre. It is pleasant, reassuring, revealing or revolting to have them demonstrated by actual living persons engaged in sequences of action which provide us, as audi-

ence, with a fuller grasp of the prevalence, orderliness, or conceivable existence of such typifications. The ritualistic element
always present in the theatre vouches for the inferences we commonly make, with more or less assurance, in our everyday
lives—particularly, as I have said, because a play reveals more of the
consequentiality of action than is usually feasible in the social occasions of everyday life, when we have to attend to the performances in which we ourselves have to engage.

This is, in effect, Souriau's point at the opening of his essay on the
aesthetics of the theatre to which I have already referred:

> The dramatis personae listed at the beginning of a play is in no
> sense a mere display of a collection of human beings selected at
> random, but a *microcosmos in process*, working out the internal
> forces contained within itself . . .
> Theatre is the art which consists in assembling people
> together in order to expose and debate what is problematic
> about their own destinies before their eyes, and to do so through
> the medium of a microcosm (of their world) in some state of
> crisis or of significant conflict between a small number of
> persons. Through the action, it incarnates, mirrors, and presents
> to the senses and the mind the condition of the larger human
> world for which, transitorily, it acts as delegate and represen-
> tative.
> The theatre . . . symbolises, in utter completeness and utter
> totality, the vast expanse of the human condition.[1]

The ritual and symbolic functions of the theatre are, as many
writers have insisted, a fundamental element of any explanation of
its existence. But there is another essential function—a different dimension of representation, so to speak—which is complementary (or
rather, orthogonal) to the first and which fixes the central point of
theatrical reality in the actor himself. This second dimension is the
almost inescapable ambiguity, vagueness, or obscurity (sometimes
deliberate) of the meaning of action. This fact of life, as Stuart Hampshire has, I think, made clear, is a subsection of the inexhaustibility
of descriptions of the reality that confronts us at any time.[2]
Specifically, there is always the possibility of variation in the accounts of actions which the agent himself, as well as other people
observing or knowing of them, might give. Following Hampshire, the
clue to meaning, in this sense, lies in the ascription of one intention
or other—a classificatory schema which prevails in particular societies or groups, and which, since it can only exist in so far as it is
accepted or shared by two or more persons, is an archetypal set of
typifications.

[1] E. Souriau, *Les Grandes problèmes de l'esthétique théâtraletaus*, trans. E.B. (Paris 1960),
    pp. 7, 8.
[2] Stuart Hampshire, *Thought and Action* (Chatto & Windus, 1959), pp. 201–4.

Now it is common knowledge that actions, besides being describable only in terms of intent (a fact which is of ultimate importance in criminal and other kinds of law) are also open to different interpretations in terms of intent, and that speech ('utterance actions') is peculiarly liable to variable interpretation according to context and situation—liable, that is, to misinterpretation so far as the speaker himself is concerned. And the ambiguity attaching to speech, and to a less obvious but equally important extent, to behaviour, is something which constantly imperils social order and our individual lives. In order to avert this danger, we constantly employ tone, gesture, facial expression, demeanour by which our references can be made more specific in relation to our intent.

I am here touching the fringe of a lengthy philosophical debate, the crux of which is nowadays taken as Russell's *Theory of Description*.

> One of the purposes of Russell's theory was to represent the meaning and the implications of any assertion of the form 'the so-and-so is so-and-so' as wholly independent of the particular intentions of any particular speaker on any particular occasion. The purpose could not be fulfilled. The variable intention of a particular speaker on a particular occasion cannot be wholly replaced by the expression of the intention in a constant form of words. Some intention, peculiar to this occasion, necessarily lies behind the words, and cannot be completely conveyed in them. It is a condition of the meaningful use of language with a definite reference to reality that a part of the user's intention in making the statement is not unambiguously expressed in the form of words that he uses.[3]

The actor, therefore, has not merely to perform a role but to 'interpret' it, to fix the words and actions presented for him in a framework of intent legible to the audience and coherent with the rest of the microcosmos of the play.

In both dimensions, performance and interpretation, the actor, as man or woman *in propria persona*, is first and foremost an interloper. He intervenes between the playwright and the audience so as to make the fictive world, *signified* by the first, a set of *signifiers* for the social reality of the latter. He acts—enacts—the rhetoric of the text by working upon 'the common stock of attitudes, of samples and conventions, of truisms and commonplaces' in the enthymemic system mentioned earlier (p. 32). In a quite real sense, he is working a confidence trick, but one in which deceit is neutralised—'earthed'—by the visibly theatrical frame in which it is worked.

He intervenes also between the *authenticity* of his own life, of his

3 *Ibid*, p. 201.

own self and its past as known to himself (and as known or assumed at least in part to the audience) and the *authenticated* life of the character he is playing. So he acts a lie, too, but a lie circumscribed and exposed, or 'earthed', this time by the relationship of trust established by theatrical tradition between the players and audience.

The relationship of trust is all-important in the theatre (as it is in all exchanges and interactions). Its importance—indeed its existence—becomes manifest only at times when it is disturbed or threatened, which is why theatrical innovations, or new forms of drama, acting, theme, or of production are always liable to provoke hostile reaction from at least part of an audience. They feel betrayed, and rightly so, since in their case too much is being demanded of them.

A relationship of trust in marriage or between friends, as well as between partners involves a mutual understanding in which each side assumes that it knows all it needs to know and that the other side will feel bound to convey that information. The point is not in 'knowing everything' but in 'knowing that one knows everything', everything, that is, one needs to know about the other. And this requires tact, a competence in handling the arbitrary lines between what the other *needs* to know, what he *does* know, and what he *should not* know, a competence, moreover, which has to be demonstrated to the other so that he is assured that the relationship of trust is in safe hands. The bodily agility, extending to control of facial muscles which is obviously out of the ordinary, and the special verbal mastery are all, therefore, much more than tricks of the actor's trade. They demonstrate his equipment of tactful competence. Bad acting is essentially a species of tactlessness—of wrong judgment which leads to the other side (the audience) getting to know either more, or less, than it needs to know.

But tact is required of the audience, too. It is, in fact, a term applicable to interaction, not merely to action by one person, or side. It inheres in what Goffman refers to as 'team play'[4]—the sustaining of a social situation by both agent and others. Social situations are sustained by the continuous exercise of discretion by others as well as by agents. Discretion consists in disregarding accidental or maladroit revelations of 'what one is not supposed to know', as well as in responding 'properly' to the rhetorical modes, according recognition to the semblances of settings and of social forces as though they were 'authentic', and recognising the indications of intent which are contained in action, utterance, demeanour, costume and personal accessories.

Hence, in discussing actors and acting, it is necessary to have regard to the particular controls which the audience exercises in

[4] Goffman, *The Presentation of Self in Everyday Life*, ch. 2.

sustaining *interaction*. Tenuous as the historical evidence is, some
knowledge of the audience's part in the theatrical occasion is essential for an understanding of acting. and, again, this understanding is
perhaps best reached by an attempt to register the changes in the
actor-audience relationship. Changes, social changes, provide an opportunity for insight by promoting a kind of binocularity—a perspective vision of the new against the background of the old. To
some extent, the task is eased (although it is also confused) by the
intervention of theatrical critics, who, in attempting to monitor the
effectiveness of playwrights and actors according to the codes of
traditional, contemporary, or coterie literature, mark some of the
changes in the relationship.

This chapter and the next are devoted to an analysis of actors and
audience, with the critic introduced not so much as intermediary or
expositor of the relationship as witness of shifts in the structure of
the relationship. But his presence is also a reminder of a more fundamental relationship in which the actor himself is truly intermediary. It is approached tangentially by Duvignaud in his
preliminary catalogue of structural relationships between 'real life'
and 'theatrical' action which he terms the *theatricalisation* of life.[5]

> The meeting of local authority councillors, a council of war, have
> a different significance; a revolutionary tribunal meeting to try
> a traitor *has to* lead to action, and sometimes to invent a sol-
> ution which will put the whole group at risk. Here too, the
> participants are each obliged to represent a role which their
> position in the group, or which the decision they make, imposes
> on them. But what they are concerned with is the preparation or
> justification of an act which they must actually accomplish so
> as to realise their socially defined task: to punish, condemn,
> pardon, declare a strike, or fight a battle. Every collectivity can
> find itself in such a situation, a situation replete with as much
> theatricality as ceremonial or re-enacted myth.
>
> In both cases, an 'effervescent social milieu', in the sense
> Emile Durkheim gave to the phrase, is turning its existence as a
> collectivity into reality by playing out the drama of its 'mythi-
> cal' cohesion or in working out its scenario for action.[6]

In a play, it is the 'mythical cohesion' of the multiplicity of roles
or potentially realisable selves, levels and systems of belief, moral
stands, and various scenarios of personal or collective or counteraction *which actually resides within one individual* which is played
out in front of individual members of an audience each of whom can
also comprehend the variety of realisable selves, scenarios, or levels

[5] J. Duvignaud, *Sociologie du Théâtre*, pp. 7–12 (trans. in Elizabeth and Tom Burns,
Sociology of Literature and Drama, Penguin, 1972).
[6] Duvignaud, pp. 8–9.

of belief *within his own self*. Each of us, in making choices, performing a role, interpreting a role, holding to an opinion or belief and so forth, is simultaneously conscious of the choices he forgoes, the roles and interpretations he neglects or surrenders to others, the opinions or beliefs he suppresses or rejects. Indeed, 'arguing with oneself', or 'arriving at a decision', or simply choosing, involves the multiplication of selves and of unrealisable possibilities which the singularity of action imposed on us by biological constraints and the singularity of intention and meaning imposed on us by social constraints forces us to reduce to the meagreness of actuality. So that a play is a ritual form of release from the need to act as undivided selves, a reaffirmation of the multiple existential potentialities we incorporate but cannot realise. This reaffirmation by a single person—the playwright—is lived out by players on a stage before hundreds of our fellows in the audience on a totally acceptable, traditionally sanctioned, and unexceptionable occasion, in buildings constructed for this very purpose, and in an institutional context which is connected with everyday existence in all kinds of manifest ways. The theatre thus reveals itself as a ritual device for the constant renewal of belief in human autonomy for individuals required constantly to submit to the vexatious necessities of consistent, recognisable role behaviour in the world of ordered social life. The actor is the visible, literally corporeal, vehicle of this ritual reaffirmation, conceived by culturally selected individuals but enacted on the stage *on our behalf*.[7]

The very appearance of critic as a specific occupational role, as reporter, commentator and evaluator of playwright, play and performance (and occasionally of audience), is testimony not only to the validity of this rendering of the peculiar semantics of the complex act of communication between playwright and auditor, but to the fact that the structured fantasies which demonstrate the opportunity costs of our actual lives have themselves taken on an institutional form. The critic, in fact, acts as umpire (not a universally popular figure) over the rules of the game being played with and for our metasocial selves, as observer of success and failure, and—at least for the student—recorder of changes in the rules of the game and of the degree of authentication accorded to such changes by contemporary opinion.

In the rest of this chapter, we shall be concerned largely with the analysis of one sector of this semantic universe inhabited by the actor.

[7] The simultaneity of presence on the stage of actors and actions is what distinguishes the drama from epic (and it is important to remember that literary tradition before and after Goethe's pronouncements, regarded epic poetry rather than ritual as the forerunner of drama) and from the novel, both of which are constructed in terms of a temporally linear narrative.

The actor inhabits four distinct domains of social reality. In the 'real world' he is a man who has adopted the professional role of actor. On the stage he is an actor who presents a character. The audience does not necessarily identify him with this role, indeed, it distinguishes him from it in his interpretation; and it is possible to admire an actor even when his interpretation seems to be wrong. In the dramatic microcosmos of the play he is a fictional character interacting with other fictional characters. Finally he rescues us from the constraints of 'the vexatious fact of society . . . a conglomeration of more or less binding, more or less particular group norms',[8] by ritually enacting and thus realising theatricalised versions of the residue of unrealisable potentialities of existence. In other words, he could be said to salvage and present to us, for a space of time, and on specific ritual occasions, the opportunity costs of the lives we have chosen, or been forced, to live.

These four aspects can be separated in this way only for purposes of analysis. The actor's social 'self', his response to the norms and constraints and his understanding of the typifications which together form the conventions of the society in which he lives, determines both the mode of presentation and the mode of interpretation of character on the stage. For this he is not, of course, solely responsible. His understanding of his role depends on the view of character and action which both dramatist and audience share with him. In performing a play by a dramatist of an earlier period he, the actor, is engaged with the producer and audience in a process of interpretation which is conditioned by a shared contemporary view of the individual's relationship to society.

The actor's occupation

A profession is thought of as one 'ideal type' or model of a fully institutionalised occupation (a craft is another). Based on the characteristics of the older professions, the ministry, law and medicine, such a model cannot be regarded as representative of all so-called professions, most of which stand somewhere on the line between ideal type professions at one end and completely unorganised occupational categories or non-professions at the other.

'Professionalisation' is a process which may affect any occupation to a greater or lesser degree. Gross has this to say about the process:

> As any occupation approaches professional status, there occur important internal structural changes and changes in the relationship of the practitioners to society at large. A useful way

[8] R. Dahrendorf, 'Homo sociologicus', in *Essays in the Theory of Society* (Stanford University Press, 1968), p. 52.

of discussing these changes is by reference to the criteria of professionalisation: the unstandardised product, degree of personality involvement of the professional, wide knowledge of a specialised technique, sense of obligation (to one's art), sense of group identity, and significance of the occupational service to society.[9]

Some importance may be attached to the fact that professionalism was forced on actors during the sixteenth century as a means of protection and survival when actors were organised into companies and came to occupy the public theatres. Because it is an activity apparently within reach of everyone and practised by some, such as confidence tricksters (and unprofessionally by social charlatans) for nefarious purposes, acting had difficulty in qualifying as an art. At a time when painters, sculptors and musicians in Renaissance Europe were revered and patronised by the powerful, actors were in danger of prosecution as 'rogues and vagabonds'.

The dangerous qualities inherent in acting are those qualities inherent in human nature, deceit, irreverent mimicry and the power to arouse in others passions and emotions normally controlled. In ordinary life these subversive powers are not usually manipulated with much skill. An actor, however, is trained to develop them and to regard his skill as an art. To some extent he comes to look upon his voice, expression, gestures and movements as instruments external to and separate from himself like the painter's brush or the musician's violin.

This externalisation of parts of the self contributed to the suspicion aroused by the pre-professional actor, the mountebank, mummer or fool. As a person who could switch from one role to another by a change of costume or demeanour his integrity was in doubt and he found himself excluded from the confidence on which the respectable rely.[10] More generally, as I have remarked, 'playing the fool' is a standard device for disrupting the conventions which maintain the symbolic universe taken as relevant by the members of any social occasion or milieu.[11]

Although the Church sponsored the earliest drama there were many churchmen who railed against the profanity of plays and

---

[9] E. Gross, *Work and Society* (Crowell, 1958), p. 77.

[10] For detailed description of the change in status of the common player see M. C. Bradbrook, *Rise of the Common Player* (Chatto & Windus, 1962), pt 1, 'Players and Society', pp. 17–119.

[11] Following Klapp and Grathoff (see pp. 123–4, above), although Shakespeare has provided instances enough to make the point clear enough to render any such laboured sociological analysis superfluous. One need only refer to the effect obtained in *Lear* by the *personnage* of the Fool triumphantly puncturing the artificial social world of his master's field of action to begin with, eventually engulfed in the tragic outcome, and thus underwriting the cosmic extension of a particular situation.

acting. Yet the Church continued to encourage and protect the performances of religious plays both inside and outside its precincts.
The players however remained amateurs: ecclesiastics in the Introit
plays and guildsmen in the Mystery cycles.

Players of secular plays at court or in the halls of the nobility were
either strollers, minstrels or *histriones*. These were either occasional
players or household servants whose duties included providing entertainment at feasts or on other special occasions. During the sixteenth
century plays and interludes became more popular than music or
acrobatics for 'occasional' entertainment, so popular that the author-
ities began to look at them askance. Their use as instruments of
blasphemy or sedition was quickly perceived, and Henry VIII at-
tacked the problem by announcing his intention of impressing for
the navy 'ruffians, vagabonds, masterless men and common players'.
Thus players were driven to seek the livery of any powerful lord
who required a large retinue. Fortunately many of these lords were
sufficiently interested in dramatic performance to encourage such
servants to develop their skills. The Elizabethan Act for Restraining
Vagabonds (1572) took a further step in the direction of creating a
profession. As all troupes had to be licensed by a nobleman or a
justice of the peace, player-servants were officially distinguished
from other household servants. Thus, although limitation and control of the players may have constricted much of the spontaneous
dramatic life (the mummings, games and dancing) of town and
countryside it did help to produce a profession without which drama
as a distinctive art form might not have developed. The loss of spontaneous dramatic activity in social life was perhaps the price that
had to be paid for this achievement.

The next necessary step towards professionalisation was the provision of permanent theatres to which all would have access. Burbage's *Theater*, and those theatres which followed it in London and
other parts of the country provided regular performances unconnected with festivals of the Church or civic occasions. In such conditions it was possible to create a regular audience which would
become familiar with the conventions of dramatic performance.
Moreover, with an enclosed building it was possible to make the
public pay (this had previously only been possible in the courtyards
of inns). This meant that the players no longer provided a utility for
their master and his guests but for a paying public which could
freely give or withdraw its support. As the takings were usually
shared by the whole company every player was aware of his obligation to please the public. The audience's response in terms of
money established the commercial basis of the acting profession in
which actors were freed from the feudal service relationship but tied
to a market in which criteria of value rested on less predictable or

less reliable social attitudes and on uncertain links with the social structure.

On this basis the profession has continued until the present day, though there have been marked changes in organisation. The sharing system, whereby the profits were shared by all members of the company after the manager and owner had taken their extra shares for expenses, broke down in the middle of the eighteenth century and left the actors dependent on salaries and even more on 'benefits'. But the prosperity of the companies in London, in repertory and on tour was always of prime importance to the actors. It depended on many things, the right choice of play, the star actor, appropriate settings but most of all on good performances from the whole company. Thus for the individual actor experience of the acting profession has always meant experience of a group of people with whom he has face-to-face relationships; and this group is a cell in a larger group which comprises the whole profession.

Like other professions the acting profession still operates through a network of formal and informal groups. Formal groups in the acting profession are now represented by the organisation responsible for the theatre, the organisation of the company, the organisation of drama schools and the actors' union. Informal groups are formed in and across companies, forming networks of producers and actors, through whose influence careers can be furthered. Although groups of this kind are also found in non-professional occupations it is in professional occupations that the interaction of social roles in these groups generates a social configuration unique to the professions, viz. a professional culture,[12] with its own values, norms and symbols. An extreme development of this normal professional tendency can be seen in theatre groups such as La Mama and the Living Theatre. Such groups live as a family and try to obliterate distinction between their professional and private selves; in fact they scarcely recognize the distinction. Life on and off the stage is supposed to display the same commitment and integrity.

The assumption of any occupational role involves changes in identity. Erik Erikson describes identity formation as a lifelong process: 'It is the identity of something in the individual's core with an essential aspect of a group's inner coherence which is under consideration here; for the young individual must learn to be most himself where he means most to others—those others to be sure who have come to mean most to him.'[13] This applies both to the large group (national,

[12] E. Greenwood, 'The elements of professionalisation', in *Professionalisation*, ed. H. M. Vollmer and D. L. Mills (Prentice-Hall, 1966), p. 10.
[13] E. Erikson, 'Problem of ego identity' *Psychological Issues*, i, no. 1 (New York, 1959), 102.

political or religious) and the small. But it sometimes applies in a peculiarly acute form to the occupational group of which he has become a member. The need to identify with this group tends to increase with the degree of professionalisation that the occupation has achieved.

Howard Becker, in his study of postgraduate students and their identification with the subject to which they have committed themselves, postulates 'the operation of certain mechanisms producing changes in identity. These mechanisms . . . consist of ways in which participation in organised groups of various kinds affects experience, and, through this, self-image. Among the mechanisms operating . . . are the development of problem-interest and pride in new skills, the acquisition of professional ideology, investment, the internalisation of motives and sponsorship.'[14]

The same mechanisms can be seen at work in the career of the actor, if slight adjustments of terminology are made. 'Problem-interest and pride in new skills' take the form of problems of interpretation and techniques of acting. 'Acquisition of professional ideology' is replaced by 'artistic integrity'. 'Investment' (and its converse, opportunity cost) remains common to both. In the case of the actor it means investment of the self (the expenditure of time and energy, the surrender of options, and financial sacrifice in payments or income forgone) in the period of training, the engagement of an agent and maintenance of a 'front'. Finally, motivations (or general dispositions, sets, or intentions) are publicly typified in the actor's new identity, qua actor, and become internalised.

Behaviour is now reoriented 'in terms of what is proper and desirable for the bearer of such an identity, in terms of the motives they consider appropriate for the kind of persons they have become'.

Sponsorship, in Becker's study, refers to the relationship of students to professors and senior members of the profession to whom they look for sponsorship. In the theatre it can be seen to operate through the actor's relationships with his agent, but more specifically with certain producers or with a theatre company which has formed a group identity, e.g. the Living Theatre, LAMDA, the Open Space, or certain tightly knit civic theatres (for example, the Victoria at Stoke-on-Trent).

Certain occupational roles, such as that of priest, doctor or policeman can for slightly differing reasons be said to be 'total roles'. It is impossible for people to discard these roles temporarily and behave like other people without being aware of some kind of moral transgression. Even on holiday the priest knows that he should maintain

[14] H. S. Becker and J. Carper, 'The Elements of Identification with an Occupation', *A.S.R.*, xxi, no. 3 (June 1956), p. 342.

his 'goodness', the policeman his respect for the law and the doctor his readiness to practise his skill. Any neglect even if unobserved can damage his relationship to his role-identification, and if observed, can ruin him professionally.

The actor's relationship to his occupational role is slightly different. There is a personal rather than a moral obligation to maintain his role, an obligation which is dependent on his desire for success. The pressure to behave like an actor is applied by other actors and by 'his public', just as the university teacher's role, by and large is constrained by colleagues and students. An individual actor usually goes to a School of Drama or joins a repertory theatre because he likes acting. But in the process of learning to act he becomes 'an actor', learning to conform to values and norms which are different from those of the rest of society. In time he feels himself to be something of an 'outsider' in ordinary society and very much an 'insider' in theatrical society. In dress, demeanour, use of language and style of living he is usually (unless he adopts a deliberate disguise) recognisable as an actor. This style is not adopted only because it helps him to feel at home with other actors but also because it helps him to 'make the grade'. He learns the right language to use with people who can be influential in furthering his career.

Although no occupational study has yet been made (in England or America) of acting as a profession, a comparable study of dance-band musicians was made by Howard Becker in America. Here, also, he is concerned with a service occupation in which the full-time activity of performers is centred on the occupation, to which they are as a rule wholly committed. The musician comes into direct personal contact with the consumers of the utility which he offers and is therefore made directly aware of the attempt made by those who are not musicians and 'do not understand',[15] to influence his art. This accounts for 'the feeling of isolation' from the rest of society that most musicians experience and the way they segregate themselves from audience and community. The feeling of difference is usually resolved as a feeling of superiority: 'From the idea that no-one can tell a musician how to play it follows logically that no-one can tell a musician how to do anything.'[16]

Actors, whose art is concerned with analysing and recreating the behaviour of ordinary as well as extraordinary people seem to feel this sense of superiority even more acutely. Professional secrecy and the creation of professional mystique are implicit in the writing and utterances (in interview) of many actors. They are usually freely informative about their personal lives but less so about their tech-

[15] H. Becker, 'The culture of a deviant group', in *Outsiders* (Free Press, 1963), p. 83.
[16] *Ibid*, p. 87.

niques. John Gielgud, at the end of an autobiographical sketch, excuses this reticence:

> No doubt it would have been better to have written in some detail of the technical difficulties and problems of the art of acting. But it is not easy to describe how actors go about their business. Perhaps it is more seemly that these mysteries should remain a secret. No one can understand the technical side of the theatre until he himself comes to practise it, and in spite of imploring letters from inquisitive enthusiasts, we actors do not encourage members of the public to watch us at our rehearsals.[17]

Other actors who set out to discuss technique still take refuge in vagueness as if they did not really know what technique was, and relied on inspiration. Michael Redgrave who, in 1958, tried to provide an acceptable guide to Stanislavski's Method, something which could be translated into an English version, and which was not too formidable, found it difficult to avoid using 'inspiration' rather than 'technique' as a key to good acting.

In spite of Gielgud's statement it seems that it might be as well for actors to let the public into rehearsals:

> It is true that many of the most exciting and true moments of the actor's work come during rehearsals. Then it is that the creative mood, the instinct that makes an actor say a line in a certain way, the impulse which prompts a certain 'unforgettable' gesture burns brightly though fitfully ... for the actor's chief and abiding problem is to find the creative mood by which he can persuade the audience that he is such or such a character and that the things he says or does are being said and done for the first time every night.[18]

In a television interview (1969) Ian McKellen reinforced the same point. He said that whereas amateurs find most interest and excitement in performing to an audience, professionals find it at rehearsals. They presumably regard other actors as their most stimulating and best qualified audience. Professionalisation, therefore, in acting as in other disciplines, tends to isolate the actor from the public, from all who are not actors.

Actors, however, who belong to experimental theatre groups and are committed to new styles of acting and production are less secretive about their art. Innovation can only be successful if new conventions are shared by actors and audience and if audience

---

[17] J. Gielgud, *Early Stages* (Falcon Press, 1938), p. 248. The reluctance of actor/producers to allow outsiders to attend rehearsals is still marked. Olivier and Miles both refused a request to attend rehearsals on the grounds that privacy was essential.

[18] M. Redgrave, *Mask or Face* (Heinemann, 1958), p. 95.

participation is desired it is essential that the audience should know
what the actor is really up to. The assumption is that all can be
actors if techniques are shared. This would be the basis of Joan Littlewood's proposed Fun Palace, where actors and non-actors would
gather to create 'theatre'. Such an experiment would go some way
towards slackening the constraints, conformities and, of course, the
mystique of professionalism.

Not surprisingly it has been producers or producer/actors who
have been most open and most interested in writing about technique.
Stanislawski, Brecht, Jean-Louis Barrault and Olivier write about and
discuss acting from both points of view, from the point of view of
the actor who can only feel what is happening and guess what it
looks like from the auditorium, and from the point of view of the
producer who sees it all as the audience will see it. Thus in *Theaterarbeit* a colleague described Brecht at rehearsal speaking to an
actor: 'This is your moment. Don't let it slip through your fingers.
Now you're the important one—the devil with the play. . . . It is in
the interest of all the performers to present the play as a unit; it is
also in your interest as an individual. It is also in your interest to
bring out certain contrasts. These contrasts are the life-blood of the
play.'[19]

It is also possible to gain a more direct understanding of the way
the actor himself works, as distinct from the way he thinks he
works,[20] from Charles Marowitz's contrast between two kinds of
actors that he calls 'trads' and 'mods', the latter being those who have
been exposed to work in experimental theatres. Although he admits
that the distinction is too rigid and probably unfair to the 'trads', the
two sets of attitudes do express some of the attitudes that are available to the actor at the present time:

Trads	*Mods*
Let's get it plotted	Let's get it analysed
Fix inflections and readings	Play for sense and let inflections take care of themselves
Plot as soon as possible	Move freely for as long as possible
Play for laughs	Play for contact
Final decisions as soon as possible	Final decisions as late as possible and always open to reversal
and so:	
My many years of professional experience convince me that . . .	Nothing is ever the same[21]

[19] B. Brecht, *Theaterarbeit* (Dresden, 1952).
[20] Cf. Hampshire *Thought and Action*, ch. 2 'Intention and action', esp. p. 118—
'Self deceit is a familiar shadow of social deceit'.
[21] C. Marowitz and S. Trussler, eds., *Theatre at Work* (Methuen, 1967), p. 180.

The actor's choice of approach, it seems, must depend on the kind of producer that he has worked with or prefers to work with, a 'trad' or 'mod' producer. This suggests that informal organisation in the profession is becoming increasingly strong. Like-minded producers and actors are hunting each other out and avoiding their opposites. This is to some extent a return to the pre-drama school tradition. Training in Schools of Drama was only firmly established in 1892 with the founding of the Royal Academy of Dramatic Art, and even now such colleges provide only one of the many routes into the profession. Training in repertory theatres, in student drama societies and occasionally 'discovery' on television are known to provide other career entries.

The existence of these various routes into the profession and the weighting of natural capacity (recognition of potential) and experience, as against certificates or diplomas, distinguish acting from other more formal professions. This is not a chance state of affairs. The most important judges of the actor are neither the governors of colleges who issue certificates, nor theatre managers nor critics (who are intermediaries) but the spectators whose power is exercised through the box office. It is therefore essential for actors to act within the bounds of the understanding and expectations of the audience. Managers of nationally subsidised theatres as much as commercial theatre have to be constantly aware of the box office takings. For the actor the audience provides the feed-back essential for the proper accomplishment of any professional role as well as the measure of his commercial success. It plays a double role as sponsor and customer. The actor is, therefore, both influenced by and an influence on the spectator. By himself he cannot *set* trends ('throw-away' style, Method acting, nudity, obscenities) but he catches their feasibility from literature and from the ordinary life of which he is a part. Then, by expressing them in a theatrical setting he provides the public with the opportunity to give or withhold sanction for their incorporation in the whole range of typified behaviour.

The actor as presenter

The actor transmutes what he sees as acceptable social action into theatrical action. He presents a character who is a fiction but who approximates to character as it is experienced in real life, from specific and reified *personnages* to ambiguous, and even improbable states of being. The character presented on the stage, therefore, belongs to the worlds neither of literature nor of reality.

Simmel attempts to describe the autonomy of the theatrical world in which the role is realised:

The orthodox theory that the way a role must be played is given by the text of the play alone signifies a literary ideal but not a theatrical one. The actor is not the marionette of the role, but between the crude representation of reality and the attempt to extract from literature what it can never produce by itself, the art of the actor stands as a third possibility deriving from its own roots, neither a derivative from reality nor from the drama, nor yet achieved by way of synthesis.[22]

Although Simmel does not succeed in clarifying this third possibility his 'art of the actor' seems to rest on the art of presentation which in the early days of drama was so much stressed. Simmel speaks of the actor 'representing' rather than realising a character. If an actor pretends that he is really the character and not the 'cheap blackguard' he really is he creates a double lie but this 'could not arise if the actor's portrayal kept us distant from the world of reality in the world of art'.[23] This conception of acting as a representation which draws from both the 'real' world and the world of art is most evident in stylisation of the traditional Japanese and Indian theatre and in what is believed to have been the style of the masked classical actors.

Although little is known about the style of medieval acting, the play seems to have been something that was 'presented' in such a way that the real world and the world of the drama were kept apart.

The function of presenting was shared, in medieval and early sixteenth-century plays and masques, with the actors by a Presenter. Moreover the actor was helped to present himself by the physical conditions of the open or round stage where he was set in the midst of the audience, with whom direct communication was natural. As we have seen the function of Presenter was reduced during the sixteenth century until he did no more than deliver a brief Prologue while the actor, himself, developed the rhetoric of presenting.[24]

The sixteenth-century actor benefited from living in a society where modes of behaviour were clearly defined both for ceremonial and ordinary occasions. The ceremonial connected with the court, the law courts, parliament and civic functions, demanded performances from the participants for which appropriate gestures and intonations were consciously learned and displayed. Players, as servants of the Queen or the nobles had access to these displays and also opportunity to observe aristocratic behaviour on both private and public occasions: 'What was livelihood for the low born—plausibility of speech, comeliness of action—was merely the aspect of the noble spirit in his superiors.'[25] This natural nobility

---

[22] Simmel, *Zur Philosophie des Schauspielers*.
[23] *Ibid*, p. 35.
[24] See chap. 5.
[25] H. Peacham, *The Compleat Gentleman* (London, 1634), p. 13.

of behaviour had to be learned by the young of gentle birth in a
school or noble household, but the fact that 'natural' behaviour
had to be learned was openly recognised and accepted. Manuals
such as *The Compleat Gentleman* and Castiglione's *The Courtier*[26]
insisted on the importance of appropriate behaviour for every occasion and the need to avoid *affectation*. The formulation of rules of
decorum did not of course imply insincerity or superficiality of behaviour (except, of course, in the case of foreign styles of courtesy).
The familiar description of the behaviour of the Earl of Essex on the
occasion of his execution suggests a 'natural nobility' of performance in which the presenting elements did not detract from the
Earl's sincerity:

> Then he put off his gown and ruff and went before the block. He
> called for the executioner who on his knees asked him pardon,
> to whom he said 'Thou are welcome to me; I forgive thee. Thou
> art the minister of justice.' Then he kneeled down on the straw
> and with his eyes fixed to heaven and with long and passionate
> pauses in his speech he prayed unpremeditatedly craving
> strength to rely to his last gasp on the promises of Christ and to
> have no worldly thought but only God before him. He then
> repeated the Lord's prayer, in which all present joined with
> floods of tears.[27]

The Earl was presenting himself, giving a performance which both
he and the onlookers understood as a conventional way of making
bearable an unbearable occasion. Performances such as this suggest
the background against which Shakespeare set his tragic scenes and
the bearing that might be expected from his actors. Thus the much
discussed suggestion that Elizabethan acting was formal or stylized
need not imply that it was not true to life.[28] We have to take into
account the great range of prescribed models for formal and informal behaviour, permissible within the scope of acceptable conduct at
this period: 'The central and distinguishing fact about behaviour in
such a (pre-industrial) society was that the whole set of roles and

[26] B. Castiglione, *The Courtier* (1528, trans. A. P. Castiglione, 1727): Castiglione
charged the Courtier to 'avoid all Appearance of Affectation. Next let him weigh each
Action and Expression, in what place he is, and before whom, how seasonable the
act is and what its Cause; let him attend to his Age, his Profession, to the end he
proposes and to the Means whereby that end may be compos'd. These particulars
considered let him prudently apply himself to what he proposes to act or speak'
(p. 118). 'Affectation' (curiositie, in the contemporary translation) seems to imply
then, as now, action which is disproportionately demonstrative—in which demonstration and instrumentality are not properly balanced. In *Hamlet* the 'affected'
Osric is more concerned to display his elegance and refinement than to accomplish
his mission.

[27] Camden, quoted in G. B. Harrison, *Last Elizabethan Journal* (Constable, 1933),
p. 163.

[28] 'What can be said is that Elizabethan acting was thought at the time to be life-
like, at any rate in the public theatres': R. A. Foakes, 'The Player's Passion',
English Association Essays and Studies (London, 1954), p. 76.

relationships available to an individual born into one particular status in it was visible and could be learned as he grew up in that status.'[29]

Somewhere between the actor in real life and the actor on the stage we find the orator, who also gave a performance, a performance which was explicitly rhetorical. Persuasion was, as it is now, its aim; but it was an aim that was then considered legitimate in a way in which it is not nowadays.[30] The successful orator required an elaborate training in the use of his voice, language, gestures and movements of the whole body. Although no one has been able to prove that actors were trained in the same way as orators the art of the actor and that of the orator are so frequently bracketed together that it seems apparent that orators and actors must have learned much from each other. Bulwer, whose treatise on Manuall Rhetoric was published in 1644, intended the publication for orators. On the title-page, however, he specified its wider application: 'The art (Manuall Rhetorique) was first formed by Rhetoricians, afterwards amplified by Poets and cunning Motists, skilful in the pourtraiture of mute poesie: but most strangely inlarged by Actors, the ingenious counterfeiters of men's manners.'[31]

Other writers confirmed this view of the relationship between actors and orators: 'In the substance of external action for the most part oratours and stage players agree.'[32] Bulwer described and illustrated a wide range of manual gestures with their precise meanings. But he did not suggest that they should be used mechanically: 'The gestures of the hand must be prepared in the mind together with the inward speech that precedes the outward expression.'[33] Thus the orator or actor was provided with an elaborate verbal and manual language whose meaning he could assume was known to most of the audience, by means of which he could present a specific character in terms of shared typifications.

It is the opposition of the terms 'natural' and 'formal' that has caused misunderstanding of the style of acting at this period. It is quite clear from Hamlet's speech to the players that both overacting and underacting were recognised faults and that a distinction was made between 'natural' and 'unnatural' acting. This does not imply that naturalness had the same meaning then as now. Natural

[29] Burns, 'Cultural Bureaucracy', p. 10.

[30] Cf. McGinnis *The Selling of the President*. The stigma which now attaches to the revelation of careful preparation, styling and rehearsal of rhetorical performance provides a curious commentary on the increasing value attached to 'naturalness' and 'sincerity' at a time when we are increasingly aware of the nature of the social self as artifact.

[31] J. Bulwer, *Chirologia: or the natural language of the hand ... whereunto is added Chironomia or the art of Manuall rhetoricke* (London, 1644), *Chironomia*, p. 34.

[32] Thomas Wright, *The Passions of the Minde in Generall*, London, 1621, p. 179.

[33] Bulwer, *Chirologia*, p. 6.

behaviour in any period is judged not by any criterion of spontaneity but by its conformity to norms that have been learned. The actor who would appear 'natural' imitates those performances in the ordinary world that are already composed to appear 'natural'. The 'natural' actor is in fact concerned more with authenticating than with rhetorical conventions. It is through authentication that he believes he can impose a character upon the audience. In fact the actor who tries to see the character he is presenting from the point of view of the audience and uses their frame of reference is mainly concerned with authentication, whereas the actor who presents the character from his own point of view concentrates on rhetorical conventions. In his choice of conventions he is of course guided by the dramatist and by the dramatist's view of the character. In the sixteenth and seventeenth centuries presentation by means of rhetorical conventions implied that the actor in collusion with the dramatist was offering not only the character but a moral view of the character which the audience should accept. In the *Character of an Excellent Actor*, published under Overbury's name this moral view of acting is suggested: 'By his actions he fortified morall precepts with examples: for what we see him personate we think truly done before us: a man of deepe thought might apprehend the Ghosts of our Heroes walked againe and take him at severall times for one of them.'[34]

In this statement we are given a general idea of the mode in which the actor was expected to present character in the fictional world of the play. It confirms the evidence, that can be derived only from drama itself, of a shift from the personification of the medieval Miracle and Morality plays to the impersonation of secular plays in the sixteenth century.

The early ecclesiastical dramatist was primarily concerned with spiritual enlightenment and therefore with the symbolic presentation of good and evil qualities. In the Miracle plays he was already provided with biblical characters who were regarded ambivalently as at the same time symbolic and historic. The outlines of the characters of Cain, Noah or Abraham were already laid down, but the dramatist was free to use vernacular speech in which to express a recognisable personality. Yet these characters were personifications of spiritual realities. There was no scope for development of character through interaction with others or through the experience of choice. The naturalism through which the characters are presented suggests rather the narrowness of the gap between ordinary life and religious experience at this time than a humanistic view of character.

Personification as an acting mode reached a clearer definition in

[34] T. Overbury, *Character of an Excellent Actor*, in *Works*, ed. E. Rimbault (London, 1856), pp. 147–8.

the Morality plays. In these the dramatist was creating an allegory. He was not concerned with biblical events but with the present and eternal condition of man. His theme was usually a variation on the struggle between God and the Devil for the soul of man. Characters were therefore personifications of vices or virtues occupied in tempting or protecting 'Mankind', 'Everyman', 'King Humanitie' or other representations of man in the world.

In the most powerful Morality plays, *Everyman, The Castle of Perseverance, Wisdom* and *The Three Estates* there was scope for realistic presentation and acting but each character was determined by the relationship between the social reality he represented and vice or virtue. Motive and intention were self-evident in the *personnage* thus created. The characters were usually established not only by their names but also emblematically by costume or appurtenances. Thus in *Wisdom* (or *Christ*) Anima enters at the beginning:

> 'as a mayde, in a wyght clothe of gold gy(n)teley purfyled with menyver, a mantyll of blake, (þer-wppe-on) a chauele(r) lyke to Wysdom . . .' Later after the corruption of Mind, Will, and Understanding, Anima 'apperythe in þe most horybullwyse, fowlere than a fende . . . here rennyt owt from wyndyre þe horrybull mantyll of þe soull vi small boys in þe lyknes of Dewyllys . . .'[35]

To the expressiveness of costume and setting the actor had to add the expressiveness of gesture, demeanour and speech.

Sixteenth-century secular dramatists inherited this form of dramatized *personnage* through personification. Instead of symbolising spiritual values derived from popular Christian doctrine, characters often personified qualities derived from the chivalric tradition and passions familiar in social life. They were no longer, as in the Morality plays, named as the vice or virtue which they personified but were presented as if they were real persons whose actions were prompted by intentions, recognisably typical of the socially real world, and were not exclusively symbolic. In this way *impersonation*, the portrayal of a person through imitation of behaviour, derived from observation and experience of ordinary life began to replace *personification*. The difference of the two modes lay in their frames of reference. Personification referred always to man in his relationship with the unseen, inferred world of spiritual reality or to universals or to spiritual beings, impersonation to the known social world. Thus although the change certainly did not denote more sophisticated or sensitive understanding of man in the world it did enable drama to become a more complex and flexible art. Allegorical drama

---

[35] *Macro Plays*, ed. F. J. Furnivall and A. W. Pollard (London, 1904), p. 186.

is restricted by the boundaries of truth and error fixed by sacrosanct tradition and sanctioned by the Church. Personified characters do not develop or even change. Impersonated characters are restricted only by the limitations of the dramatist's knowledge and that of the society in which he writes.

The essential conception of personification, that man has an inner and an outer being (a self and a 'front') and that while the 'inner' being is in control of his action the 'outer' often attempts to disguise it, is in itself a dramatic idea. It is therefore not surprising that forms of personification have, as we shall see, survived as possible means of presenting character, in spite of the predominance in post-Renaissance drama of impersonation.

Impersonation as opposed to personification implies that the character who is represented on the stage has been conceived by the dramatist in accordance with his view of the ways in which men do act, not only of the ways in which they should act. *Personnages*, predetermined characters, personifications of virtues or vices of spiritual good or evil, are endowed with credibility in a society dominated by a single common religion and also bound by an unchallenged hierarchic social order. Together the sacred and secular values determine the kind of personality appropriate to different estates. It is the erosion of stable religious and social values and the dissolution of the boundary between the sacred and the secular consequent upon the Renaissance and the Reformation that renders personification inadequate as a mode of representation. Without consensus the emblematic *personnage* becomes meaningless and its interpretation impossible.

During the sixteenth century, in place of the person who judged his own value and that of others in terms of a relationship with God and *sub specie aeternitatis* appeared the individual who saw himself free, autonomous and possessed of a unique character. Burckhardt saw this happening much earlier in Italy (beginning in the thirteenth century). The individual appeared as the *subjective* counterpart of the *objective* view of the state, as something fabricated by man in the world: 'Man became a spiritual individual and recognised himself as such', no longer as a member of some general category, 'race, people, family or corporation.' The aim of the civilised individual was to become *uomo sigolare* or *uomo unico*, instead of the humble spirit who looked to God for instruction before every act.[36]

In painting and sculpture this change in the concept of the person is expressed in the portraits and portrait busts, which were usually commissioned by the sitter himself or by some member of his family. They presented him in dress and setting that accorded with his status. The appearance of the donor in many religious paintings at

[36] J. Burckhardt, *The Civilization of the Renaissance* (Phaidon Press, 1945), p. 81ff.

this time signifies the individualisation of the self in its spiritual role. A man can take a place, humble and yet proprietary, beside the sacred images of Christianity. In drama the tragic hero appears, a man who is defined not only by his actions but also through the thoughts which he addresses directly to the audience. He is recognised as the being responsible for his actions and to a large extent for his destiny.

It was not only Renaissance humanism but also the spirit of Protestantism that, in England, later contributed to the view of man as an individual responsible for his own actions and destiny. The penetration of domestic, secular life by religious values under Protestantism[37] led those who believed in the supremacy of God's will in every aspect of life to rate highly individual achievement and endeavour in those places in life to which they had been 'called'. Although according to Calvinist doctrine the rewards of the 'elect' were reserved for the after life, excellence in this life was regarded as a testimony to one's submission to God's guidance and to his supremacy over the individual's destiny. Calvinism was not a religion for the humble in spiritual or worldly terms, but for those who would soberly reflect God's glory in dedication to their 'calling', and the duties that it imposed.

For different reasons the godly and the godless were committed in the sixteenth and seventeenth centuries to the development of character and individuality. As secular drama began to gain in popularity over religious drama interest began to shift from didactic purpose and symbolic meaning to the human interest that could develop in fiction or history. Characters were presented as impersonations of possible human beings rather than personifications of predetermining virtues, vices or passions.

Impersonation, as a term, therefore, emphasises imitation of character, as it can be known, rather than the incarnation of qualities. It allows, firstly, for autonomy, secondly for the mixture of good and evil qualities and thirdly for change through interaction with others. Interest in what is now called psychology emerged in the late sixteenth and early seventeenth centuries as an interest in 'character', based on the medieval theory of humours, but brought up to date and formulated in such books as Philip de Mornay's *Knowledge of man's Owne Self* (1607), Wright's *Passions of the Minde* (1601) and the now famous *Anatomie of Melancholie* of Burton.

The humours, which were regarded as predispositions of character, were yet thought to be subject to a man's will, and to some extent form a bridge between personification and impersonation.

[37] See Max Weber, *The Protestant Ethic and the Spirit of Capitalism* (1904), for an analysis of the ethos of Protestantism, and its manifestations in social life.

Both modes of expression were available to the dramatists of the period and were adapted to their uses. Before Shakespeare, however, full and consistent use of impersonation never seems to have been truly achieved. Instead, other dramatists developed progressively more effective ways of relating personification to the world of known social realities. In the 'drama of blood', with its emphasis on the action of the plot, quasi-emblematic personifications of vices and virtues are discernible. But they were clothed and styled as plausible members of feasible social worlds. The expressiveness of personification rather than its exemplariness was stressed.

In Kyd's *Spanish Tragedy* (c. 1585) the excitement of sensational events and tragic action gave scope for the presentation of a kind of enriched *personnage*. Kyd and other writers of 'revenge' or violent tragedy, Peele, Greene and Chapman still presented characters in the traditional mode of personification although their purpose was to excite pity and terror rather than to instil moral precepts. Kyd's Hieronimo is a two-dimensional character in the grip of events that are not of his making. He is memorable mainly for his capacity to express his violent emotion. But the expression of this emotion is itself an enlargement of character.

In the plays of Marlowe, the transition from the exclusive use of personification to the presentation of a person who seems to be responsible for choices and decisions which affect his own actions and those of others is progressive. Such characters develop in the course of the play both through their own actions and by submitting to the influence of others. In *Dr Faustus* Marlowe succeeds in presenting an 'impersonated' hero within the structure of the traditional Morality play. Faustus emerges as a complex character, driven, not by a single passion, but by a desperate awareness of the inadequacy of a destiny accomplished in terms of satisfying either the carnal or intellectual passions which govern moral existence. The interest of the play does not lie in the morality theme of the battle between God and the devil for Faustus's soul but in the presentation of a desperate man who deliberately damns himself. As the chief protagonist, Faustus, unlike the main actor in the Morality plays, seems doubtful of the reality of the dangerous game in which he is involved. He doubts hell: 'Come I think hell be a fable.' His cynicism and the trivial use that he makes of his great powers suggest that he is closer to the atheistic spirits of the time, with whom Marlowe, himself, consorted than to the christian of medieval drama.

In Shakespeare's early plays the same character is often transformed from personification to impersonation in the course of the play. Characters such as King John and Richard III seem, in their undisguised evil, to be very close to the vices of the Morality plays. Richard introduces himself in the guise he is to wear throughout the play: 'I am determined to prove a villain'. The only motivation he needs is his desire to overcome the stigma of his deformity and the determination to prove himself as successful as those he envies. Throughout the play he impresses this image on the audience. He is 'the plain devil' with 'dissembling looks', the villain who advertises his own villainy and uses it to account for his actions with very little attempt to claim more subtle motivation. Yet the personification is merely projected to the audience through rhetorical conventions, the 'aside' and the 'direct address'. In interaction with others, with Lady Anne and with Buckingham, his behaviour is a subtle impersonation of a convincing hypocrite. He presents himself as a personification of evil but acts as an impersonated character.[38]

This kind of double character who practises what Brecht later calls 'alienation' is the prototype of most of Shakespeare's later villains, Don John, Edmund, and Iago. Their behaviour reflects an individual social reality, even though it occurs within the stereotyped frame of the jealous or disappointed man. The heroes of the tragedies are even more complex characters and the frame is in fact jettisoned. Macbeth's ambition, Othello's jealousy, Lear's vanity and Hamlet's self-disgust are spurs to action, but are not personified in action. Their soliloquies are not self-descriptions like those of Richard, but revelations of their thoughts which the spectator overhears. Even in modern realist plays where rhetorical conventions are covert no other dramatist has achieved Shakespeare's complete mastery of the impersonated character, representing apparent autonomy in confrontation with the social realities conjured up by the play.

For Shakespeare's contemporaries and immediate successors impersonation became a familiar mode, defined in these terms. But personification, still visible in the early seventeenth century, underwent a subtle change. The medieval view of man as a soul possessed by a good or evil passion was replaced by the Jonsonian view of 'humours' as governing behaviour, speech, thoughts, indeed the whole being. Jonson treated humour as a psychological bias which a man could struggle with or modify or deliberately nurture (as people now sometimes cherish neurotic symptoms), 'a gentleman-like monster, bred in the special gallantrie of our time, by affectation; and fed by folly'.[39] The interplay of humours and the manipulation of

---

[38] W. Clemen, *English Tragedy before Shakespeare*, ed. T. S. Dorsch (Methuen, 1955), p. 290: 'At every turn in Shakespeare's early and middle plays we encounter conventional usages, forms of style, literary artifices and dramatic features which have their origins and many parallels in the pre-Shakespearian drama. . . . Nonetheless his work as a dramatist is not to be understood merely as a logical continuation or a further development of the dramatic art that we meet with before his time, for already in his early plays, from Richard III onwards, we constantly find ourselves in the presence of something entirely new and unexpected.'
[39] Ben Jonson, *Every Man in His Humour* ed. C. H. Herford and P. Simpson, Oxford University Press, 1927, Act III, 2.

others through their humours provided Jonson with a technique
adapted to satire in a realistic milieu. In *The Alchemist*, Dol, Face and
Subtle represented social types recognisable to all who knew the
raffish sectors of London life and were labelled as such by their
names. Similarly in the Induction to *Bartholomew Fair* Jonson suggests, by contradiction, that real characters may have been the
models for his most scurrilous types. He warns the spectators that
they should not search out 'who was meant by the Ginger-bread
woman, who by the *Hobby-horse-man*, who by the Costard monger
... what *Mirror of Magistrates* is meant by the Justice, what great
lady by the *Pigge-woman*, what *concealed* States-man by the Seller
of Mouse-trappes, and so of the rest.'[40] Jonson also employs a translation of types on which so much literary and graphic parody rested
in the seventeenth century. Thus in *Volpone* he uses animals as
symbols of human attributes, man-beasts of a kind that are found in
the sketches of Le Brun and Grandville and later in eighteenth century caricature.[41]

Although the delineation of characters as humours is so closely
related to personification it is at the same time a form of impersonation. Once it was accepted that stage characters were of interest
as social *personnages*, as visible social types, not only as expressions
of a moral quality, thematic emphasis was placed on action which
could illuminate social behaviour. It has never been possible in any
form of literature to suggest the being of a person in a social vacuum.
There is however a specificity of technique to be found in the plays
of this period that makes it difficult to imagine the characters translated into other social settings. Volpone's miserliness and hypocrisy
are of course qualities observable at any period but the opportunity
for his practices and the scale of his operations belong to fantasy
world only conceivable in Jonson's time.

When Jonson drops the metaphorical style of *Volpone* to deal
directly with the rogues and semi-criminals of London, in *The Alchemist* and *Bartholomew Fair* his characters are less reified representations of vices and humours, and yet depend for their effect
on the acceptance of a particular social world. The fact that
Dol, Face and Subtle, in spite of changes in language, seem to us
recognisable (whereas Kyd's Hieronimo belongs to a world of values
from which we have become historically estranged) may indicate the
durability of structural features in western society rather than universality of types. The thieves' world, with its private language and
special code of behaviour, still exists, as one can tell from reports

---

[40] *Bartholomew Fair*, 'Induction'.
[41] Cf. Illustrations by Le Brun from C. Lévi-Strauss, *The Savage Mind* (Weidenfeld
& Nicolson, 1966).

of such cases as that of the Kray[42] brothers in 1968 as well as professional studies of criminals.[43]

Although Jonson does not present characters who seem to impersonate real people in the sense that they develop in interaction with others and become autonomous beings, he creates a social world in which there is a dynamic or social 'density' in Durkheim's sense, i.e. a complex of role relationships involving the individual members of a given social milieu which generates further specific and distinctive kinds of roles and role behaviour. Moreover, Jonson is more explicit than most of his contemporaries about the range of parts which each person can play. Mosca in *Volpone* can 'change a visor swifter than a thought', and in *The Staple of News* Picklock makes a similar claim:

> *Picklock:* Tut, I am *Vertumnus*,
> On every change, or chance, upon occasion,
> A true *Chamelion*, I can colour for't.
> I move upon my axell like a turne-pike
> Fit my face to the parties, and become,
> Streight one of them.

A similar 'social density' can be found in those plays of Massinger, Marston and Middleton that deal with middle and lower class characters in London and various country towns. In many of these plays the stereotyped plots do not give scope for full impersonations. But the characters respond to each others' roles in such a variety of contexts that an overall simulation of real life is created.

In *A New Way to Pay Old Debts* Overreach, Greedy and even Welbourne are all confined within a mode appropriate to their type and function in the plot, but within its bounds develop social identities even to the point of self-knowledge. Sir Giles Overreach in the last scene, as he is overcome with madness, has a sudden clear vision of the personality that has been built up throughout the play:

> Why is not the whole world
> Included in my selfe? To what use then
> Are friend and servants? . . .
> . . . Ha! I am feeble:
> Some undone widdow sitts upon mine arme
> And takes away the use of't; and my sword
> Glew'd to my scabbard with wrong'd orphans teares
> Will not be drawne . . .
> . . . no, spite of fate

---

[42] It was very clear from reports (*The Times*, June-July) of the committal hearing that a great many people outside the gang understood the power of 'the firm' and the significance of such sentences as 'They gave him five injections in the nut', and 'he has gone for a sea voyage'.

[43] e.g. E. Sutherland, *The Professional Thief* (Chicago University Press, 1937).

> I will be forc'd to hell like to my selfe
> Though you were legions of accursed spiritts
> Thus would I fly among you.[44]

Such a character demanded from the actor an understanding not so much of reactions to a range of social situations as of possible states of mind to be encountered in all people, states of mind to some extent equivalent to modern psychological types. But in the same way that a modern actor needs no detailed knowledge of Freudian psychology to interpret pathological personalities, but depends rather on observation, so the Jacobean actor could depend on his knowledge of types or characters, which were part of a literary and social tradition.

Dramatists were, therefore, able to use a technique of personification, originally intended for the symbolic portrayal of the virtues and vices, for a relatively more clinical treatment of the passions. It is this sense of the determinacy of a man's conduct, based on his physiological and psychological make-up, that conflicts with the equally strong Renaissance view of man as a free emancipated creature. These two views are represented in the drama by a wide range of characters (the 'revenger' can be as free a character as Hamlet or as restricted as such 'malcontents' as Vindice or Bosola) demanding from the actors a correspondingly wide range of techniques between personification and impersonation.

From this time however the fully developed impersonated character has gradually come to dominate the fictional world of the play. Personifications are still discernible in the high tragedy and sentimental comedy of the eighteenth century and in nineteenth-century melodrama. But for serious drama Shakespeare remained a model, not so much by virtue of his verse, which was seriously mutilated, but more for the creation of 'real', living, natural characters. Most of the poetic drama of the nineteenth century had little success in the theatre. But one finds in Shelley's *Cenci* and Byron's *Cain* no return to personified or stereotyped characters.

The actor as interpreter

Actors from Garrick onwards were valued for their 'natural' acting, their ability to present three-dimensional, autonomous characters. It was for this reason that the 'great' actors of the nineteenth century came to dominate the theatre often at the expense of the minor characters and the play as a whole. The actor himself derived prestige from the prestige of the live character. He relied on natu-

[44] P. Massinger, *A New Way to Pay Old Debts*, ed. A. H. Cruickshank (Oxford University Press, 1926) V, i.

ralness as a means of realising both the character and his own personality so that the audience would remember Kean's Hamlet,
Kemble's Macbeth or Irving's Shylock.

'Natural behaviour' on the stage is, clearly, as much an artifact as
stylised or rhetorical acting. The actor's style is a response not only
to the expectations of the society in which he lives but also to the
demands of the dramatist who 'writes in' the degree of personification or impersonation required for his characters. Although it
is possible to present a stylised rather than a natural St Joan just as it
is possible to present Macbeth as a complete personification of evil
rather than as a complex personality struggling with good and evil
impulses, this can only be done by deliberate departure from the
dramatist's apparent intentions. The dramatist is, of course, himself,
influenced by, as much as an influence on, social modes or conduct.
In adapting his concept of character the actor is presenting the audience with images that, however much transformed, must be recognisable.

The producer as interpreter

In the last decades of the nineteenth century the actor's role as
presenter and interpreter was to some extent preempted by the producer who emerged as an important new force in the theatre. As yet
another intermediary between dramatist and audience, he performed
the function of editing and coordinating the multiplicity of selves
realised by individual actors and, above all, defining the tone of the
whole action. His criterion was and still is a purely personal idea of
the play, either approximating closely to what he believes the
dramatist means or to what the dramatist can be made to mean in a
different period or social milieu. He covers the whole range of possible interpretations from reconstruction of ideas, intentions and behaviour (of the dramatist and his age) to translation of these into the
contemporary forms. Even in the case of a contemporary play,
meaning has to be 'developed' and 'printed' with more or less verisimilitude according to the dramatist's transparency or opaque-
ness.

We have little detailed knowledge of attempts made by dramatists
or chief actors to 'produce' (in the modern sense) in the sixteenth and
seventeenth century theatres. From the time of Garrick on to the
nineteenth century the successful actor manager paid more and more
attention to the production as a whole. But he still had the actor's
view. He could not share the spectator's vision of himself, taking
part in the action. The call for an independent person in control of
the actors and responsible for the action as a whole coincides with

the political and social changes that took place in the advanced industrial societies of the nineteenth century.

It has been suggested that:

> The decay of a universal system of values and a traditional way of life at the beginning of the modern era deprived the theatre of its homogeneous and representative public and of its accepted conventions for mirroring a shared human experience. As the audience lost its collective emotion, the diverse arts of the theatre lost their internal cohesiveness and the fragmentation of society and hence of the theatre called for a producer who could impose some form of unity on it and find a collective focus for theatre in an atomised society.[45]

Apart from the self-contradictory nature of this statement, which suggests that an 'atomised' society yet supports an institution (the theatre) which is aware of a need for unity, it fails to account adequately for the producer's social and artistic function. If the idea of fragmentation is replaced by the growing awareness of the complexity of roles played by individuals in interaction with others in urban society, particularly in the heterogeneous community of London where most theatres were situated, then the producer's synthesising function, which aims at presenting a coherent image to the audience, is understandable; he becomes an organisation man keeping the simultaneously multiplied selves of the playwright within bounds for the single audience member with whom he is communicating.

The rise of the producer also coincided with the rise of the expert specialist in society and the accompanying development of professionalisation, a part of the diversification and patterning of occupational roles within industrialised, urbanised society. As the acting profession moved in step with other professions in the nineteenth century, experts began to proliferate, each making his contribution to the performance—the producer, stage-designer, lighting expert, costumier and sound effects man—although some of these jobs were performed by the same person. The degree of independence which the producer allowed the actor, designer or choreographer varied. But the most successful as well as the most ambitious seem to have felt that all components of the production should be under their control.

The prototype of the modern producer, the Duke of Saxe-Meiningen, first appeared with his company in London in 1881. He produced three of Shakespeare's plays at Drury Lane and displayed what was recognised as a new realism. He concentrated on historical accuracy of scene and costume, gestures and style of action appropriate to the period of the play and paid close attention to the

[45] T. Cole and H. K. Chinoy, *Directing the Play* (Peter Owen, 1954), p. 19.

movements and effectiveness of minor as well as major actors. The Duke's influence was not immediately apparent here, but his influence on Stanislavski and Antoine, who saw his troupe acting in Europe, set in motion a new approach to production and encouraged a long line of autocratic producers, among them Meyerhold, Reinhardt and Komisarjevsky, whose work became influential here. Although producers in the English theatre never attained such power and eminence the necessity for the one man who stands outside and directs the play was firmly established at the beginning of this century and shows little sign of decreasing in importance.

In the modern English theatre the 'great man' producer is no longer encouraged. The contemporary producer is inclined to co-operate with his actors rather than treat them after the manner of Gordon Craig or Prampolini[46] as marionettes. A more fashionable stance is that of Tyrone Guthrie, who believed that the producer should receive the impressions the actor gives and give them back: 'His function at its best is one of psychic evocation.'[47]

Yet the producer is still regarded as mainly responsible for the performance. He is firmly established as the man who interprets, and while good or bad acting is usually credited or debited to the actor, the total effect of the performance is attributed to good or bad directing.

The effect of the development of a new profession, that of producer, on the older acting profession has on the whole advanced its prestige and encouraged more experiment. This is partly because many directors have been and often still are actors and therefore have experience of the making of a play both from inside and outside. One result, however, of treating producing as an art or technique, in itself, has been to give increasing emphasis to 'interpretation'. Every performance of a Shakespeare play is now regarded as a 'challenge' to the producer and to the chief actors to offer a new interpretation, or occasionally, as in the Mermaid *Macbeth*,[48] what he believes to be an old interpretation.

The need for 'interpretation' suggests that there is not sufficient information in the text for a definitive portrayal of a person, and sometimes leads to a somewhat frenetic search for fresh emphases and new meanings. As Susan Sontag has said of literary criticism,

---

[46] Prampolini came to consider the actor 'a useless element in theatrical action and one that is dangerous to the future of the theatre . . . the appearance of the human element on the stage destroys the mystery of the beyond', quoted in N. Marshall, *The Producer and the Play* (Macdonald, 1957), p. 43; cf. Alfred Hitchcock's notorious remark: 'Actors are cattle.'

[47] Tyrone Guthrie, 'An audience of one', quoted in Cole and Chinoy, *Directing the Play*, p. 255.

[48] Production of *Macbeth* by Bernard Miles based on B. L. Joseph's research on Elizabethan rhetorical gesture (1952) see *Elizabethan Acting*, Oxford University Press, 1951.

'modern styles of interpretation excavates and as it excavates destroys: it digs behind the text to find a sub-text which is the true
one'.[49] But this practice may be less dangerous in the hands of the
critic than in the hands of the producer who presents his interpretation to the audience as definitive. Interpretation is, of course, impossible to avoid in any performance, even if there is no producer.
The producer, however, gives authority to one particular reading
and may mask alternative ones. Brecht tried to combat this by training his actors to demonstrate the 'not but'—the moment of
choice—the possibility of alternative interpretations.[50]

The producer's role is now firmly established in the theatre except
in recently formed companies which have moved towards partial or
complete forms of improvisation. These, in involving the audience
actively in the performance, leave no place for an intermediary. This
development seems, however, to be closely connected with another
concept of character that rivals the traditional forms of personification and impersonation in the modern theatre.

The actor as constructor of alternative existences

Just as personification was a product of the hierarchical religious
world of the Middle Ages and impersonation of the individualist,
humanist world of the Renaissance, a new concept of character or
substitute for character seems to have emerged in modern industrial
secular society. I am going to call this concept *depersonalisation*.
Although this term is defined as 'deprived of personality' (O.E.D.) I
do not wish to stress the process of deprivation but rather the state of
being without the continuous, coherent, identity we associate with
the idea of 'character'; no other word seems to serve.

During the last decades of the nineteenth century 'character' was
becoming a more suspect concept both in life and in literature.
Freud's writings, as they became part of the currency of literate
discussion, both articulated and reinforced new awareness of the
precariousness of identity, the fact that it is not 'given' but sought
and created through experiences which from birth onwards provide
the material from which personality is fabricated. In spite of the
suspicion and dismay with which it was at first regarded, Freud's
analysis of personality signalled (rather than created) the erosion of
the accepted humanist view of the individual as an independent
being whose choices and achievements were rationally motivated.
Changes in intellectual attitudes became apparent in literature, at

[49] S. Sontag, *Against Interpretation* (Delta Books, 1967), p. 5.
[50] B. Brecht, 'Short description of a new technique of acting', in *Brecht on Theatre*,
trans. Willett, p. 137 (see supra p. 59).

first in the novel. The dominant, apparently autonomous, characters created by Dickens can no longer be found in the novels of James, Conrad or Hardy. These novelists are more concerned with people in social groups and the ways in which they react to and against the conventions of the group, than with the 'great' or eccentric individual. They are interested in the ways in which people stimulate and control each others' actions, the ways in which they ennoble or corrupt each other.

Freud's writings themselves did not make their full impact on a wide public until after the First World War. By the 1920s the war, and violent change in political and social life had sapped the confidence in personal endeavour and achievement that had characterised the nineteenth century. In literature a deliberately fractured image of the person emerged in the novels of Joyce and in the poetry of Eliot and Pound.

But in England the change in the drama was slower in coming. The strength of theatrical tradition, strong because it is passed down informally from one generation of actors to another, and the dominance of middle-class audiences delayed any response in the theatre to social and intellectual change. Although Jarry had experimented with non-realist forms in the theatre in the 1890s and had started a new movement which demanded a completely different spectator attitude to the performance and performers, this movement, carried further by Artaud in the 1920s, made no impact in England until the plays of such European writers as Ionesco, Arrabal and Adamov became popular here after the Second World War.

It was in fact Pirandello who first introduced the new concept of the elusive identity in place of the realised character to the English stage. Although he had already used the theme of identity-crisis in *Right You are (If You Think So)* his first two plays on the same theme to be performed in England were *Six Characters in Search of an Author* (1920) and *Henry IV* (1921). The former was concerned with the large theme of the relationship of art to life and hence of the relationship of the fabricated to the 'real' person. The latter dealt with the fabrication of illusion in real life and made the dangerous assumption that people not only assume masks but are obliged to assume them and cannot be detached from them. Henry IV with his accidentally discovered ability to be mad or sane finds himself a saner person than his friends who are trapped in the theatrical behaviour which the norms of their society have forced upon them. He is isolated in his sanity.

Audiences in England were puzzled by Pirandello's manipulation of character. Outside the universities his plays were seldom performed before 1945 and he had little influence in the English theatre, where realism reigned.

The next attack on character presentation on the stage came from Brecht. Although his plays contained such powerful characters as Mother Courage, Galileo and Joan (*Saint Joan of the Stock-yards*) he hoped by teaching the actors his 'alienation technique' and abrogating the empathy of the audience, to reduce their importance as personalities and awake the consciousness of the spectators. It was action and the social conditioning of action that he considered important. In the *Messingkauf Dialogues* the philosopher (Brecht himself) explains to the Actor and *Dratamturg* what is wrong with realistic characterisation:

> You can't give a realistic picture of the character you are putting forward for identification (the hero) without making it impossible for the audience to identify itself with him. A realistic picture would mean that he would have to change with events, which would make him too unreliable for such empathy; he would also have a very limited viewpoint which would mean that the spectator who shared it would not see far enough.[51]

Brecht's Marxist view of the individual as the product of his position in the social system is the logical basis for his 'alienation' technique, a deliberate device to devalue the importance of individual character and to deprive the hero of his *mana*. Yet Brecht's plays, as written, could be presented traditionally. It is very easy to make a 'character' of Mother Courage, of Galileo or of Saint Joan. It is only careful attention to Brecht's instructions, worked out in the course of production, that prevents producer and actors from impersonating these characters at the expense of the new rhetoric of the play as a whole.

Brecht's formulation of acting and production technique coincided, however, with non- and anti-realist plays which also seem to require this style of acting. Ionesco, Genet and Beckett are all concerned to reduce the importance of personal identity but because they regard it as unknowable, not because they regard it, like Brecht, as inappropriate or a distraction. In the plays of these writers the actor is given very little freedom of interpretation. The presentation of a personality that is not self-explanatory depends upon a close attention to the dramatist's directions, which ensure that his meaning is expressed by every actor on the stage and that the total effect is more significant than the individual action. It is difficult to imagine two very different interpretations of Winnie in Beckett's *Happy Days* that would remain faithful to the author's directions, which take up almost half the space in the printed text. Action, gesture, expression and tempo are all controlled in such passages:

WINNIE (*Pause. She takes up mirror*): I take up this little glass, I

[51] Brecht, *Messingkauf Dialogues*, trans. Willett, p. 26.

shiver it on a stone—(*does so*)—I throw it away (*does so far behind her*)—it will be in the bag again tomorrow, without a scratch, to help me through the day (*Pause*). No one can do nothing (*Pause*) that is what I find so wonderful, the way things ... (*voice breaks, head down*) ... things ... so wonderful. (*Long pause, head down. Finally turns, still bowed, to bag, brings out unidentifiable odds and ends, stuffs them back, fumbles deeper, brings out finally musical box, winds it up, turns it on, listens for a moment, holding it in both hands, huddled over it, turns back front, straightens up and listens to tune, holding box to breast with both hands ...*)[52]

Winnie is an extreme example of a character buried in her situation interacting not with other characters, but with contextual objects. But an actress who has successfully played Winnie should be capable of understanding the demands of other modern writers who eschew traditional characterisation.

The ceremonial of Genet's plays requires a highly organised synthesis of direction, design and acting. *Les Bonnes* was acted in 1963 in Cambridge and six months later the same production was performed in Edinburgh. Only the part of Solange was performed by a different actress, but this change was enough to upset the whole balance and meaning of the play. The new actress brought an idea of character to her part instead of the empty persona that changed constantly under the pressures of the situation.

The style of depersonalised acting required by avant-garde dramatists approximates to the gestures and intonations of an incident seen from a distance through a window. The style can often be detected in performances of Shakespeare or other classical drama where it is not always appropriate. The National Theatre production of *Much Ado About Nothing* in London (1966) presented Don John, not as the traditional seventeenth-century malcontent, but as a depersonalised neurotic who might have slipped out of a Pinter play. In fact the atmosphere of the production in spite of its rollicking pantomime style suggested an indefinable menace more in keeping with the comedies of Pinter and Joe Orton, then fashionable, than of Shakespeare, whose dramatisation of evil is never vague, but sharply defined in all his villainous characters.

The contemporary style of depersonalised acting also vitiated some performances in the National Theatre's 1965 production of *The Master Builder*. The neurotic elements in the play, which are certainly there, were transformed into presentations of alienated or non-persons, especially in the portrayal of Sölness who appeared not as a man whose spirit was slowly dying but as one whose spirit had never been alive. Only his wife emerged as a fully realised

[52] S. Beckett, *Happy Days* (Faber and Faber, 1963), p. 30.

character, suggesting, by controlled performance, the history of her development. Ibsen demands this sense of history from his characters. They must be able to express the half-hidden past in the present.

Characters in the plays of Genet, Ionesco, Beckett, Pinter, exist only in the present or outside time, and depersonalisation is an effective form of presentation. In Pinter's *The Caretaker*, in construction his most traditional play, there is no time for the characters to develop, no room for them to act on each other more than momentarily. They move choreographically from one configuration to another, sometimes repetitively, never progressively. Davies, the tramp, approaches the dimensions of a traditionally authenticated dramatic character, but it soon becomes apparent from the little of him that is revealed that he is being used not as a catalyst for the unresolved situation between Mick and Aston, but as a reflecting mirror for their attitudinising. Pinter, himself a professional actor, exploits this new style of acting in all his plays, and relies on the audience's recognition of a new convention of authenticity in the patter of banal language and awkward gestures to overcome the sense of 'let down' which the unresolved themes induce. He is concerned with the actors' mimetic powers, not with their ability to interpret. The technique that he requires is near to that of the clown, the buffoon, who challenges the social reality of his audience, not to the creator of character.

In the plays of the new dramatists, Ionesco, Beckett, Genet, Adamov, Weiss, and others less well known in this country, the actor is offered a part similar to the distorted figures of Picasso or semi-abstracts of Henry Moore, a part which suggests certain human qualities but also the implied comment. Lucky's interminable nonsense speech in *Waiting for Godot* is the expression of the mute voice of slavery rather than that of a single character. Genet's maids, much more explicit, acting out their roles again and again, become progressively demoralised.

The style of acting required for plays of this kind has been worked out in many experimental group theatres. Charles Marowitz, who, with Peter Brook formed the Theatre of Cruelty (modelled on Artaud's specifications) in 1963, gives a clear account of the principles of acting that lay behind performances of *Hamlet*, Genet's *Les Écrans* and *Marat/Sade*:

> One of the main objects behind the work was to try to create a discontinuous style of acting; that is a style which corresponded to the broken and fragmentary way in which most people experience contemporary reality. Life today is very much like the front page of a newspaper. The eye jumps from one story to another; from one geographical location to another; from one

> mood to another. A fair in Hoboken; an election in Paris; a coronation in Sweden; a rape in London; comedy, passion, ceremony, trivia—all flooding one's consciousness almost simultaneously. The actor, however, through years of training and centuries of tradition moves stolidly from point to point. His character is established; his relationships develop; his plot thickens and his conflicts resolve . . .
>
> To break the progressive logical beginning-middle-end syndrome one uses improvisation (i.e. personal and organic material rather than theatrical *donnés*) and uses it simply as rhythmic matter.[53]

Although the underlying assumption of this statement—that the quality of experience has been subjected to some revolutionary change by what are called the mass media—is dubious, the kind of depersonalised acting that is suggested does seem to fit the requirements of the anti-realist play. Instead of working out an impersonation of an ideal model the actor tries to produce a series of personae appropriate to each separate situation. There is of course an extreme end to the process of depersonalisation, when the actor finds himself without persona, part or theme, and required to improvise a whole performance.

So much of the training of actors in workshops and experimental groups, both here and in America, has been concerned with improvisation and semi-improvisation (i.e. with a script from which the actors can depart) that it was a natural step to make such practice scenes into performances. In such improvisations there is of course no place for impersonations of consistent developing characters. Instead the actors concentrate on gestures, movements and words which grow out of ideas which the actors have begun to work out in rehearsal. In a sense there is no final definitive performance as the actors continue to innovate and respond to each other's changes.

Improvisation calls for creative actors who can dispense with both dramatist and producer. It requires moreover a recovery of some of the arts of presentation. If the actor is to stimulate an unrehearsed response from other actors or from spectators as participants he cannot take refuge in naturalism. What impact the acting of the La Mama group in Paul Foster's unemphatic play *Tom Paine* (1967) had was due to the rhetoric of their speech and movements. Much of what they did and said seemed to be *both* instrumental and symbolic. (For example, the miming of Tom Paine's journey across the Atlantic, represented both his physical discomforts and his spiritual struggle to find stability.)

Whatever the success of improvisations and semi-improvisations as a form may be they seem to have forced the actor to a rather more

[53] C. Marowitz, S. Trussler, eds., *Theatre at Work* (Methuen, 1967), p. 168.

serious consideration of acting as interaction with the audience (as against the guarded or inarticulate pronouncements of the older generation). This preoccupation seems to have produced some curious paradoxes, in that the presentation of alternative realities to the audience points sometimes in the direction of mystical representation of human destiny stripped of all recognisable social reality, sometimes towards an embarrassed defiance of moral conventions and sometimes to the assumption of a kind of quasi-charismatic political, spiritual and moral leadership carrying with it a rather hermetic, or fuddled, sense of unlimited responsibility—sometimes to the considerable discomfiture of the audience and indeed of the playwright. David Caute's rueful account of the walkout of the company which had undertaken to produce his 'revolutionary' play *The Demonstration* has a full-blooded irony for which it would be difficult to find a parallel in drama:

> One day last December it seemed as if everyone had forgotten my birthday until, at about six in the evening, the phone rang. Seizing the instrument in high expectation, I was told to stand by for a call from Stuttgart. 'David', said the familiar voice, 'we have bad news.' There was a pause. Then the voice almost cracked with grief. 'It has all stopped, David. At midday the last actor walked out.'
>
> Precisely what had occurred in terms of personal rivalries and intrigues I shall never know. But in essence the birthday message from the Staatstheater, Stuttgart, was that a play of mine, after six months of meticulous German preparations and four weeks of full rehearsals, had been boycotted by its actors. Because it was politically reactionary. I didn't happen to agree, nor did the director, a Marxist who had worked with Brecht in East Berlin, nor indeed did the theatre's chief *Dramaturg*, whose painful duty it was to break the news to me on the telephone. But the younger actors of the company insisted that *The Demonstration*, as the play is called, would give comfort to a bourgeois audience. The vast majority of the regular patrons of the Staatstheater are, of course, bourgeois, and no one, not even the young Turk actors, wanted them to become one bit less regular, but the main thing, apparently, was never to afford them any comfort.
>
> The play itself is to do with a political revolution carried out by student actors against the opposition of their professor, an intellectual of the old Left; that art had therefore anticipated life was an irony not lost on me, but none of my local shopkeepers regard irony as a convincing currency. In fact, my only consolation has been to relate the story to British professional actors and to enjoy their inevitable reaction of scornful outrage. 'Good God, how unprofessional,' they say. 'You can't run a theatre that way.' I nod in solemn agreement while inwardly

recalling, and not without a grimace, a line spoken in the play
by a young revolutionary student, one of the characters: 'Actors
are no longer obedient puppets. A threat to you, no doubt.' He is
speaking to his professor—but also, it would now seem, to me,
his creator, his author.[54]

At all events, the implication is clear: the audience too is given a
role and supposed to contribute to the making of the play into a
performance. Sometimes only verbal participation is asked for. In
the La Mama performance of *Tom Paine* (1967) the actors, halfway
through the performance, sat at the front of the stage and tried to
conduct a seminar with the audience on the historical and political
significance of Tom Paine. More active and physical audience participation can take place in specialised theatres where the audience
knows what is expected of it. In the Performing Garage in Greenwich Village the Performance Group made one of the most ambitious
attempts of this kind in *Dionysus—69*. Here, without stage or auditorium, the play took place in the midst of the spectators, who themselves were cajoled into becoming followers of Dionysus, joining in
the 'orgy' and the baiting of Pentheus. Leaving aside the effect of this
experiment on the role of the spectator, the effect on the actor seems
to be one of enlargement of his role. He is not only responsible for
the free development of a not-too-clearly defined role but also for the
casting of roles for those who are not normally actors. He has to
think his part out as he goes along, and suggest to the spectators
appropriate responses.

The happenings—improvisation movement is not merely a reaction against the rigidity and sterility of playwriting and acting which
people remember from the 'thirties. It is more significantly an attempt to involve the spectators in the unreal world of the theatre and
to make the theatrical performances recreate everyday life. The
Living Theatre on a recent occasion (1969) led a naked audience out
into the streets of New Haven after a tryout of *Paradise Now*.

In one rather restricted sense the wheel seems to have come full
circle. An avowed reason for taking the Corpus Christi procession
out of the church was to confront ordinary people and the shared
typifications of everyday social reality with the transcendent realities of the Christian faith. Missionary zeal enters into both occasions and the *confrontation* itself has symbolic meaning, but equally
evidently it is a new life style which is now being exported into the
streets, not a set of beliefs which transcends life. Nudity, as usual
nowadays, was supposed to stand for freedom, but was not merely
symbolic. The naked spectators as well as the actors were presumably liable to arrest for an offence against public decency and
order. It is, moreover, the declared aim of the Living Theatre to

[54] David Caute, 'Actor's theatre', *The Listener* 3rd June, 1971, pp. 700–1.

to make the spectators rush out and change society and their presence in France during the 'May events' involved them to some extent in this process. As Julian Beck, founder of the theatre has said: 'We have gone on to a theatre of answers.' This is a much more ambitious claim than that of Shaw and Brecht, who wanted to make spectators think. Neither of them dreamt of confusing the world inside and outside the theatre.

This attempt to blur the distinction between the two worlds could result in the devaluation of the actor as professional. As David Caute's remarks indicate, an 'actors' theatre' may increase the power of the actor, but at the expense, at present, of playwright and producer. But control over the audience, inherent in the ritual base and the conventional tradition, may also be lost. Once the spectator swallows the bait whole and jumps on to the stage and begins to initiate his own action the actor will become one of the crowd, no longer in control.

Even if things never reach this point, because producers may realise the danger of creating playgrounds rather than performances the threat to the 'acted' character remains. In improvisations and in the new 'obscure' or 'open-ended' plays (plays whose meaning cannot be shared by actors and spectators because clues to meaning are withheld and shared typifications abjured as in, for example, the plays of Megan Terry and Rosalyn Drexler), the actor is deprived of theme, persona and even social identity as actor. He is being reduced to the primitive role of the mime who can reproduce sequences of behaviour that need not be related either rationally or interactionally to those of others. He can no longer depend on the theatrical context to establish for him a significant identity.

When the conception of acting as something conjured from ordinary life and given meaning in the theatrical world is lost, a category of meaning is lost. It is the separation of the two worlds that has in the past enabled them to illuminate each other. There can be no question of returning to the ritual origins of the theatre, rooted in a common religion and ethos. At the same time that there is loss there may be gain in expressiveness of action both inside and outside the theatre. The present movement which involves the conflation of acting on the stage with acting in real life is symptomatic of a new attitude to personality and character, an attitude which has implications for dramatists, actors, producers, spectators and for all members of society. But for the actor himself it is the latest (and perhaps final) stage in a long cyclical process of change.

On the stage this transmutation of the actor from personifier to impersonater to depersonalised element, expressing the dramatist's meaning at his own expense, can be explained in several ways. Throughout his history the actor has animated changing conceptions of man. From the medieval concept of man as a battleground for the warring forces of good and evil, a personification of virtue or vice, he emerged as Renaissance man learning to control himself and his environment, developing through stages of sophistication and self-consciousness into modern man analysing his thoughts, motives and actions. This development as we have seen has not been constantly progressive. Periods of stagnation and regression have occurred, especially in the eighteenth and nineteenth centuries, at times when the theatre has been neglected by the intelligentsia as writers or spectators. As Jarry says in *Douze arguments sur le théâtre*: 'Maintenir une tradition même valable est atrophier la pensée qui se transforme dans la durée; et il est insensé de vouloir exprimer des sentiments nouveaux dans une forme conservée.'[55] At such periods the theatre has failed to provide for the spectator through living conventions an extension of life and he has turned for this to poetry or the novel. Today there are signs that the theatre is recovering its organic function in society. In most contemporary drama the actor is again in a dialectical relationship with the audience, although he is now much more dependent on the dramatist than he has been throughout his previous history. He is also using techniques of presentation that everyone tries to learn in his daily life, and therefore exposes himself to more informed criticism than his predecessors.

[55] A. Jarry, 'Douze arguments sur le théâtre', in *Tout Ubu* (Livre de Poche, 1962), p. 150.

10

Spectators and critics

Saniette represents a distinct type of audience—smart, sophisticated, sensitive yet hard-boiled, art-loving frequenters of the
little theatres. I am their particular kind of a performer. Some
day I will obtain my revenge by writing a play for one of their
art theatres. A theatre patronised by the discriminating few: art-
lovers and book-lovers, school teachers who adore the grass-
eating Shaw, sensitive young Jews who adore culture, lending
librarians, publishers' assistants, hard-drinking newspaper men,
interior decorators and the writers of advertising copy.

In this play I shall take my beloved patrons into my
confidence and flatter their difference from other theatre goers. I
shall congratulate them on their good taste in preferring Art to
animal acts. Then suddenly, in the midst of some very witty
dialogue the entire cast will walk to the footlights and shout
Chekhov's advice:

'It would be more profitable for the farmer to raise rats for
the granary than for the bourgeois to nourish the artist, who
must always be occupied with undermining institutions.'

In case the audience should misunderstand and align itself
with the artist, the ceiling of the theatre will be made to open
and cover the occupants with tons of loose excrement. After the
deluge if they so desire, the patrons of my art can gather in the
customary charming groups and discuss the play.[1]

There is a conflict that lies at the roots of the relationship between
dramatist, actors and producers on the one side and on the other side,
the audience. The more closely they are drawn together the sharper
the discrepancy between their interests, the more damaging the representation of the real in terms of the theatrical world.

During the course of the history of the theatre first dramatists,
then actors and, at the present time, producers have been in ascend-
ance. But the position of the audience, however much its social

[1] N. West, *The Dream Life of Balso Snell*, 1931, Penguin, p. 187.

structure may have altered, has remained constant. Although at different periods it has been less or more articulate, either vocally or in writing, it has always held the power of making or breaking a play by attendance or abstention, and has always been ultimately responsible for sustaining the performance. In the larger society from which the audience is drawn, the theatre depends for its being on the preservation of a conception of drama that assigns it to some position central to contemporary culture.

It is this centrality that the critic seeks to exploit. He is, in fact, not the spokesman of inarticulate spectators but a self-appointed mediator between the value system signified or articulated in a play and the values obtaining in contemporary society. In the necessary conflict between stage and auditorium, however, he cannot be neutral. Involved with both he hopes to establish for himself a position in which he can manipulate the two and display almost as much detachment as Nathanael West's 'performer'.

The history of theatrical criticism is an overtone of the history of the changing relationship between society and the theatre. The critic not only codifies and interprets dramatic conventions, but, by imposing his own literary judgments, influences the nature of these conventions. As we have seen, the Elizabethan spectator was accustomed to the same kind of acting on public occasions as that which he saw on the stage and, therefore, accepted the artifice of behaviour both outside and inside the theatre. He could apply the same criteria in either place. The eighteenth-century spectator, on the other hand, had been taught by critics and authors of treatises to see acting on the stage as a distinctive art. Criticism trained the audience to compare one actor's performance with another's and to recognise certain standards of stage behaviour far removed from those applicable in ordinary social life. Since then the critic has continued to contribute to the theatrical tradition.

Criticism emerged at the end of the seventeenth century as the voice of a small section of society, already intimately connected with the theatre, and expressing the attitudes of dramatists and performers rather than those of the audience. Richard Steele, Aaron Hill and Addison wrote with much of the strained goodwill and eagerness to appeal to the cultured reader that a public relations officer now employs. Since that time the critic's close ties with the theatre have been broken, and he is now part of the audience, although he, no more than his predecessors in the eighteenth century, can claim to voice its opinions. He has, rather, become a professional expert intent on establishing and enhancing his own profession by the formulation of criteria and values which society can respect.

He is still a P.R.O., but for his own profession, not for the theatre.

It is, however, significant that the theatre critic's function, unlike that of the literary critic, has always been primarily justificatory. The literary profession has always been accepted, and books respected as objects. Only the value of their content has been questioned. But the theatre as an institution has always been under fire from a large section of society. It is constantly asked to justify its financial, emotional or intellectual extravagance. The critic can seldom concentrate exclusively on aesthetic judgments.

During the early period considered in this study, the sixteenth and first half of the seventeenth century, comment on the theatre was sporadic and for most part only critical from a narrowly moral point of view. The theatre was regarded with suspicion by the Church, the government and the middle-class law-abiding citizen. Queen Elizabeth, in spite of her partiality for dramatic performance, understood the political dangers of allowing uncontrolled performances in the public theatres. Although it had been the practice of her father to encourage Interludes as a means of spreading Protestant doctrine, it was considered safer, in her reign, to remove the drama altogether from the fields of religious and political controversy.

In 1559 Elizabeth issued an important proclamation, codifying the rules by which municipal officers, lord lieutenants and justices of the peace should supervise the licensing of plays, 'that they permit none to be played wherein either matters of religion or of the governance of the estate of the Commonwealth shall be handled or treated'.[2] This accounts for the difficulty of tracking down topical allusions in the plays of Shakespeare and his contemporaries. The hidden dynamite that can only now be guessed at was probably eagerly seized on by audiences that had few other sources of licit information or public comment.

Other ordinances followed, including one, in 1574, prohibiting performances coinciding with times of divine service, both morning and afternoon.[3] Not only the performance but the congregation of spectators was considered to constitute a danger. Although performances were only forbidden in times of plague there was constant criticism from citizens living in the vicinity of the theatres, and their pressure was eventually successful in getting the theatres shifted outside the city boundaries.

Far more virulent, were the attacks of the Puritans and other moralists who regarded dramatic performance as evil in itself. Philip Stubbes in his *Anatomy of Abuses* dealt almost as severely with plays of divine as of profane matter. The former he regarded as sacri-

[2] V. Gildersleeve, *Government Regulation of the Elizabethan Drama* (Columbia University Press, 1908), p. 15.
[3] *Ibid*, p. 158.

legious: 'For at no hande it is not lawfull to mix scurrilitie with divinitie, nor divinitie with scurrilitie.'[4] Profane plays, on the other hand, are self-evidently condemned by the nature of their content. The arguments are concerned with: 'anger, wrath, immunitie, crueltie, injurie, incest, murther, and such like, the Persons or Actors are Goddes, Goddesses, Furies, Fiends, Hagges, Kings, Queenes or Pottentates. Of Commedies the matter and ground is love, bawdrie, cosenage, flattery, whordome, adulterie: the Persons or agents, whores, queanes, bawdes, ...'[5] The virulence of these attacks, of which there are many from Stubbes's *Anatomy* to Prynne's *Histriomastix*, called forth defences of the theatre of an equally high moral tone, of which Thomas Heywood's *Apologie for actors* is one of the better known. Here one finds the apologist defending the moral lives of the players rather than their skill, and the moral precepts of the dramatists rather than their artistic accomplishment.

Overbury's *Character of an Excellent Actor* and Shakespeare's criticism in *Hamlet* of contemporary acting are among the few assessments of acting from a non-moral point of view that have been recorded. Yet early in the seventeenth century when the private theatres were catering for a more select, and, on the whole, more educated audience than the public theatres, they stimulated a considerable amount of vocal criticism at the time of the performance. A good deal of this was destructive and ill-informed. In fact its main purpose was to enable the 'critics' to take part in the performance by exchanging badinage with the actors from their vantage point on the stage. Jonson, who waged constant battle against the gallants who paid two shillings for a stool on the stage, made their intentions clear. Such spectators come, as he says in the dedication to the *Newe Inne*: 'To see and to bee seene. To make a generall muster of themselves in their clothes of credit; and possesse the Stage against the Play. To dislike all and marke nothing. And by their confidence of rising between the Actes, in oblique lines, make *affidavit* to the whole house of their not understanding one Scene.'[6] Such performances were designed to rival those of dramatist and players. Their success was admitted by Dekker who described the dependence of many dramatists upon the favour of the gallant, who 'by spreading your body on the stage, and by being a justice in examining of plays, you shall put yourself into such true scenical authority, that some poet shall not dare to present his muse rudely upon your eyes, without having first unmasked her, rifled her, and discovered all her bare and most mystical parts before you at a tavern.'[7]

[4] *Anatomy of the Abuses in England* (1583), ed. F. J. Furnivall (London, 1877), p. 141.
[5] *Ibid*, p. 143.
[6] Ben Jonson, *The Newe Inne*, ed. P. and E. Simpson, Oxford University Press, 1938.
[7] *The Gull's Hornbook, Old Book Collector's Miscellany*, ed. G. Hindley (London, 1872), ii, 56.

Yet the dramatists and actors were not wholly at the mercy of the audience. The boys' companies were notorious for the scurrilous tone in which they slandered and abused society to such good purpose that many spectators brought their table-books with them to note down scraps of gossip or slander on which they might 'dine out'.[8] At this time the theatre provided, at least for Londoners, a forum where they might exchange and enlarge on views of topical interest. The comparative smallness of the metropolis enabled writers such as Jonson and Marston to remain popular while engaged in a private warfare. A sufficient number of the audience understood what the 'war of the theatres' was about; the rest could derive entertainment from the knowledge that some of the protagonists were on the stage, some in the auditorium.

Out of this coterie atmosphere written criticism might well have developed, but for the closing of the theatres in 1642. During the interregnum the few players who were not enlisted by the Royalist forces went underground and the necessity for keeping their performances secret prevented the development of criticism.

The theatres that reopened at the Restoration had a good deal in common in size and exclusiveness with the earlier private theatres. Restoration theatres were small with a picture stage behind the proscenium arch and a forestage curving out into the auditorium. They made use of elaborate scenery and stage machinery, and attracted an audience drawn from the court, the town, their servants, and a raffish section of the disreputable of both sexes. They were also influenced by the French stage and the tastes of the King, who, with his brother, the Duke of York, controlled the theatre as a personal hobby. Such an audience and such patrons seemed to call forth a kind of entertainment in which wit, sentiment and some tragic grandeur predominated, to the neglect of more intellectual or imaginative themes.

This theatre displayed behaviour that could by no section of the society be regarded as exemplary so that its effect was, inevitably, to incite amongst the educated a debate concerning the values of the drama, a debate out of which criticism was to grow.

The tradition of vocal criticism during the performance recalled from the prewar private theatres reached its peak in the Restoration and early eighteenth-century theatre. It was further stimulated by the fact that so many of the wits who thronged the pit were themselves rival playwrights, at least of amateur, if not professional, status. The sport of maiming or killing a play at its first performance

---

[8] 'that brings his Table-books
to write down what again he may repeate
At some great table to deserve his meate.'
quoted in W. Armstrong, 'The audience of the Elizabethan private theatre', *Review of English Studies*, x (1959), 244.

became the serious business of faction.[9] The term 'critic' was at first applied to anyone who could make his opinions or abuse heard during the performance as well as to those who thronged the coffee houses afterwards to dissect the play. But the proliferation at the end of the seventeenth century of general news-sheets in which some theatrical notices were included, and the appearance of news-sheets devoted exclusively to the theatre at the beginning of the eighteenth century, soon provided space in which opinions took the form of written criticism. As soon as criticism was written down it was bound to seem more authoritative. In these early news-sheets, the critic was spokesman for the theatre rather than for the audience. The term 'theatre' in this sense includes all those connected with it as owners, actors or dramatists. The critic spoke as a colleague and addressed his colleagues directly, the audience indirectly. In addressing the audience his intention was to inform it of the criteria by which it should learn to judge a play.

The emergence of this new profession of criticism coincided with the increasing professionalism of the actors' companies to which it was parasitically attached. When they lost the direct patronage of the court, at the beginning of the eighteenth century, and had to rely on their patents, the actors had to increase their concern with the actual running of their companies. Their subsequent struggles with the Lord Chamberlain's censorship and the restrictions of the Licensing Act (1737), in which they were forced to rely on the business competence of the theatre managers, made them dependent on those managers in all aspects of their professional lives. Managers not only administered the theatre and selected their plays. The best of them, such as Henry Giffard at Goodman's Fields and later Lincoln's Inn Fields (1731–43), gave their actors a 'thorough apprenticeship in the technique of acting, thorough rehearsals, and a systematic regimen of production'.[10] Actors, no longer the servants of the great, could now apply for employment to the manager who seemed to them the most competent or most likely to further their careers. Foote, Fielding, and Macklin, all had their distinctive methods and styles of training their actors. A profession, laying down certain standards of training and qualification, offered its members an autonomy and range of choices that they had lacked completely as servants of the

---

[9] 'Prologues and epilogues of the Restoration and eighteenth century give eloquent testimony to the presence and power of an army of critics in the London theatres which when occasion or faction or malice demanded could on the opening night, launch an attack on a new play so fatal as at once to destroy all present or future chance of its success, and to leave the unfortunate author with reputation in ruins': D. F. Smith, *The Critics in the Audience of the London Theatres* (New Mexico University Press, 1953), p. 16.
[10] A. H. Scouten, *The London Stage* (Illinois University Press, 1962), Part 3, p. lxxxi.

court. It also exposed them to informed criticism rather than to the personal animus or whims of the King and his friends.

The influence and importance of criticism in relation to dramatists was recognised as early as 1670 when Dryden ascribed the superiority of post-Commonwealth to pre-Commonwealth drama to the critic:

> They who have best succeeded on the Stage,
> Have still conform'd their Genius to their Age.
>
> They rose, but at their height could seldome stay.
> Fame then was cheap, and the first comer sped;
> And they have kept it since, by being dead.
> But, were they now to write when Critiques weigh
> Each Line and ev'ry Word, throughout a Play
> None of 'em, no, not Jonson in his height
> Could pass, without allowing grains for weight.[11]

At this time most criticism was directed to the play itself. The Pit critics were more interested in the script than in acting or production. The Prologues, which had become so prominent that eminent writers or dramatists were often engaged to supply them for the plays of others, were used to soften the severity of these critics. They reflect the nervousness of the playwright at his première:

> What various thoughts a Poet's Breast divide
> When brought before an Audience to be try'd:
> Guilty of scribbling, with beseeching Hands,
> Before your Bar the Malefactor stands.
> Now hopes 'twill please, now doubts 'twill prove but dull:
> Mourns a thin Pit, yet dreads it when 'tis full.[12]

Much less attention seems to have been paid on these occasions to the performers on whom the production depended. Prologues and epilogues were retained as bridges on which the dramatist could make contact with an audience, rapidly changing from a body of people eager to be entertained to one more ready to find amusement in hostility. The audience was felt to be safer if kept at arm's length but had to be given the illusion of contributing to the performance.

Styles of acting as well as types of play came under critical scrutiny, less in written criticism, more in the satirical plays, of which Buckingham's *Rehearsal* was the first to be well known. Many others followed: D'Avenant's *Playhouse to be Lett*, a pastiche of opera and tragedy, Arrowsmith's *The Restoration*, again burlesquing heroic tra-

---

[11] J. Dryden, Epilogue to *Conquest of Granada*, in Complete Poems (Oxford University Press, 1935), p. 215.
[12] Prologue to J. Trapp's *Abra Mule* (1704), quoted in *The London Stage*, ed. E. L. Avery (Illinois University Press, 1960), vol. ii, p. clviii.

gedy, and, in 1673, a series of plays by Thomas Duffet which travestied popular successes. Plays of this kind were produced all through the eighteenth century, culminating in Sheridan's *Critic*, but seem to have been most forceful in the last decades of the seventeenth century. The theatre of the Restoration was sufficiently new and self-conscious to find endless interest in analysing its forms and modes of expression. It had also to contend with the rival attractions of opera and spectacle, and needed to define its values as clearly as possible.

Although only the Comedy of Manners has survived from this period, to be appreciated by later generations, this type of play had only a limited vogue at the time. The heroic tragedies of Dryden and lesser playwrights' sentimental comedies and farces remained predominant. As Allardyce Nicoll says: 'By 1676 the age was moving steadily in the direction of sentimentalism, pure intellect was being banished by feeling, emotion was taking the place of wit.'[13] But it becomes clear when one reads Pepys's comments on the many performances he saw that there was as yet no firm line drawn between a highbrow and lowbrow theatre. It was still possible for him, as a man of taste, to appreciate Jonson's *Bartholomew Fair*: 'It is an excellent play; the more I see it I love the wit of it',[14] and yet go at least nine times to the Italian puppet farce *Polichinello* 'which is prettier and prettier and so full of variety that it is extraordinary good entertainment'[15]; of a puppet show *Whittington* at Southwark Fair he remarks: 'how that idle thing do work upon people that see it, and even myself too'[16], and in spite of an appreciation of *Macbeth* he could rate *An Adventure of Five Hours* above *Othello*. But Pepys's comments belong to his private diary. In this he expresses quite candidly his own tastes and predilections. There is a marked contrast between these statements of a spectator's casual opinions and the professional criticisms of Hill and Steele who were, some years later, concerned to formulate standards and values for the theatre. By these means they hoped to institutionalise the profession of dramatic critic. Steele's professed scorn of the critic can be seen as an attempt to monopolise the profession by men of the theatre like himself, men who were also concerned with ownership, production and the writing of plays.[17]

[13] *Restoration Drama* (Cambridge University Press, 1940), p. 227.
[14] *Pepys on the Restoration Stage*, ed. H. McAfee (Oxford University Press, 1916), p. 110.
[15] *Ibid*, p. 206.
[16] *Ibid*, p. 208.
[17] 'Every body in Town knows that the dullest and most stupid Writers, we had had, have set up for criticks, and after abusing the most celebrated and bright Personnages of the Age, have made Reproofs and Answers needless, by some undeniable Evidence of their Inability in Publications of their own': R. Steele, *The Spectator*, no. 502, in *Works* (Oxford University Press, 1965), iv, 282.

In 1702 the first daily newspaper, the *Daily Courant* was published and from then on there were occasional notices of plays and of the affairs of the theatre. But this space was limited, and certainly did not allow for regular reviewing. A wider field of criticism was opened up by the news-sheets devoted exclusively to the theatre. The earliest of these, Richard Steele's *The Theatre* 1720, and Aaron Hill's *The Prompter* were both written by men deeply involved in the theatre, as managers and playwrights, as well as critics. Steele used his journal to defend both his personal position and that of the theatre. Several numbers were devoted to his quarrel with the Lord Chamberlain, Newcastle, with whom he was politically involved. But amongst these polemics were interspersed serious criticism of plays, actors and spectators. Hill, however, devoted his paper almost exclusively to theatrical criticism and, with the help of Popple, laid down standards for production, regular rehearsals, acting and audience behaviour. He also published a treatise on acting, which enumerated the 'ten dramatic passions that could be portrayed, as joy, grief, fear, anger, pity, scorn, hatred, jealousy, wonder, love,'[18] and described the muscular movements of face and body needed to express them. He, like John Hill, Richard Steele and many less known critics, was taking a progressive interest in the theory and principles of acting. But emphasis was still laid on oral imitation of the great orators and actors of the past, and the visual imitation of sculpture and historical paintings. Their most valuable and innovatory suggestions concerned the movement towards professionalism. Aaron Hill constantly demanded more thorough and better attended rehearsals. In his treatise on acting he drew attention to certain abuses:

> A great and general mistake among the players at *rehearsal*; where it is their common practice, to mutter over their parts inwardly; and keep in their voices; with a mis-imagined purpose of preserving them, against their evening acting. Whereas the surest natural means of strengthening their delivery would be, to warm, dephlegm and clarify the thorax, and the wind-pipe by exerting (the more frequently the better) their fullest power of utterance.[19]

In *The Prompter* he dealt more specifically with interpretation of character. A whole number (57) possibly written by Popple, was devoted to the usual interpretation of the character of Polonius, which he considered falsified by buffoonery. The whole conception of the falsification of character—as against an ignoble or inflated rendering of language and demeanour relative to the rhetoric of the play or the standing of other characters—which is all that Hamlet is

---

[18] Aaron Hill, 'An essay on the art of acting', in *Works* (1753), iv, 355.
[19] *Ibid*, p. 397.

concerned with in his address to the Players—introduces a new dimension into theatricality. One can assume that social awareness of the new set of commitments of playwright, players and audience to the staged world antedates this mid-eighteenth century critique, but the measure of the change is now clear and articulate in the identification of the way in which the 'reification' of Polonius as a stock buffoon figure changes not merely 'the character' of Polonius but the meaning and significance of the whole play.[20] Even so, Hill seems generally to have understood the art of impersonation but did not regard it as the ultimate end of acting. Like most writers then, and in the following century, he was concerned more with the rhetorical dimension, thinking that the actor's duty lay in the elucidation of the 'moral meaning of the play as a whole' rather than that of a single character. Of Mr Holman he wrote: 'It is very evident he, by his every action, his every look, his every tone, has made it his business to enter into the core of the author's mind and extract the very soul of his own character.'[21]

By the time that Garrick had become the foremost actor the importance of a more sensitive presentation of the acted self was beginning to be accepted by audiences and acclaimed by critics. Garrick prepared the way for greater social realism, first by clearing the stage of beaux with their stools, secondly by using historical costumes for historical characters, at least in Shakespeare's Roman plays, and thirdly by insisting on more careful rehearsals and attention to detail in the production. But according to the critics and other commentators, his greatest innovation was the naturalness[22] and unrhetorical tone of his own acting. Fanny Burney's heroine in *Evelina* is overcome by this manner: 'I could hardly believe he had studied a written part, for every word seemed to be uttered from the impulse of the moment.'[23] Johnson, who regarded Garrick to some extent as his protégé stressed his mimic power, his mobility of countenance: 'When he speaks one minute he has quite a different countenance to what he assumes the next. I don't believe he kept the same look for half an hour together in the whole course of his life.'[24] A more technical account of his style is given by Joshua Steele, a pioneer in the science of phonetics, who had attempted to produce a written notation for speech, which he applied to stage diction. He contrasted Garrick's rendering of Hamlet's soliloquy, 'To be, or not

---

[20] See above, p. 122.
[21] A. Hill, *The Prompter*, no. 10 (1734).
[22] This naturalness was of course an artifact. Joshua Reynolds's 'character' of Garrick does not lack malice but is confirmed by others: 'Great as Garrick was on the stage he was at best equal if not still superior at the table, and here he had too much the same habit of preparing himself as if he was to act a principal part': Joshua Reynolds, *Portraits* (Heinemann, 1952), p. 86.
[23] F. Burney, *Evelina* (Dent, Everyman, 1958), p. 22.
[24] F. Burney, *Diary*, i, 57, 58.

to be', transcribed with this notation with that of any 'ranting actor'. Garrick, he found 'delivered it with little or no distinction of *piano* or *forte* but nearly uniform; something *sotto voce* or *sempre poco piano*'.[25]

The movement towards social realism in acting was not exclusively Garrick's personal innovation. Macklin at Drury Lane instructed his company explicitly to avoid the pomposity and the 'singsong' delivery of Quin and other popular actors. John Hill in *The Actor*, in 1750, claimed that he 'founded for us a new method of delivering tragedy from the first rate actors, and banished the bombast that us'd to wound our ears continually from the mouths of the subordinate ones.'[26]

Yet John Hill, whose treatise on the art of acting shows an interest and understanding of techniques in advance of his time, is one of the few critics who ventured any adverse criticism of Garrick's acting. He considered that Garrick showed too much of his own personality which he was incapable of submerging in a fictional character. He also observed that in spite of his acquaintance with polite society he fell short in representing gentlemanliness on the stage, because 'while he has the example he is teaching himself not to imitate it (polite society) but to play the part of an inferior'.[27] Hill, however, recognised Garrick's artistry in basing his 'natural' acting on careful study of the rules by which intonation and gestures can be made to appear natural on the stage. He was apparently judging Garrick by the criteria that Garrick himself had created.

From this time until the last decades of the nineteenth century it was the actor rather than the dramatist who defined levels of illusion and modes of presentation. He came to be accepted as an 'interpreter' of the dramatist's idea of character.[28] This necessity for interpretation was to a large extent formulated and insisted upon by the critics. Their interest for the reader lay in their ability to compare and evaluate different interpretations and to categorise styles as 'old' or 'new'.

The curious juxtaposition of the new and old style of acting is clearly brought to light in Richard Cumberland's account of a performance of Rowe's *Fair Penitent*. While Quin, as Horatio, and Mrs Cibber, as Calista, adhered to the older style of elaborate dress, heavy gesture ('a sawing kind of action') and monotonous delivery, Garrick, as Lothario, and Mrs Pritchard, as Zarina, introduced the new 'natural' and varied style. But Cumberland asserts that the former

[25] Joshua Steele, *An Essay towards establishing the Melody and Measure of Speech* (London, 1775), p. 47.
[26] John Hill, *The Actor* (London, 1750), pp. 194–5.
[27] *Ibid*, p. 71.
[28] See above, p. 146.

pair were more in favour: 'in the dialogue of altercation between Horatio and Lothario (the audience) bestowed far the greater show of hands upon the master of the old school than upon the founder of the new.'[29] Eventually, of course, Garrick's personal popularity enabled him to persuade the audience to accept the style he wanted to impose. It is apparent, however, from both favourable and adverse critics, that it was the interpretation of the main characters that interested him rather than the rendering of the play as a whole, hence his merciless adaptations of Shakespeare.

Inevitably therefore this aspect of theatre tended to become the focus of audience attention. In 1753 a critic in the weekly *Gray's Inn Journal* says: 'The Art of constructing the dramatic study should always be subservient to the Exhibition of Character, our great Shakespeare has breathed another Soul into tragedy which has found the way of striking an Audience with Sentiment and Passion at the same time.'[30] From this time on the critics pay more and more attention to the delineation of character, and the actor seems to be given increasing scope. Garrick himself 'improved' Shakespeare's plays with the public intention of facilitating the audience's appreciation of the great dramatist, but in the process it was the great actor who came off best.

In any case during the eighteenth century and early nineteenth the main piece was never allowed to dominate the performance. The evening's entertainment was a careful arrangement of play, dancing, singing and farce or harlequinade, during which the main actor appeared at the moment when the audience was expected to be most attentive. An 'Account of England' for the *Town and Country Magazine*, April 1772, gives this account: 'The entertainment of the English Theatre consists of a prelude of music, a play, whether tragedy or comedy, with music or dancing between the acts and is concluded with a petit piece either farce or pantomime.'[31]

G. W. Stone, who quotes this passage in *The London Stage*, lists the playbills for a number of seasons, of which the following is typical: 'Drury Lane, Dec. 1st, 1752. Every Man in His Humour also The Double Disappointment. Dancing, several entertainments by Devisée, Mad August, Ferrere, Mad Auretti, Etc. and at Covent Garden, Jan. 6th 1753 the Tragical History of King Richard III. Also the Dragon of Wantley. Dancing (by Desire) Grand Scots Ballet.'[32] In such programmes, with an audience that could not be relied on to come at the beginning and leave at the end, it must have been

[29] R. Cumberland, *Memoirs* (London, 1806), pp. 59–60.
[30] *Gray's Inn Journal*, 1753.
[31] G. W. Stone, *The London Stage* (University of Illinois Press, 1962), pt 4, vol. ii, p. ccxi.
[32] *Ibid*, p. 335.

difficult for any actor to build up a character integrated with the action of a play which had in any case already been cut to show him to his best advantage.

By the 1770s a new play could be expected to be reviewed in a dozen daily or weekly papers, of which the foremost were *The Morning Chronicle* and *Morning Post*. Progressively criticism had become less concerned with the maintenance of high moral standards and more with the technicalities of acting and producing, although the great actor rather than the production as a whole remained the focus of attention. The critic no longer identified himself with the audience in the pit, or provoked riots in favour of rival playwrights, but as a member of a new profession preserved a distance from both actors and audience, addressing the wider public of newspaper readers.

The honesty of reviewing at this time is hard to judge. Apart from some evidence of absentee reviewing[33] there is evidence of managers paying for 'puffs' masquerading as reviews. Even Garrick, who owned stock in many newspapers, was suspected of improving his reputation through these interests. Yet his personality alone was enough to give a fillip to criticism. His performances drew the most attention of any actor's and were discussed both for their own merits and for comparison with those of Barry and other leading actors.

By the time Sheridan and Goldsmith were publishing *The Theatrical Review* in 1771, regular reviewing was the rule and a standard form for criticism well established. The popularity of criticism in general at this time is underlined by Goldsmith *The Citizen of the World*:

> To what purpose was the book then published, cried I?
> *Bookseller*: Sir, the book was published in order to be sold; and no book sold better, except the criticisms upon it; which came out soon after. Of all kinds of writing that goes off best at present, and I generally fasten a criticism upon every book that is published.[34]

Dramatic criticism was in one sense part of the same fashion. It was, however, also fulfilling the audience's need to take a correct attitude to the theatre. Society has always been suspicious of the theatre's ability to provide fun, and eager to find a formula to appease this suspicion, particularly acute in an age of decorum, constantly threatened by crudity.

[33] George Ann Bellamy recounts a visit paid to her in the Green-Room by John Hill, editor of the Grays-Inn Journal, who confessed that he had written a critique of her Juliet 'from what he had heard at the Bedford and never till that evening had one opportunity of seeing it'. She adds: 'I believe most of the praise or censure we read in the papers is put in by the partisans or enemies of performers': *Apology for the life of George Ann Bellamy* (London, 1785), iv, 184.
[34] *Citizen of the World*, Letter li (Oxford University Press, 1966), p. 216.

There was now an increasing tendency to try to codify traditional conventions as rules and principles. G. Austin's *Chironomia, or A Treatise on Rhetorical Delivery* restated the principles of Bulwer, Betterton and Aaron Hill, but was more practical, expressing the need for a notation of gesture for painter and actor as well as a notation of intonation, which he himself attempted to supply. Lacking any technique for recording he points out that:

> If great actors would themselves note their most successful efforts and mark their ideas of the conduct of favourite scenes ... these would go down to posterity as memorials of their requirements in their art and as models for the improvement of posterity. And the aspiring actor would not be obliged as at present almost before he can emerge from obscurity to invent for himself an entire system of action.[35]

The idea that training can only be based on models was in keeping with the traditional educational principles of the eighteenth century, which had not yet given way to the ideas of spontaneity, intuition and imagination that were later to emerge from the romantic movement.

A nineteenth-century survey of dramatic criticism shows the critic more firmly entrenched in his own profession. His newly-won security meant that he could attack or defend performances from outside. It was now the man of letters, such as Hazlitt, rather than the man of the theatre, who had his column in the newspapers, although some had already sunk from a literary to a journalistic level. Hazlitt himself, writing in *The Examiner, The Champion, The Times* and *The Morning Chronicle* concentrated more on acting and interpretation than any previous critic. His best criticism was concerned with productions of Shakespeare's plays. As they needed little reassessment as plays, he could concentrate on the performance. The poverty of contemporary playwriting gave him much less scope although he often attempted to give significance to the commonplace: 'Mr Kenney's new comedy called *The Touchstone or the World as it Goes* has been acted with great success. It possesses much liveliness and pleasantry in the incidents and the dialogue is neat and pointed.'[36] Hazlitt was inclined to pay considerable deference to 'success' and the judgment of the audience: 'His (Mr Dimond's) pieces have upon the whole been exceedingly popular, and we think deservedly so: for they have all the merit that belongs to the style of drama to which he has devoted his talents—a style which is a great favourite with an immense majority of the play-going public.'[37]. His interest in acting, however, produced much more informed and intelligent

[35] *Chironomia or A Treatise on Rhetorical Delivery* (London, 1806), p. 286.
[36] W. Hazlitt, *Works* ed. P. P. Howe (Dent, 1930), v, 368.
[37] *Ibid*, p. 366.

criticism of the technique of individual actors, particularly of the re-
doubtable figures of Charles Kean, Kemble and Mrs Siddons. Filled
with romantic interest in character he judged these actors in Shakespearean roles according to his own conception of their parts. Criticising Kean's Macbeth (1814) in *The Champion* he says:

> He did not look like a man who had encountered the Weird
> Sisters. There should be nothing tight or compact in Macbeth, no
> tenseness of fibre, nor pointed decision of manner. In the fifth
> act in particular, which is in itself as busy and turbulent as
> possible, there was not that giddy whirl of the imagination—the
> character did not burnish on all sides with those flashes of
> genius of which Mr Kean had given so fine an earnest in the
> conclusion of his Richard III.[38]

He also gives some indication of the gap now visible between Garrick's 'naturalism' (the ability to move an audience in a succession of
ad hoc impersonations), and the new demand for rhetoric and authenticity which would serve for the play as a whole. Of Kean's Richard III he said:

> Mr Kean's manner of acting is on the contrary rather a per-
> petual assumption of his part, always brilliant and successful,
> almost always true and natural, but yet always a distinct effort
> in every new situation, so that the actor does not seem entirely
> to forget himself, or to be identified with the character ... Mr
> Kean's acting in Richard, as we before remarked in Shylock,
> presents a perpetual succession of striking pictures. He bids fair
> to supply us with the best Shakespeare Gallery we have
> had.[39]

This tone by which the critic lays claim to superior knowledge of
what the dramatists and the actors are about is to be found in the
writings of most nineteenth-century critics culminating later in the
century in the pontifical tone of reviewers in *The Quarterly*, *Black-
woods*, *The Theatre*, and *The Times*. These critics were writing for
middle- and upper-class readers who might visit the theatre very
seldom on account of its vulgarity and ill-repute but who liked to be
well informed of its activities, and who treated outstanding actors,
whose pictures and life stories were often published, as popular idols.
Later in the century, William Archer, in his introduction to selec-

---

[38] *Ibid*, p. 204.
[39] *Ibid*, p. 204. Diderot made the same point much earlier, and in a positive form.
In his *Paradoxe sur le comédien* (1770) he examined the means by which an actor
should simulate emotion and concluded that it should not be too strongly felt:
'Les gestes de son désespoir sont de mémoire, et ont été préparés devant une glaçe:
... L'acteur est las, et vous tristes; c'est qu'il s'est démené sans rien sentir, et que
vous [le spectateur] avez senti sans vous démener.' (Paris, Plon, 1929, p. 39.)
Diderot recognised at this early stage the necessity for some degree of alienation in
the technique of acting if the actor were to succeed in building up a three-dimensional character, detached from the author, who had put him in motion.

tions from Leigh Hunt's *Dramatic Essays* (1894), did not acknowledge any dramatic critics before the beginning of the nineteenth century. The critics, Hill, Steele and Murphy, who had been so much involved with the theatre and concerned for its reputation, were disregarded. The successful critic of the nineteenth century did not possess his predecessors' power to make or break a play. Instead he had a steady readership to rely on. The critics of this period, however, had some responsibility for the sterility of the contemporary theatre. Most of them made no attempt to make their readers' taste more adventurous or to encourage innovation or experiment. The depths to which taste was allowed to sink in the travesties and burlesques of Shakespeare's plays can be partly blamed on the complacency of these critics.

The interdependence of the elements that contribute to theatrical performance, the dramatist, the actor, the audience and the off-stage voice of society, that comes through the critic, is most apparent in a period of innovation. Such a period occurred at the end of the nineteenth century when realistic impersonation was regarded as the true aim of the actor. A new concern with realism was already becoming apparent in the plays of Robertson, Pinero and Wilde, but the themes and settings still belonged to the upper-class London world that was for most people as unreal as that of the Elizabethans or the Romans. It was the introduction to the English theatre of Ibsen's plays, by Bernard Shaw and Archer, backed up by Gosse's criticism that called for the creation of new conventions, on which the actor could rely in communicating with the audience. The characters were expected to 'reveal' themselves without any direct or indirect presentation. The educated spectator, schooled by the novelist to discover what thoughts and motives lay behind explicit action, was prepared to dispense with the older rhetorical convention in favour of behaviour that, once again, appeared 'natural' (i.e. authentic).

The introduction of Ibsen to the English stage and the practice and theory of the Russian producers woke both critics and audiences from their lethargy. Archer and Shaw in the 1880s forced the public to take notice of Ibsen's plays and to facilitate their performance at the Independent Theatre. Shaw was the first to see the full implications of dramatic criticism. In his *Advice to a Young Critic* addressed to Reginald Golding Bright he said: 'To be a critic you must be not only a bit of an expert in your own subject but you must have literary skill and trained critical skill too—the power of analysis, comparison etc.'[40] Previous critics had assumed that their gentlemanly education entitled them to criticise performances without any more expert knowledge. But Shaw, Archer, and Beerbohm

[40] *Advice to a Young Critic*, 1894 (London, 1933), p. 13.

formulated criteria that enabled them to place plays and actors in relation to the audience. Shaw spoke always to the spectator sitting in the theatre, not to the newspaper reader in his own home. He declared himself from the first a partial, crusading, critic. In 1906 he wrote: 'I must honestly warn the reader that what he is about to study is not a series of judgments aiming at impartiality but a siege laid to the theatre of the XIXth Century by an author who had to cut his way into it at the point of the pen and throw some of its defenders into the moat.'[41] This declaration is much closer to the spirit of early eighteenth-century criticism than to that of the nineteenth or twentieth century. In this spirit he decried drawing-room comedy and 'the cup and saucer' school of acting, and championed Ibsen and those actors, such as Sullivan and Forbes Robertson, who attempted a more heroic style. But his aim was not so much to reform the theatre as to give it a central position in contemporary culture. He wrote:

> The theatre is growing in importance as a social organ. Modern civilisation is rapidly multiplying the class to which the theatre is both school and church, and when the dramatic art is practised rightly, when it is all pervading, all pestilent romance is swept out of it, the natural importance of the theatre will be as unquestioned as that of the army, the fleet, the church, the law and the schools.[42]

The realistic 'New drama' that Shaw and Archer coaxed the audiences of the 'nineties to take seriously was in no way revolutionary. The increasingly middle-class audience that the growing number of secondary schools and evening classes were producing was sympathetic to the middle-class values that Ibsen dramatised—respect for the individual, honest dealing and social conscience. At the same time it was beginning to condemn the bourgeois vices that he castigated—hypocrisy and self-assertiveness. Ibsen was intent on clearing up the bourgeois mess, but he was not subversive except perhaps in matters of sex and private relationships, which have always been a middle-class obsession. Characters, such as Lövborg in *Hedda Gabler* and Brendel in *Rosmersholm* who try to live by a different anti-bourgeois code, are exposed as rotten and self-indulgent. Thus, although the public that Shaw and Archer tried to educate were easily shocked they could respond to this kind of realism. Shaw would have been less successful had he tried to attract

---

[41] *The Author's Apology*, quoted in M. Meisel, *Shaw and the Nineteenth Century Theatre* (Princeton University Press, 1963), p. 66.
[42] 'The stage and its critics', *Blackwood's Magazine* clxiii (1898), 872. This opinion was held up to ridicule by the dramatic critic of this journal who defended theatre 'of mere amusement mere sensuous distraction', and believed that this was what the growing audience wanted.

them to the hyperrealism of Strindberg or the anti-realist drama with which Jarry and his friends were then experimenting in France. The force of this movement, with its followers in the tradition of what has been called the 'Theatre of the Absurd', was not felt here until after the last war when more people began to explore the possibilities of the theatre without groping for the guiding hand of the critic.

Criticism for Shaw was a total activity, apparent in his life, his politics, and his plays as well as in his theatrical criticism. He never allowed his readers to be ignorant of the duty they had to perform as listeners or readers. This was the kind of critic that the audiences of the 1890s seemed to need. The intelligentsia and the educated middle classes were slowly returning to a theatre that had been for a century the preserve of the vulgar or disreputable. They were looking for the kind of satisfaction that they had previously found in poetry and the novel. They needed help in bridging the gulf between themselves and the artificialities of the stage world. Drama which was close to religious ritual and based on familiar cosmic realities had needed no critics. Sixteenth-century drama that relied on the patronage and the taste of the aristocracy had needed none. But an audience where consensus is riven by class distinction and differing levels of education seems to require a new set of standards and criteria provided by a member of a profession which specialises in this activity. The success of Shaw as a critic lies, however, not so much in the fact that he was influential in persuading the audience to accept new conventions of dramatic thought and action in Chekhov's, Ibsen's, Strindberg's and his own plays, but in his conversion of a large section of the audience from passive acceptance to active criticism.

This change in the audience has been recognised by dramatists who, following Shaw's lead, now address the audience directly, not only in plays but in criticism. Brecht and Ionesco, both dominant figures in the modern theatre, have written explicitly about their criteria and intentions and provided the audience with the tools of criticism. Brecht in demonstrating the 'alienation' effect demands critical actors as well as a critical audience. Ionesco addresses the audience as critic: 'What then should the critic do? Where should he look for his criteria? Inside the work itself, its universe and its mythology. He must look at it, listen to it, and simply say whether it is true to its own nature ... A work of art is the expression of an incommunicable reality that one tries to communicate and which sometimes can be communicated.'[43] The possibility of communication presumably rests on the maintenance of a dialectic between dramatist and audience of which the language is a developing series of symbols. These can too easily be deadened. As Ionesco says

[43] *Notes and Counter Notes* (Calder, 1964), p. 96.

in his essay on the avant-garde: 'As soon as a form of expression becomes recognised, it is already out of date. A thing once spoken is already dead, reality lives somewhere beyond it and the thought has become petrified.'[44]

The breakdown of traditional religion and morality during this century has produced an audience undaunted by the kind of moral challenge and shock tactics offered to earlier audiences by Ibsen, Strindberg and Shaw, but bewildered by the challenge to rationality offered by Adamov, Beckett and Ionesco: 'images drawn from dreams, realities that have been dreamed'.[45] To help the audience chart its way through these unmapped territories modern professional critics have resorted to categorising terms: 'theatre of the absurd', 'comedies of menace', 'theatre of cruelty', 'angry' or 'kitchen sink' plays, 'committed' plays. This rhetorical form of criticism makes explicit the conventions but establishes spurious criteria.

In the category of 'absurd' plays are included any plays that do not conform to conventional rules of cause and effect, from Beckett's to N. F. Simpson's, as well as a spate of 'pointless plays' by Giles Cooper and his imitators that have become vogueish on television. Even writers of satirical propaganda, such as Mrozek, have been included on account of their oblique and slightly mystifying technique. The existentialist idea of 'absurdity' explicit in Sartre's *Hui Clos*, implicit in *Waiting for Godot*, and in most of Ionesco's plays has been misconstrued.

Antonin Artaud's conception of a 'theatre of cruelty' as an attitude to reality, has also been misunderstood. Artaud wrote: 'Nous voulons faire du théâtre une realité à laquelle on puisse croire, et qui contienne pour le coeur et les sens cette espèce de morsure concrète que comporte toute sensation vraie.'[46] Yet 'theatre of cruelty' has been used as a label for any play emphasising violence, from *Titus Andronicus* to *The House of Ginger Coffey*. It refers to those dramatists who dwell on unbearable situations, as Weiss does in *Marat/Sade*, or who, like Bond in *Saved* take an amoral stance in the face of brutality. Plays, such as Arden's *Serjeant Musgrave's Dance* that do not fit neatly into any of these categories often receive summary and contradictory treatment from the critics, even when the audience is enthusiastic.

The implication of contemporary criticism is that plays that have been sorted into appropriate categories correspond to conditions of society or of man in society. This view of the theatre as a reflection

---

[44] *Ibid*, p. 41.
[45] *Ibid*, p. 115.
[46] A. Artaud, *Le Théâtre et son Double, Works* (Gallimard, 1964), iv, 17.

of a static situation is a long way from that of Bernard Shaw who, at
the beginning of this century, saw drama as an energiser of social
change. Antonin Artaud, examining the nature of its dynamism,
spoke of the theatre in these terms: 'Toute vraie effigie a son ombre
qui la double; et l'art tombe à partir du moment ou le sculpteur qui
modèle, croit libérer une sorte d'ombre dont l'existence déchirera son
repos ... Mais le vrai théâtre parce qu'il bouge et parce qu'il se sert
d'instruments vivants, continue à agiter des ombres ou n'a cessé de
trébucher la vie.' But a consensus for such dynamic theatre depends
upon an audience which has learnt to interpret these shadows, and is
willing to be carried step by step with the dramatist who can, as
Artaud suggests: 'Briser le langage pour toucher la vie, c'est faire ou
refaire le théâtre; ... Ceçi amène à rejeter les limitations habit-
uelles de l'homme et des pouvoirs de l'homme et à rendre infinies les
frontières de ce qu'on appele la réalité.'[47]

Twenty-five years after it was written, this attitude now finds
more and more acceptance in the avant-garde theatre. It is discernible in the way in which audiences respond to Brecht, Genet,
Ionesco. They see these dramatists using different methods to break
into ordinary life and create bridges between the territories of the
stage drama and the world outside the theatre in both of which
expressive performance takes place. Unfortunately most critics isolate these three dramatists in their separate categories and do not
recognise Brecht's 'a-effect' in the ceremonial 'acting out' of Genet's
characters in *Les Bonnes* or *Le Balcon* or in the splintered identities of
Ionesco's figures in *Victimes du Devoir*.

The critics, in fact, endanger the usual process of making
and changing conventions between dramatists and audience by
sub-dividing recognisable modes of expression. The tendency of
such categorising is to create even more rigid barriers between an
intellectual and popular theatre, barriers that the cinema
and television often overcome by making popular such plays as
The Caretaker, and *Waiting for Godot*, and incorporating their
technique in such easily acceptable films as *The Knack*, and *The
Servant*.

It is no longer to the critic that the spectator looks for instruction.
It is first to the dramatist who often supplements his works with
critical writing. Many people who have never seen a play by Brecht
or Ionesco, may be familiar with their theories in *Brecht on Theatre*,
and *Notes and Counter-Notes* or from newspaper interviews or other
secondary sources. They look secondly to a producer who has often
collaborated with the dramatist. Becket gave detailed advice on the
production of *Play* and *Happy Days* and usually sees his plays right
through from the first draft to the performance. This surveillance is

[47] *Ibid*, iv, 18.

essential for plays such as these, which depend so much on the intellectual, moral or spiritual context of the linear sequence of utterances. Dramatists and producers frequently supplement this control
by communicating directly with their audience by writing articles or
giving television and radio interviews and talks. The dissemination of
creative and critical ideas has produced an audience that responds
much more readily to new forms. The popular concern with 'absurd
behaviour', derived from a diluted background of existentialist philosophy, and familiarity with sociological terms such as 'alienation'
and 'anomie' has helped to encourage spectators to dispense with
plot, narrative, character definition, and relationships and accept
any idiosyncratic form that a new dramatist may impose. The readiness to accept the new forms has its dangers, but seems preferable to
the unwillingness of nineteenth and early twentieth-century audiences to break with old forms or judge for themselves without the
guidance of a professional critic. As W. Archer told them in 1912:
'Any movement is good which helps to free art from the tyranny of
a code of rules and definitions.'[48]

It begins to look as if the professional dramatic critic (at least in
Europe) has a very slight function, little more than the provision of
Sunday reading matter, or the taking of sides on controversial
matters of censorship. Kenneth Tynan, one of the most widely read
critics since the war, is now literary adviser to the National Theatre,
and can only write occasional criticism. As in the eighteenth century
the critic now seems to need some involvement with the theatre
while the business of making or breaking plays returns to the audience. The fact that a very large part of society has turned its back on
the theatre for the sake of cinema, television and other forms of
entertainment, has left for the theatre an audience of choice that is
prepared to give it the same kind of informed and devoted attention
as the connoisseur gives to pictures or music.

This audience is increasingly concerned with developing critical
attitudes to the theatre. A spectator can scarcely feel that he has
enjoyed a play until he has taken some kind of critical stance. This
perhaps constitutes the biggest contrast between the audience of the
sixteenth century and the audience today. The modern spectator sees
himself professionally in this critical role. His reactions and opinions
seem as important as what goes on on the stage. He no longer competes with the actor on the stage as he did in the seventeenth and
eighteenth centuries, but competes for first place as critic, either pri-
vately or publicly.

The critic has cut away some of the ground under his own professional feet by educating the audience and revealing the process by
which criteria are formed. He now finds himself disliked by some

[48] 'Dramatic and undramatic', *Playmaking* (Dodd, 1912), p. 32.

directors[49] and mistrusted by much of the theatre-going public. He speaks to and on behalf of a newspaper public which reads his reviews with the same attention that it gives to reviews of books it never reads, pictures it never sees. Criticism has become comment, of a superior but peculiarly detached nature. Thus critics no longer provide a medium by which dramatist and spectators can interact, but much more often, serve merely to signal the arrival of cultural innovations or changes in fashion.

At the same time, the recognition of spectatorship as a role essential to performance in the theatre does not disguise the fact that there is a discrepancy between the interests of dramatist, actors and producer on the one side and, on the other side, the audience. The performers are concerned to transform real experience into rhetoric and emphasise the separation of the real and theatrical worlds. Even when they demand audience participation they are attempting to 'theatricalise' the audience. The spectator, however, cannot accept truth or authenticity in drama unless it can be related to his own experience of theatricality in ordinary life. He himself, outside the theatre, is a trained performer and is obliged to exercise some of the skills of dramatist, producer and actor. Thus the tensions that are set up between performers and spectators rest on and react on the maintenance and style of theatrical behaviour in daily life.

[49] William Gaskill's rejection of newspaper critics was reported: 'I do not', he says, 'consider the work of a serious theatre to be a subject for sensational news items which is all most critical notices amount to.' He was seriously considering excluding dramatic critics from the first night audience. *The Guardian*, 27th October, 1966. Later in 1968 the Royal Court stopped inviting critics to first nights.

11

Themes: ceremony and significance

'It is not moral that any system of thought be judged wholly by its own criteria.' Colin Cherry.

There are still a few kingdoms left in the world; so, occasionally, we are offered the opportunity of attending or watching the ceremonial inauguration of a new sovereign. No doubt there are sizeable differences between the performance of a coronation ceremony and the contextual pageantry in, say, Britain, the Netherlands, Sweden, or Jordan, but there would be little room for doubt that they were all ceremonies of the same kind. The more frequent and less dressy affair connected with the swearing-in, or installation of a new President in any of the far more numerous republics in the world, would be equally recognisable for what it was. There are 'deep' similarities and 'superficial' differences.

The question arises of how it is that we know the 'deep', significant, essential similarities running through such affairs so that we can see them as of the same type, and can disregard, or regard as interesting, amusing, or curious but inessential, the multitude of linguistic and other differences. One fashionable answer to the problem of how it is that the recognition of 'what is going on here?' at a coronation or a presidential installation (or a wedding, or a funeral, or a greeting ...) is to invoke one or other of the analytical models created within the last generation by linguists. These models are attempts to explain the ground rules which underlie every language, and by which native speakers are able to construct meaningful utterances and compose sentences, and are also able to distinguish them from nonsense, and from incomplete or wrongly composed sentences:

> How then [remarks Edmund Leach] can we distinguish between the basic grammatical principles—the rules of the game which

allow us to say that these performances [he cites a series of English weddings] are all 'proceedings of the same type'—and the subsidiary contingent rules which allow for individual variation? I do not know the answer, but it seems highly likely that the investigation of linguists in the field of generative and transformational grammars will provide very profitable analogies for the Anthropologist whose concern is with the transformational rules which govern custom. And of course what goes for weddings goes for any other kind of institutionalised sequence of events which you care to mention.[1]

The central concern of this book could be read as the attempt to demonstrate the unprofitability of any such endeavour. It is unrealistic to try to separate the notion of the conventions of social action from the intentions of the actor and the understandings of the audience, the explicit from the implicit.

To return to the instance with which I began, it is imaginable (and, for all I know, actually the case) that the coronation ceremony performed in 1953 for Elizabeth II replicated exactly that which occurred in 1559. But the full significance of the ceremony for both performers and society were for the most part, utterly different on the second occasion from what obtained four hundred years before—different in terms of the consequences of the performance itself, of the actual consequences for the performers and for contemporary society, and of the meaning which it held for them. The similarities of meaning in so far as they relate to social action (the 'deep' structure, to follow the linguistic analogy) are confined to the religious ritual and its moral significance, in Durkheim's sense, for English society at both times. A complete replication of either coronation ceremony *on the stage* would, again, have utterly different significance for performers, audience, and society, and this time the difference would include a difference in the moral significance, because, simply, the rituals performed would be essentially non-religious (or even irreligious). The moral significance attaching to the theatrical performance—equally composed, equally ceremonious, equally ritualised—would derive from the generalised intention of the play as a whole directed towards a specific set of audience understandings—from, in short, the play's *theme*.

The equivalences and distinctions between scene, setting, exposition and role-playing inside and outside the theatre are not difficult to identify. But the composition in accordance with specific intentions and understandings of conduct and events in everyday life in more or less ritualised form corresponds with theme in drama. Events are composed of actions which are neither conceived nor

[1] E. Leach, 'Language and anthropology', in Noel Minnis, *Linguistics at Large* (Gollancz, 1971), p. 156.

perceived as isolated. They are perceived as causally connected and therefore as consequential. But identical sequences of action interpreted according to different sets of values and norms can express completely different meanings. These interpretations are expressed in social life in the form of ceremonial and ritual specific to particular social groups. Ritual is in fact a system of communication, a 'language' of conventions.

Ceremony is a limited form of ritual. It can be used to refer to those collective actions, required by custom, performed on occasions of change in social life. Thus a ceremonial consists of a specific sequence of ritual acts, performed in public.[2] Much public ceremonial that has been retained is quasireligious, such as coronations, the investiture of the Prince of Wales, weddings, funerals, and so on. But occasions of non-religious ceremonial, the Trooping of the Colour, the opening of parliament and of High Court trials, for example, are observed with just as much reverence and formality. These are in fact all ceremonies that stress some aspect of social organisation. The equivalence, in this respect, of both religious and non-religious ceremonies is in keeping with Durkheim's view that society is a moral community whose religion is a means of asserting and reaffirming its collective solidarity and its sacred character.[3] According to Radcliffe-Brown the application of 'ceremony' to secular occasions is very old. Confucian philosophers of the second and third centuries B.C. spoke of it as the orderly expression of feelings appropriate to a social situation.[4] In ceremonies the expression of 'appropriate feelings' always takes a symbolic form. Stylised forms of the language of movement or gesture, such as bowing, presenting arms, or removing the hat, may be used in conjunction with symbolic objects, flags, chains of offices, chalices, traditional costumes, etc. Some of these may have little significance in themselves, or their significance may have been forgotten, but in combination they form the significant language of ceremony which is close to the expressive language of the theatre. There are, however, varying degrees of theatricality acceptable as ceremonial at different periods and on different occasions.

Ceremonial depends essentially on distinctions of rank, status or class. It indicates and emphasises where power lies. Its manifestation is therefore as significant in political as in religious terms. In periods when the hierarchical structure of society was generally accepted ceremonial played an important part in politics. Throughout the

---

[2] J. Goody, 'Religion and ritual', *British Journal of Sociology* (June, 1961), p. 159.
[3] See E. Durkheim in *Elementary Forms of the Religious Life* trans. J. W. Swain, (London, 1915), pp. 415–47.
[4] J. R. Radcliffe-Brown, *Taboo* (Cambridge University Press, 1939), p. 33.

fourteenth and fifteenth centuries royal entries, progresses and the reception of foreign ambassadors were the occasions for demonstrating power, security and peaceful or aggressive intentions. During the Tudor period, ceremonial reached an unparalleled grandeur and elaboration. The coronation and marriage of Henry VII were occasions not only for display but also for assurances, depicted allegorically and declared in verse, of the new security and strength of the monarchy. But Henry VII was not, it is said, inclined to display. It was Henry VIII who developed ceremonial with all its pageantry and semi-dramatic interludes as a political implement. The lavishness of the progresses, entries and tournaments, the entertainment of foreign rulers culminating in the meeting with Francis I at the Field of the Cloth of Gold, were not mere wanton displays of extravagance but carefully calculated political moves.[5]

Henry's children continued to manipulate ceremonial, with the same kind of political intention but with less success. Even Elizabeth, who had inherited much of her father's taste, was hampered by a dislike of extravagance. Much of the pageantry during her reign took the form of 'offerings' presented to her and partly paid for by her courtiers, especially on the occasions when she visited them in their country estates. On such occasions poets and scholars devised dramatic entertainments with heavily stressed allegorical overtones.[6] Although these elaborate pageants were distinct from the traditional ceremonies attached to the daily life of the court it is apparent that the line between reality and fiction was often blurred. When the students of Gray's Inn presented the Queen with an extended masquerade in 1559 the 'Prince of Purpoole' and his retinue were entertained by the Queen with much the same attention and ceremonial pomp that would have been provided for a real foreign prince.[7]

Although James I continued to make progresses they were accomplished with less pageantry, and the most elaborate masquing seems to have taken place at court or on visits to the universities or the Middle Temple. These masques, in which his Queen took much delight, entailed extravagant expenditure on costume and mechanical device. This was private entertainment for the magic circle of courtiers and for distinguished visitors such as the King of Denmark.[8] This became still more marked in his son's court. Charles I had even less sense than his father of the political value of

[5] See S. Anglo, *Spectacle, Pageantry and Early Tudor Policy* (Oxford University Press, 1969), p. 125.
[6] Bradbrook, *Rise of the Common Player*, p. 247ff.
[7] 'Gesta Grayorum', quoted in G. B. Harrison, *Second Elizabethan Journal* (Constable, 1931), pp. 4–8.
[8] Pageantry in the city for the visit of the King of Denmark in 1606 was presented elaborately in the tradition of Tudor ceremonial: see G. B. Harrison, *A Jacobean Journal* (Routledge, 1941), p. 327.

maintaining a public relationship with the citizens of his realm.[9]
Although traditional ceremonial was maintained it was losing its
force as a public or political gesture, partly perhaps because the
'orderly expression of feelings appropriate to the social situation' obtaining between the sovereign and his subjects had manifest risks
attaching to it, partly because of the discretion which the spread of
puritanism enforced on display.

Under the Stuarts the court gradually became a more private
place. The demonstration of power or friendship either towards
foreign princes or towards the king's subjects had to assume a more
substantial form. In the court of Charles II the masque was often
revived but all other forms of pageantry were reserved for state
occasions.

Since the seventeenth century ceremonial has played a progressively less important part. In its fictional or make-believe form,
as the masque, it gave way to more formal dramatic entertainment,
which no longer involved the courtiers as participants. Thus declarations of loyalty or pleas for favour could no longer be made in
the form of 'play'. Moreover the semiotic significance of non-
fictional ceremonial became more rigid, defined as a routine and
ruled by traditional usage. Although the political significance of a
coronation or investiture is still apparent these ceremonials have
only one set of long-accepted meanings. The sovereign is no longer
able to exercise his will or display specific meanings (as Tudor
monarchs still could) through the manipulation of ceremonial.
Symbolic meanings are no longer proliferated but accepted as
fixed.

The ceremonial of state occasions, today, has therefore become a
historical re-enactment. With the loss of most of its instrumental
aspects only its symbolic aspects are left, and this means, as we have
seen, that it has moved nearer to a theatrical show. Moreover much
of the symbolism has been diluted. At the coronation the Queen's
sacred office is represented on the same terms in which it was represented when the monarch had real political power. As Queen she
represents at the same time the historical idea of monarchy and of
the state, to which political power has now shifted. She herself is
seen as a symbol (or, as she is often called, 'a figurehead') of power,
although she cannot wield it.

The dilution of meaning in traditional ceremonial has been accompanied by the loss of 'play' forms or 'make-believe' ceremonial.
The masque was itself a game made out of the relationships which

[9] In a letter from William Murray, groom of the bedchamber, written to Sir Henry
Vane, 1631, the court is described as 'like the earth, naturally cold, and reflecting
no more affection than the sunshine of their master's favour beats upon it', quoted
in D. Mathew, *Social Structure in Caroline England* (Oxford University Press, 1945),
p. 35.

court ceremonial reflected. At court functions from the early eight-eenth century on, its place was taken by the formal dance and later by a benign interest in the theatre. But even Queen Victoria pre-ferred to attend the public theatre rather than summon the actors to court. Dilution of the meanings of ceremonial is apparent not only at court but also in all relationships where distinctions of status and class have changed or shown a loss of power. Thus in this century, a period which has seen the dissemination of democratic ideas and lip-service paid by most people to the principle of equality, there has been a reduction in the number of ceremonial occasions which give scope for overt theatricality. Yet when they do occur, the coronation, the investiture of the Prince of Wales or the Troop-ing of the Colour are as carefully rehearsed as any theatrical occasion.

It is also significant that the most fully rehearsed and best per-formed regular ceremonial is military. Although parades are often dressed in costumes and trappings far removed from the operational uniform and equipment of the modern army, they do represent this institution (the armed forces) which still has real power and effectiveness. This also applies though less spectacularly to the cere-monial of the law courts. Costumes, ritual behaviour and forms of address are not inappropriate though they may often seem to verge on self-parody, in that they carry the implication of the permanence and perhaps the rigidity (and thus, in Weber's sense, sanctity) of legal procedure over a long period of history. But, overridingly, they denote authority and power.

In expected contrast, Church ceremonial, in England, having lost its meaning for the majority of the population, is seldom brought out of the church setting, and, except on royal occasions, is unstressed in national life. The retention of any ceremonial in a society that stresses informality and secular values does, however, need some ex-planation. It can be distinguished as a theatrical/historical event from its original *ritual* form.

In a fully rehearsed event, such as a coronation, we are presented with a ceremony which depends for its meaning on beliefs and in-terpretations shared by all present. Now that many people do not believe in the effectiveness or authority of the ritual connected with the crown this consensus is weakened. Ritual always implies that something happens. According to tradition the Queen is given a sacred charge by God and really becomes a more powerful person, a sacred person, when the crown is placed on her head. If this is not believed the actions merely symbolise the fact that she has become Queen (she has in fact become Queen some months before and is already endowed with as much authority as she will ever have). This kind of symbolism which is descriptive rather than effective is theatrical.[10] It lacks the combination of instrumentality and effectiveness that characterises religious ritual.

On the stage the symbolic aspect of actions, which in real life would be indissolubly connected with their instrumental intention, loses this *ad hoc* instrumentality and becomes bound up with the drama's audience-directed intention. For example, murder in a play is neither a real action nor merely the imitation of a real action. It is a symbolic representation which can arouse reactions similar to those aroused by the real thing, but does not result in action. The reactions are purely emotional. They seldom cause the spectator to leap on the stage to seize the murderer, or call for a policeman. The action is *affective* but not *effective*. It is through the presentation of action on the stage, the stressing of certain actions at the expense of others, the implied quotation marks that accentuate certain meanings, and the use of rhetoric, that the meanings of actions are synthesised into a general statement to which the audience can react. It may be merely with 'how funny', 'how cruel', 'how stupid' or 'how like us', but it is impossible for any play, however bad, to make no statement at all, to carry no 'message' or to receive no response as if no statement had been made.

In ordinary life ceremony serves the purpose of distinguishing an important event or of endowing an ordinary event with dignity or mystery. The instrumentality of action is 'weighted' with symbolism. Many non-religious people want to have a church wedding or funeral because there is no comparable secular ceremony with which to dignify the transaction at the registry office or at the burial ground. Renunciation of ceremonial on such occasions places a heavy strain on the emotional content of relationships. New forms of celebration or of expressing grief are required, and their sincerity can only be tested by personal testimony.[11]

Although ritual acts form a part of every ceremony they can also be observed in other contexts that are not normally recognised as ceremonial. Ritual has been defined by Edmund Leach as denoting 'those aspects of prescribed formal behaviour which have no direct technological consequences. The "prescription" is ordinarily pro-

---

[10] The closeness—and the still significant gap—between the coronation ceremony and theatrical performance was clearly articulated in the famous *gaffe* of the Minister of Public Works who was responsible for the 1953 coronation arrangements. He could not, he said, have asked for a better 'leading lady'—a remark regarded by many at the time as vulgar and offensive.

[11] Another function of ceremonial is suggested by Freud in his comparison of neurotic with religious ceremonial. He suggests that it is a means of control based on repression and can represent 'the sum of the conditions subject to which something which is not yet absolutely forbidden is permitted just as the Church's marriage ceremony signifies for the believer a sanctioning of sexual enjoyment which would otherwise be sinful': 'Obsessive actions and religious practices' in *Sociology and Religion*, ed. N. Birnbaum and E. Lenzer (Prentice-Hall, 1969).

vided by cultural tradition, but may in some cases be a spontaneous invention of the individual.'[12] This definition comprehends behaviour considered appropriate for both public and private, major and minor social occasions, ranging from the formal reception to the informal party with friends, from annual celebrations of the New Year, birthdays or anniversaries to the daily rituals connected with greeting or parting from a guest, making introductions or the first steps in forming friendships.

Ritual is not, however, confined to 'occasional' observances. Ritual, as a language in constant use, provides a key to our perception of, and interpretation of, social reality. 'It operates not by trial and error guided by observation but by symbolism and drama.'[13] It provides the forms through which children are socialised both in their homes and later through the institutional life at school and other social establishments. Although in modern Western society initiation ceremonies—christenings, confirmation, coming of age— are given little social importance and are often neglected entirely, the child's future is still usually presented to him as a series of tests and challenges. Entry to primary and later to secondary school, initiation into adulthood, into university education or a career, is still recognised and discussed as an important and difficult process accountable for many strains which might be relieved by more overt recognition of the rituals which are entailed:

> Initiation is so tightly bound to modes of being in human life that a considerable number of the gestures and actions of man in contemporary life re-enact themes of initiation. Often 'the struggle of life', the 'trials' and the 'difficulties' which impede vocations or careers seem to some extent to re-enact the trials of initiation. It is through the 'blows' he receives, his 'sufferings' and the moral or even physical torture to which he is subjected, that a young man 'proves' himself and realises his possibilities—becomes conscious of his powers and eventually becomes spiritually adult and creative (here 'spirituality' is meant in the sense in which it is understood in the modern world).[14]

These observances are part of a process which is going on all the time, a process of communication. The 'occasional ritual' emphasises loudly and clearly what is constantly felt or what it is thought should be felt. A child's behaviour to his mother, however sincere, is inevitably ritualised. Until he is ten or eleven he treats her in a way that shows he knows she is stronger, more powerful (she

[12] Edmund Leach, 'Ritual' in the *Dictionary of the Social Sciences*, ed. J. Gould and W. L. Kolb (Tavistock, 1964).
[13] J. Beattie, 'Ritual and Social Change', in *Man* i, no. 1 (March 1966).
[14] Mircea Eliade, *Le Sacré et le profane* (Paris, 1965), p. 176–7 (my translation, E.B.).

can give or withhold food) and has more knowledge than he. Whether he is obedient or disobedient his actions show that he is aware of his subordinate position as well as his filial attachment. Even the spoilt child has to work for indulgence, by currying favour, throwing tantrums or developing some attractive trait. These ritual sequences of action can culminate on the occasion of the mother's birthday in a ceremony, performed by most if not all children in Western countries. The mother is given a present or a card or at least some expression of affection. If a special meal is prepared the mother will perhaps be allowed to sit back and be given special attention. This is the kind of behaviour that is commonly recognised as cere-monial because it is repetitive and expressive. But it is only express-ing in a stylised way those feelings and attitudes that are normally expressed by deference, obedience and the occasional caress, also by the rebellions and affronts that by no means contradict the domi-nant-subordinate nature of the mother–child relationship. If there is a lack of affection on either side the ritual seems to be 'empty'. But this may only mean that either mother or child is in daily life trying to hide from or escape from the essential nature of the relationship.

Raymond Firth clarifies the distinction between ritual and cere-mony in a slightly different way. He suggests that ritual is enforced by mystical standards and ceremony by conventional standards.[15] If 'mystical' can be used to describe such emotions and beliefs as the love and the trust that most people experience, relationships such as the mother–child relationship mentioned above can be seen to be related to ritual as well as to ceremonial.

A ritualistic view of individual life presents not only a structure of initiations, tests and goals that appear to provide meaning and value to what might otherwise be an anomic day-to-day existence but also a dramatic picture of the individual engaged in social interaction.

In primitive societies it is possible to observe the ways in which ritual really works in daily life so that action is in practice overtly related to beliefs and ritual observances. In his study of Ndembu village life[16] V. W. Turner uses the concept of 'social drama' to classify sequences of behaviour in which a breach of custom (neglect or deliberate distortion of ritual) resulted in a crisis situation, followed by redressive action and subsequent reintegration or recognition of schism (the offenders would withdraw to found a new village). By its revelation of the ways in which the rules of conduct can be tested and sometimes manipulated the 'drama' can be seen as either the 'index or a vehicle of social change'. The reading of such social dramas depends on the appreciation of consensus in such

[15] R. Firth, *Tikopia Ritual and Belief* (Allen & Unwin, 1967), p. 73.
[16] V. W. Turner, *Schism and Continuity in an African Society* (Manchester University Press, 1956), p. 161.

a society at all levels from deeply held beliefs to superficial deportment.

In contemporary society, riven by religious and political disagreement and segmented by specialisms and by social class, it is impossible to rely on a code which will enable one to understand the meanings of the many elaborate social dramas that do occur. Instead such dramas have to be interpreted in the context, seldom of society as a whole, but of the isolated situation, at work, in the family or some other social group, in which crisis occurs. The discovery made by psychotherapists that trouble in one milieu is usually connected with pressure in another (the child psychologist usually wants to find out what is happening to the 'difficult' child at home as well as at school) seldom succeeds in completing the drama. One is presented with fragmented scenes in which neither motives, intentions nor goals can be disentangled with any confidence. Yet the difficulties of interpretation do not invalidate the dramaturgic intentions of the protagonists. Each person, whatever his frame of reference, is concerned with carrying out, and demonstrating that he is carrying out, a course or courses of action as well as merely satisfying material needs or desires.

The terms used in the passage from Mircea Eliade are heavily suggestive of the agonistic forms on which drama, especially tragedy, depends. It is a function of socialisation to urge individuals to compose their lives not only in terms of roles and settings but also of courses of action. In the primary stage of socialisation parents are mainly concerned with teaching their children to behave as they themselves do or as they think they should. Standards of cleanliness, politeness and morality are usually based on the norms of the class to which the parents belong or believe themselves to belong. But when the child goes to school and begins to meet adults from other institutions, the church, youth clubs, or families of other children who belong perhaps to other social classes, parents and teachers are usually concerned to stress the kind of choices that confront him and the responsibility that he bears for working out a future for himself. Each change of school, choice of course at school, decision to take exams or to leave school at a particular time is presented to him, even at this early age, as something that is going to determine his future. Similarly, moral criticism is usually based on future, not present, contingencies. He must control his conduct so that he will not grow up to be dishonest, bullying, cowardly, extravagant or dissipated. In this way a person learns to regard his life not merely as a series of disconnected events, but as a series of consequential actions in which every decision to act has a series of predictable and unpredictable consequences. This becomes apparent when people look back on their lives and distinguish right or wrong decisions which have rendered the 'story' sad or happy, successful or unsuccessful. They are able, however, to compare this 'story' with others they have been able to observe and about which they knew something even before they began to act. Possible patterns of action are presented in ritual form to every member of society.

Thus the decision to get married involves a series of traditional sequences of action—getting to know a particular person, courtship, engagement, finding a place to live—all leading up in ritual stages to the actual ceremony. Ways of obtaining recognition as a couple and orienting to each other's relations and friends are also involved. The ceremony is thus a private manifesto. By engaging in any kind of ritual, such as a degree ceremony, a wedding or a funeral, people announce that they are passing through a stage through which others have passed. They declare their membership of a category whose implications others are expected to recognise.

Even those who avoid formal rituals find themselves involved in informal and sometimes private rituals of the kind mentioned above. These too, concerned as they are with the making of friends or enemies, declarations or betrayals of principles, also announce positions and membership of categories on a micropolitical scale and of classes on a macropolitical scale. Life styles are reflected not only in choice of settings but also in performance of rituals. At work people can be seen to adopt certain prescribed rituals both in their relationships with their co-workers and with outsiders. But in leisure activities which ostensibly allow for more freedom they can also be seen choosing patterns of ritualistic behaviour for specific occasions.

There is a distinction to be made between routines and rituals. A routine is a formalised way of dealing with recurrent actions and events which a person regards as necessary (i.e. has learned to regard as socially incumbent) but with which he does not feel deeply involved. Whitehead has given a lucid and compelling exposition of the place of routine in social life:

> Routine is the god of every social system; it is the seventh heaven of business, the essential component in the success of every factory, the ideal of every statesman. The social machine should run like clockwork. Every crime should be followed by an arrest, every arrest by a judicial trial, every trial by a conviction, every conviction by a punishment, every punishment by a reformed character. Or, you can conceive an analogous routine concerning the making of a motor car, starting with the iron in the ore, and the coal in the mine, and ending with the car driving out of the factory and with the President of the Corporation signing the dividend warrants, and renewing his contracts with the mining Corporations. In such a routine everyone from the humblest miner to the august president is exactly

trained for his special job. Every action of miner or president is the product of conditioned reflexes, according to current physiological phraseology. When the routine is perfect, understanding can be eliminated, except such minor flashes of intelligence as are required to deal with familiar accidents, such as a flooded mine, a prolonged drought, or an epidemic of influenza. A system will be the product of intelligence. But when the adequate routine is established, intelligence vanishes, and the system is maintained by a co-ordination of conditioned reflexes. What is then required from the humans is receptivity or special training. No one, from President to miner, need understand the system as a whole. There will be no foresight, but there will be complete success in the maintenance of the routine.

Now it is the beginning of wisdom to understand that social life is founded upon routine. Unless society is permeated, through and through, with routine, civilization vanishes. So many sociological doctrines, the products of acute intellects, are wrecked by obliviousness to this fundamental sociological truth. Society requires stability, foresight itself presupposes stability, and stability is the product of routine. But there are limits to routine, and it is for the discernment of these limits, and for the provision of the consequent action, that foresight is required.[17]

Routines are characterised by repetition and inexpressiveness. Ritual, on the other hand, consists of a series of actions, considered appropriate to certain situations and capable of generating appropriate reactions from others. They are as we have seen characterised by instrumentality and expressiveness. Most people devise their social life, visits to the pub or club, cultural or athletic activities, protection of privacy or demonstrations of accessibility, in such a way that what at first sight may appear to be routine turns out to be a series of rituals. For instance the man who spends regular evenings in a pub, greeting and conversing with friends, is not merely seeking drink, warmth and conversation, he is also demonstrating both to himself and others his amiability, popularity and conversational ability.

This kind of demonstration is of central importance both to himself and to the continuity of social life. Durkheim specified ritual, whether secular or religious, as a form of, or at all events a preliminary to action. As the main function of ritual is to stimulate faith (ultimately in society) that of faith in turn is to stimulate will. 'For faith is above all an impulse to act and knowledge, however far it is driven, always remains far from action.'[18]

[17] A. N. Whitehead, *Adventures of Ideas* (Cambridge University Press, 1933), pp. 113–14.
[18] Durkheim, *The Elementary Forms of the Religious Life*, p. 615.

The form ritual takes is determined by the manipulation of
symbols through action. It is in this way that drama is so closely
related to ritual. Action on the stage is a representation of action in
ordinary life which has already been given a meaning in its ritual
form. These meanings are made manifest in the themes of drama,
where they are not only restated but enlarged through the dramatic
action. When the rite is recapitulated as drama a great many changes
take place. It is no longer a performance in which all are concerned,
a performance with an exclusive 'actor-reference'. Added to it is a
'spectator-reference'. The symbolism of action on the stage is, therefore, doubled.

In ordinary life when one man hits another he not only damages
him but expresses anger or disgust or some similar emotion. His act is
both instrumental and symbolic. The same action on the stage symbolises both aspects of the action in real life, the instrumental and the
symbolic. The putting out of Gloucester's eyes in *King Lear* represents the physical act, the cruelty of Goneril and Cornwall, and the
symbolism of the whole act which can be interpreted in a number of
ways (his moral blindness becomes physical; an old man becomes the
victim of the young; he learns to see the truth after his physical sight
has gone).

In ordinary life people do not react simply to the actions of others
but to what they think to be the meaning of these acts. To return to
the example above, he who is hit interprets the blow according to the
other signs, the words, stance, demeanour of his attacker and the
context in which it has occurred. Two blows can be equally hard but
one interpreted as an angry attack and the other as play. The recognition of this process has given rise to the term 'symbolic interaction'
used by many social-psychologists and sociologists to describe the
social activity that characterises society: 'Human interaction is mediated by the use of symbols, by interpretation or by ascertaining the
meaning of one another's actions. This mediation is equivalent to
inserting a process of interpretation between stimulus and response
in the case of human behaviour.'[19]

It is the whole process, the act, the interpretation, the response and
the consequences of action that is mimed in drama, and interpreted
by the spectators. The spectators therefore perceive *themes* rather
than isolated acts. A theme is a sequence of acts, interpretations and
responses reinterpreted as a whole, by the spectator. It is, as in music,
recognised in the overall pattern of events, not in a single event but
in the relationship between events. The interpretations are not the
same for each member of the audience, still less for members of
different audiences. Action that is performed on the stage is more

[19] M. Blumer, 'Society as symbolic interaction', in *Symbolic Interaction* ed. J. G.
Manis and B. N. Meltzer (Boston, Allyn, 1967), p. 139.

difficult for a spectator to interpret than action in a face-to-face relationship. On the stage the spectator's interpretation is an amalgam of the interpretations that he imputes to those characters involved in a situation. It is at the same time conditioned by his experience of the social structure which forms the context of his own life.

It is very difficult[20] for a modern spectator to interpret the themes of *Hamlet* definitively because he is obliged to articulate consciously the norms and values which the Elizabethan audience took for granted. It has been suggested that the main theme of *Hamlet* is concerned with the struggle between honour and religion as manifested in conscience, which Hamlet tries to resolve.[21] Yet it is very hard to tell how a contemporary audience would have weighted this against the theme of loss of religious conviction expressed in his definition of man as a 'quintessence of dust', of disgust with the world or of the anomie, which may have been equated with madness, or of many other themes that can be discerned.

Themes are of course subject to the dramatist's manipulation in the interests of dramatic effect. The dynamism of Greek tragedy seems to us to arise from the theme of the fatefulness of man's relationship with the gods. If the hero offends the gods he sets in train a sequence of actions in which the fate of many individuals is implicated. He can also be used, on account of trivial transgression, like that of Philoctetes, as a pawn in the quarrels of the gods. Yet Aristotle's words suggest that this was by no means a normal view of action even for those who retained a religious view of the world. It was rather a dramatic device:

> 'But again, Tragedy is an imitation not only of a complete action, but of events inspiring fear or pity. Such an effect is best produced when the events come on us by surprise; and the effect is heightened when, at the same time, they follow as cause and effect. The tragic wonder will then be greater than if they happened of themselves or by accident; for even coincidences are most striking when they have an air of design'.[22]

Thus the ordinary motives, intentions and consequences represented in the plays can be distorted by the dramatic design and it is difficult for us at this distance of time to relate the themes of Greek tragedy to the rituals of social life, although we can assume that the design of the dramatist seemed to the spectators possible if not probable.

[20] Impossible, Colin Cherry would say, for 'we can but speculate': C. Cherry, 'Language and extra-linguistic Communication', in Minnis, *Linguistics at Large*, p. 279.
[21] B. L. Joseph, *Conscience and the King* (Chatto & Windus, 1953).
[22] Aristotle, *The Poetics*, trans. H. Butcher (Macmillan and Co Ltd), Fourth edn. 1936, p. 39.

In an exegesis of Sophocles' *Antigone* David Robinson has stressed the fact that the play does not show a conflict between right, represented by Antigone and wrong, represented by Kreon. What it demonstrates is the inevitable results of wrong actions, actions which offend authority, in this case the gods. Kreon suffers not because he is cruel but because he fails to bury a dead body and allows the city temples to be polluted by it. He suffers because he breaks rules, and rules, unlike moral principles, need not be understood but must be respected.[23] The consequences of transgression are known and this knowledge contributes to the sense of fatefulness and inevitability which underlines action in all Greek tragedy.

Different ways of achieving this sense of inevitability have modified similar themes throughout the history of the drama. In medieval religious drama themes stressed man's relationship with God. In the Moralities, where plots were no longer taken from the Bible, the patterning of themes and events emphasised the fatefulness of decisions and actions in relation to the sacred, not the secular world. The symmetry of the conflict between God and the devil fighting for the soul of man was all important for the drama. But the audience reaction to this theme cannot be deduced. The Church itself seems to have had doubts about the value of expressing such ideas through the 'unreal' forms of the drama.[24] The allegorising nature of medieval modes of thought meant that the stage offered a third unnecessary level of symbolism which might detract from truth.

In the secular drama of the sixteenth and seventeenth centuries themes are based for the most part on the relationship between man and man not between men and God, though religious pressures as well as political and social pressures can still be brought to bear on action. The sense of inevitablility is on the whole reduced even when such powerful forces as honour, ambition, power or love are invoked as motives for action. Horatio observes in the tragic scene at the end of *Hamlet*, not inevitability or a higher will, but:

> . . . accidental judgements, casual slaughters,
> Of deaths put on by cunning and forc'd cause
> And in this upshot purposes mistook
> Fall'n on the inventors' heads.

Accident plays a large part in most of Shakespeare's tragedies, in Romeo's arrival at the sepulchre before Juliet has revived, in Cor-

---

[23] D. Robinson, 'Antigone', *Recordings* (Edinburgh University, 1967).
[24] Religious drama was under attack from many clerics, even at the time that it was performed and organised within the Church. Grosstête in 1348 issued a prohibition against such plays and the Dominican preacher Bromyard referred to the 'Miracles' of 'foolish clerics'.

delia's death which Edmund could have stopped had he repented sooner, and in the convenient coincidences that enabled Iago to carry out his plot. Such accidental circumstances are seldom related to fate or to any external agency.

In his comedies accident and coincidence are manipulated in such a way that they provide the structure of many of the plots. Confusion over twins, mistaken identity, letters sent astray and a general distribution of misinformation underlie the comedies from the *Comedy of Errors* to *Twelfth Night* and *The Tempest*. The artificiality of the comic convention allows accident to replace motive legitimately. But the darker side of accident in tragedy does suggest that there was at the time little general reliance on the remorselessness of cause and effect or on a general overriding design. In Western European drama from this time until today (except in plays based on classical themes) emphasis has been placed on choice and accident rather than on inevitability and consequence. How far does this reflect a shift in the perception of events in ordinary life and how far is it merely a new kind of dramatic device?

At least it is evident that the medieval view of the universe as a hierarchy in which correspondences and analogies related the spiritual to the physical world was losing ground from the sixteenth century onwards although many traces of it remained even in the writings of the more sceptical writers such as Francis Bacon and Sir Thomas Browne, throughout the seventeenth century.[25] For many ordinary people the theocentric view of the universe persists even into the twentieth century, in spite of scientific explanations of cause and effect.

In the seventeenth century many Protestant sects persisted in the belief that God's will could be felt, even if it were hidden, in all sectors of daily life; and they not only opposed the theatre but ostracised all those who took part in it. It is therefore not surprising that motivation and action in the drama at this time is based not on God's directives but on the Renaissance image of the free and autonomous individual. Such a person free to choose was nevertheless not all-powerful and therefore subject to accident. Failure was the result of his own weaknesses or mistakes. Consequential action came to replace the transgressions of God's laws. Thus the tragic flaw was no longer related to force outside the protagonist but was personal and private, a weakness caused by overdeveloped passions—pride, ambition, lust for power—whose origins did not have to be accounted for. As Lukács has said of the 'modern poets' of the late nineteenth century: 'What once was destiny has become character for the

---

[25] Even Bacon in his *Nine Books of the Dignity and Advancement of learning* (1623) accepted 'some astrology' as capable of 'predictions' and 'elections', as a necessary part of natural history.

modern poets.'[26] It is easy to see that they derived the nature of
their themes from Shakespeare and his contemporaries. Lukács saw
this situation as a danger to tragedy as he saw the only possibility of
universality in 'what comes from without'. In place of destiny he
found pathology (the sick hero, e.g. Oswald, Rank) creating consequentiality but not achieving universality. What he did not recognise
was the diminution of the tragic hero since the seventeenth century.
Throughout the nineteenth century the individual was becoming
aware of being controlled by society whether he felt himself to be
conformist or non-conformist as regards its rules. Although the
concept of alienation was most clearly defined by Marx, non-Marx-
ist writers such as Carlyle, Mill and Arnold were aware of the erosion
of individual freedom in the newly transformed industrial society.

Tragic dramatists at the end of the nineteenth century, such as
Ibsen, Strindberg and Chekhov, dealt with these themes. The pressures of society to make them conform, deceiving themselves or
others, replace destiny or moral dictates to ensure the tragic fates of
Rosmer, Hedwig, Miss Julie and Konstantin. Ibsen's own preliminary
notes for his plays emphasise the part played in his theories by social
conflict rather than personal weakness. *Hedda Gabler* is supposed to
be about: 'the insuperable . . . longing and striving to defy convention, to defy what people accept'.[27] It is not enough that his
heroes are imperfect, that Borkman is filled with grandiose ambition
that overrides his moral scruples, that Rosmer is afflicted with a
desire to seem to himself always in the right or that Gregers Werle
believes he has a messianic mission. Many other people have contributed in the past and the present to the situations in which they
find themselves. In fact Ibsen seems to have been attracted by the
idea that the individual has no personal responsibility for his fate.
Oswald is a model of such a hero whose fate has been determined
long ago by the actions of his parents. Yet congenital faults, unlike
the curse of the gods on the House of Atreus, cannot call from the
hero a response of any grandeur.

Many of Strindberg's themes deal with similar social conflicts but
are focused more often on personal than on social situations. He
took, however, a less materialistic view of society. He claimed that
'an event in life—and that is rather a new discovery—is usually oc-
casioned by a series of more or less deep-seated motifs, but the spectator usually chooses that one which his judgment finds simplest to
grasp'.[28]

In the themes of both Ibsen and Strindberg accident and chance

[26] G. Lukàcs, 'Sociology of Modern Drama', trans. Lee Baxendall, in *Theory of the
Modern Stage*, ed. E. Bentley (Penguin, 1968), p. 449.
[27] Ibsen *Letters*—ed. Sprinchorn, Letter to Moritz Prozoc.
[28] A. Strindberg, Preface to *Miss Julie*, in *The Plays*, ed. M. Meyer (Secker &
Warburg, 1964), ii.

are often overridden by the emphasis placed on personal responsibility for choice and decisions. Hedda, Sölness, Rosmer and Rebekka, Strindberg's Edgar and Alice (The Dance of Death) and Miss Julie sacrifice or destroy themselves because of the principles or passions that sustain them and drive them to oppose society. Thus while Ibsen was still using traditional themes, the heroic sacrifice for a principle (Dr Stockman), the fate of the outcast from society and of the victim of society (Oswald, John Gabriel Borkman), the struggle to achieve eminence and maintain power (Sölness), amongst many others, he was also introducing completely new themes that have come to dominate later drama. The most important of these is the search for definitions of reality and the implicit search for identity. These themes attempt to establish meaning and a standpoint. For the dramatist they provide a way of relating the action of daily life to criteria of coherence which take the place of God's authority.

The rhetorical conventions of medieval and to a large extent of sixteenth- and seventeenth-century drama were used to define illusion. Religious consensus made the definition of reality unnecessary. Reality belonged to the spiritual world and the shows of the physical world could only be accepted as 'real' in relation to it. Scholastic realism referred to universals, and assumed that the secular had no reality in itself. Philosophical interest in 'reality' in the modern sense dates from the writings of Descartes, Locke, Berkeley and, especially, Hume. But it does not appear to have become a question that could be dealt with in literature until the end of the nineteenth century. As God came to be more openly questioned the vexatious problem emerged. The reality of the sacred was in doubt and reality had to be redefined in physical terms.

Ibsen cast doubt on reality by suggesting the different ways in which actions can be assessed by different people, also by suggesting in a purely secular way the symbolic quality of many actions. His use of symbolism was not only a theatrical device. It was not merely a short cut to interpretation but an illumination of the way in which people seem to think about things.

Although the allegorising cast of mind is no longer the natural outcome of religious upbringing and education it has been replaced in the modern world by an intellectual interest in symbolism and a loose employment of Freudian symbols. Ibsen knew nothing of Freud, though he was interested in psychiatric research and seems to have known Freud's teacher. When Aline in the *Master Builder* mourns her dead dolls and Hedda Gabler destroys Lövborg's manuscript because it is the 'child' of Lövborg and Mrs Elvsted he is dramatising psychological patterns of conduct of a kind that Freud was to turn his attention to. In society he saw both good and evil, the force of liberation and the force of conservative repression. Thus his themes are concerned with the ways in which the individual reacts to this dichotomy. Where Marlowe's Dr Faustus chooses between God and the Devil, Rosmer is faced with the choice between traditional conservatism and the new liberalism which he sees as a way of liberating and ennobling his countrymen. The same sort of choice faces Dr Stockman in *An Enemy of the People*.

Yet Ibsen makes more of a division between the public and private person than sixteenth-century dramatists did. Whereas the Shakespearean character had one role, that of king, prince or general, which dominated his other roles, the modern hero is doubtful which should take precedence amongst conflicting roles. Thus Rosmer's choice of political duty in the public world is disturbed by the guilt that arises from his treatment of his wife and his association with Rebekka, also from his established position as pastor at Rosmersholm.

Traditional themes concerning honour and vengeance, ambition, power and love were translated by Ibsen from the public (universal) world to the private and domestic. He did however attempt to imply a universal interpretation of his themes through heavily weighted symbolism. *The Wild Duck* is not merely a study of Hjalmar's weakness and self-deception and Greger's messianic view of his mission to transform his fellow-men. Although all that many contemporary critics saw in it was 'a dreary record of provincial meanness and pessimism' it is apparent that Ibsen was interested in exposing the different levels on which a theme can exist. The central theme of the play seems to be the discrimination of the different levels of reality and the distinction often so hard to make between reality and illusion. In *The Wild Duck* three worlds are suggested, the outside world represented by Werle's house and office, where money is earned and lost, the private world of the Ekdals' home where bread is earned by photographing reality, and the play world of the attic where Ekdal and Hjalmar go hunting and where the sacred object, the wild duck, lives out its days. It is in this play world that serious metaphoric meanings can be grasped.

Strindberg was also preoccupied by the definition of reality. In his later plays, *A Dream Play* and *The Ghost Sonata*, events are disregarded and only the 'deep-seated motifs' are represented. Reality lies in the evil background to ordinary life. The rest is '*schauderhaft* ... When the veil falls we see *Das Ding an sich*'.[29] Strindberg who spent some time in Paris was of course aware of forms of anti-realist literature, of expressionism and symbolism, and was more influenced by the currents of this new European mode of presentation than Ibsen. Thus although both techniques were symptoms of the same attempt to grasp new aspects of reality, Ibsen's symbolism (perhaps

[29] A. Strindberg, Preface to the *Ghost Sonata*, in *The Plays*, ed. Meyer, i, 420.

because it was too close to the more authoritative symbolic interpretation of Freud) seems to have been much less influential in the European theatre than the 'absurdity' of Strindberg's *Dream Play*, and *Ghost Sonata*, where apparent symbols cannot be definitively interpreted.

The 'realist' dramatists of the first half of this century, Galsworthy, Granville Barker and many other writers of 'problem' plays chose the kind of situations that Ibsen had dealt with but failed to suggest more than one level on which action could take place. Nor were they interested in the definition of reality in itself. They seemed to accept reality on the level of common discourse. If certain social conventions concerning marriage, work or conformity are generally accepted then they need not be questioned.[30]

Explicit treatment of the theme of the definition of reality was introduced to the English theatre by Pirandello (who confessed to his admiration of Ibsen). Like Ibsen in his last play, *When We Dead Awaken*, he was much concerned with the theme of the relationship of reality to artistic truth. But before he tackled this theme in his trio of plays on the theatre he had approached the problem of reality in real life which he saw as in itself a theatrical display. In *Right You Are (If You Think So)* the situation, in which it is impossible for anyone to ascertain who is sane, or who is mad, is based on the theme that truth and, by implication, reality, are not objective. Mr and Mrs Ponza have, as Laudisi says: 'created, she for him, he for her, a world of fantasy that has all the substance of reality itself'. Pirandello insists on the theme that appears many times in his later plays that Mrs Ponza is, as she says, 'just whoever you think I am'. Yet in spite of his juggling with different levels of reality, reality on each of these levels is defined by Pirandello in much the same way. The logic of causal connections rules the world of Henry IV's madness as much as the world from which Belcredi and Matilda have come. Pirandello sees ambiguity in all actions and relationships but he does not suggest irrationality either in the order of things or in the conduct of persons. Like Ibsen his themes are concerned with the definition of kinds of reality not of the laws of reality. The strange realisation of the 'oddness' of the composition of everyday life, of the arbitrary nature of the norms that constrain behaviour and make social life possible was something that Pirandello prepared his audiences for but did not express. Instead he presented characters, Don' Anna in *The Life I Gave You*, Signor Ponza in *Right You Are (If You Think So)* who live in an imaginary world hedged about by the same kind of constraints that obtain in the real world.

---

[30] Galsworthy and Granville Barker, like Ibsen, were much concerned with the exposure of hypocrisy in social life, but not with the perception of different codes of morality.

The theme of the search for reality was approached in another way by Jarry at the end of the nineteenth century. His influence was not felt in the English theatre until the writing of Artaud became known and the plays of Ionesco, Arrabal, Adamov and many other European anti-realist dramatists were produced here in the 1950s. Ionesco explained his first play, *La Cantatrice Chauve*, as 'the expression of a feeling for the strangeness of everyday things, a strangeness that appears at the heart of the most outworn commonplace'.[31] He hoped in this way to present universal rather than particular themes and arrive at a reality that was new and presumably unrecognisable. The existentialist term 'absurd' has been used to describe his technique although it is the theme itself that is really 'absurd', the theme repeated in all his plays that reality lies in disconnected actions not in consequentially composed sequences of cause and effect. He seeks, as non-representational painters do, 'a clashing of forms and lines . . . abstract antagonisms without psychological motivations'.[32] Thus the search for reality is the central theme of *Le Leçon*, *Les Chaises*, and *Victimes du Devoir* although the method of presentation contradicts and assaults all the accepted conventions on which conduct in the ordinary world is based. Ionesco's use of irrational actions, the disconnected incidents, the impossible events, like the growing corpse in *Amedée*, the personal transformations and exchanges of identity that occur in *Victimes du Devoir* seems to be a method of alienating experience in Brecht's sense. It is an analysis that seeks to expose the reality behind the reality.

This theme is treated more obliquely by Beckett. In *Waiting for Godot* the implication is that the real (which is the foundation of 'meaning') is undiscoverable. There are in fact no sustained sequences of action in Beckett's plays, only states of being, waiting, searching, suffering, and dying, states which have no articulated cause or aim. Yet the suggestion of a search for the definition of reality and identity lies behind *Waiting for Godot*, *Play*, *Happy Days* and *Endgame* and most of the other plays. Beckett's refusal to articulate these themes clearly gives a static quality to the plays and perhaps accounts for the terse style and restricted form, a style and form which culminate in *Act Without Words, A mime for one player* (1958). This mime, except in its length and careful composition (no allowance is made for improvisation) is not far removed from the 'acts' of the circus clown, music hall comedian or mime. But the title is significant. The absence of words is a positive factor in the complete isolation of the one character. The success of Beckett's plays depends on the readiness of the audience to accept the meaning of the appar-

---

[31] Ionesco, *Notes and Counter Notes*, trans. D. Watson (Calder, 1964), p. 172.
[32] *Ibid*, p. 225.

ently meaningless, the ambiguities of definition, the uncertainty of reality.

The effect of such an underlying theme has been to make drama more expressive, less concerned with meaning in the traditional sense. The theatre of happenings and improvisations where there is either no written text or a text that is plundered for effective moments constitutes this kind of theatre. Where there has been political commitment as in *U.S.*, *Tom Paine* and *America Hurrah* the themes are distinguishable, appeals for freedom, hatred of oppression and disgust with the treachery of society. But political or social criticism is more often achieved by eliminating or attacking themes. Grotowski's 'archetype' which is equated with 'symbol, myth, image, leitmotiv', is really a theme set up only to be destroyed. The self-sacrificing hero is stripped of his *mana* so that he is made to appear absurd. Grotowski sets up myths not as themes but as models that can be broken down. Similarly, perhaps more crudely, the Living Theatre is a 'shock theatre'. It does not try to present a theme to the audience, to show them anything. It tries to stimulate them to action, or as they might say, to drive them to reality. The theme of the search for reality has reached its apotheosis as a dramatic theme in the sense that it is now used to show that reality can only exist outside the theatre, not, as dramatist and actors have previously assumed, in the imagination of the spectators. Julian Beck said of *Paradise Now* 'we wanted to make a play which would no longer be an enactment but would be the act itself . . . an event in which we (the actors) would always be experiencing it (the play) not anew at all but something else each time.'[33] In the same tone Tom O'Horgan has spoken of theatre becoming 'a way of life' for the La Mama group. He attempts to use the actors' own personal relationships for action in the play context.

The attempt to substitute theatrical experience for experience in the outside world seems to be a new form of the didacticism that has always haunted the theatre. Apologies for the theatre in the seventeenth century frequently stressed its exemplary function. A play such as *The Murder of Gonzago* could always be resorted to to stir conscience or less drastically to set up models of behaviour. Yet the nature of many plays of this period when the good triumphed only after the attractions of evil had been sensationally demonstrated betray the perfunctory nature of the claim. Today the statements of the Becks, Grotowski, O'Horgan and actors of other avant-garde groups display a fervour that links moral and artistic standards. They

[33] 'Containment is the Enemy', Judith Malina and Julian Beck interviewed by Richard Schechner, *Tulane Drama Review*, Spring 1969, xiii, no. 3, p. 24.

also aim at injecting myths and ritual into ordinary life. Yet myth and ritual can only arise from ordinary and repetitive human experience. The theatre cannot remake ritual in this way. Through incantation, dance and stylisation of movement it can only reproduce ritual forms in theatrical terms, imitations of religious or political ecstasy (Brook's *Oedipus*, Schechner's *Dionysus*) love or war.

Drama which keeps much more closely to ordinary speech and action such as *The Brig* or *The Connection* accentuates the ritual forms that are already there, the ways in which hatred, domination, servility are expressed. Although conduct in these plays seems to be presented photographically (as if in real life) the mechanism of staging and performance puts the emphasis on the symbolic aspect of every word, action and movement. Moreover the audience is supposed to attend to everything that happens on the stage. In ordinary life the spectator selects the characters and events to which he will pay attention. But for the theatre audience the selection is of course made by dramatist, producer and performers. The spectator responds to their sign language and accepts their version of reality. The effect of *The Brig* is to emphasise the fabrication of reality and to show that the more spontaneous a character is the more he is an actor.

However disparate the interpretations of signs or symbols in the drama these symbols are 'heavily infused with ideas and images of social order',[34] as well as with the ethics and associated doctrines of religion. The theatre is always a place in which symbols, whether stressed or unstressed, can be displayed in a form that is more potent than that of other kinds of literature. The response of the audience, even if some of the spectators dissent from it, suggests through laughter, sighs or tears the kind of interpretation that messages have been given—the action or words are funny, sad, or shocking. When a play (sometimes categorised as 'black comedy') such as Edward Bond's *Saved* makes some of the audience laugh, some unhappy, some angry, some shocked and some merely puzzled, it exposes the discrepant values of the audience, but it can still be effective because of its semiotic complexity.

Reactions to novels, poetry or essays are less immediate and often mediated by discussion. This suggests that although reactions in a theatre may be cruder, less thought out, and less expressive of an individual mind, they are the kind of reactions that are likely to be encountered in ordinary life. Even outside a mob people do act in accordance with the actions of *some* others, those with whom they consider themselves like-minded and they do use rituals of behaviour as guides to appropriate action. These rituals range from the almost

[34] H. D. Duncan, 'The development of Durkheim's concept of ritual', in E. Durkheim *et al.*, *Essays in Sociology and Philosophy* (Ohio State University Press, 1960), p. 112.

theatrical behaviour of an orator's audience, which may laugh, clap, boo or hiss or even on occasions throw things, to the behaviour of friends or one friend, listening to an anecdote or confidence. To maintain the speaker's confidence in his performance the listener must show at least by facial expression that he is in touch with the speaker. Going to sleep or becoming intent on some other occupation, reading or listening to the radio, is as much of a rebuff as leaving the room. This attention is not only necessary, as is sometimes suggested, to keep things going. Attention is variable in degrees capable of precise definition. So attention is a functional, instrumental, element in social interaction, defining boundaries of agreement and disagreement, establishing common values and the lines of divergence which may or may not be explored.

In the theatre this situation occurs only more formally and with a less even balance between those involved. Even in the most recent experiments in the theatre it has still been the actors, producer and (if there is one) dramatist who have been dominant in the sense that they both stimulate and limit audience participation. In the traditional theatre the rules are of course more explicit. The audience responds to what it is offered. It can be obstructive, abusive or leave the theatre but it cannot change the action or initiate new action. Yet this situation is only an enlargement of the real life one and has an added dimension. The rules and rituals of ordinary behaviour have been formulated and codified and can be watched occurring on the stage and responded to. When people said that they wanted to get up on the stage and hit Jimmie Porter because he insulted his wife, when Victorian audiences called out to warn the heroine of danger, they did not merely identify with one of the characters but displaced the whole scene from one thematic level to another, as well as from the symbolic to the actual.

It is in the drama that different kinds of ritual, those connected with family life, public life or individual experiences of an emotional or interpersonal situation can be observed and interpreted according to the spectators' values. It is there, because of his lack of real involvement, his inability to initiate action, that the spectator becomes most aware of the symbolic aspect of action. The ferocious domestic quarrel in *Who's Afaid of Virginia Woolf?* may be outside the range of experience of most people. But its stages, 'Fun and Games', 'Walpurgisnacht', and 'The Exorcism' follow the familiar lines of manipulated situations with which any pairs, husband and wife or friends are familiar, though they may deal with them less hysterically and according to different social values or codes. The subsidiary theme of the secret and its betrayal to others, whether the secret be a phantom child or a secret game of bears and squirrels, also generates a series of incidents and crises which take a ritual form.

The privacy and security of domestic life in the contemporary world, the predominance of the small family unit over the more open extended family, tends to inhibit the development of new or transformed rituals. The stereotyped rituals of family life are reproduced in the many domestic comedies and 'soap operas' shown in the theatre and on television. But in the last fifteen years the introduction of themes and settings from working-class life, from work milieux and from the milieux of subcultures, such as criminal or deviant groups has expanded the range of available rituals. It is not only the accents and manners of the characters in Wesker's *Roots*, Arden's *Live like Pigs* or Delaney's *Taste of Honey* that differ from those of the characters in the middle-class worlds of Maugham, Robert Bolt or Enid Bagnold. Much more significant differences lie in the values and goals of the people represented and the accepted relationships of husband and wife, parents and children, and workmates.

Although the working-class 'attitude' and its implied values has also become to some extent stereotyped, so that there is now an anticipated and reliable reaction to the behaviour portrayed in many of these plays, the shifting of viewpoint from middle-class to working-class has added another dimension to theatrical reality. It has also drawn people's attention to the fabricated nature of much of the behaviour that is represented as authentic. In *A Taste of Honey*, which deals with a disreputable drifting working-class mother and daughter, the attempt of the mother to adhere to certain norms and values, to have a settled home, to show family affection, and to despise at least one kind of person (the coloured boy) and so remain not quite at the bottom of the pile, demonstrates a model of the way in which people try to give even the most disorganised lives coherence and meaning, in fact, to ritualise their social behaviour.

The equivalences between role playing, inside and outside the theatre, between manipulation of settings on stage and off, and between themes in the drama and ritual in ordinary life, suggest that the dramatisation of life is an activity in which everyone is involved. This does not mean that drama loses its value as an art, as something which enlarges experience and intensifies meaning. Drama offers experience of limited but complete cycles of situations in which the consequences of choices, decisions, and actions are explored and selected.

Action in a play is however not only contrived but also normative. The normativeness of drama is a heritage from ritual, which, as V. W. Turner says has an 'exemplary model-displaying character: in a sense they (all rituals) might be said to "create" society in much the same way as Oscar Wilde held life to be "an imitation of art".'[35] The success of a play depends in part on the dramatist persuading the audience to take a particular standpoint, to adopt certain standards by which actions and characters can be judged as good or bad, successful or unsuccessful, conforming or deviant. The spectator judges from a position which he can never occupy in ordinary life, that of someone who sees and knows everything that it is necessary to see and know.

Thus the audience is engaged in an ideal making and remaking of moral life. For this reason the banality or triviality of a play is far more ennervating than that of a novel. The audience is required not only to keep the play going but to relate it to its own experience of life outside the theatre, even if it is relevant to only one milieu, to the upper-class society of the Restoration court or the grey houses of a north-country slum.

The drama itself emerges through the experience of the dramatist and performers from the perceived theatricality of ordinary life. But this involves a constant feed-in and feed-back between art and life. As suggested at the beginning of this book, theatrical possibilities can only be perceived when division between performers and spectators, at however primitive a level, has occurred. The composition of events, the focusing on situations and individuals, is part of reality which everyone experiences in ordinary life. But fiction allows one to reflect upon this experience, freed from the tensions which the need for decisions or actions give rise to. Drama, moreover, is a heightened form of fiction which depends on the involvement of the audience so that real action is to some degree simulated. Even in the traditional theatre the spectator is within the performance in a part that he can discard when the play ends. He is always to some extent conscious of the spotlight that in *Les Nègres* Genet would like to train on him.[36] It is because of the involvement of the audience that the theatre can be regarded as *existential*. In the theatre the audience is at the same time contributing to the ceremonial of a performance and observing life converted into ceremonial forms on the stage.

> Ceremonial, polarisation of the setting and the choice of a special individual are the factors common to the theatre and social life. But they also divide the two domains: social ceremony actually accomplishes action which is deferred and sublimated in the theatre; the distribution of social space between two groups which exchange beliefs and rituals, becomes, in the

[35] V. W. Turner, *The Ritual Process* (Routledge, 1969), p. 117.
[36] 'Toujours Village: lorsqu'il commence la tirade: "Marchez! vous possédez ce soir la plus belle démarche du royaume ... il faut allumer toutes les lumières, y compris les lustres de la salle, *Les spectateurs doivent inondés de lumière*".' J. Genet, *Les Nègres* (Paris, 1959), Introduction.

theatre, the participation which helps to create an image of the person.[37]

This tension between the groups inside the theatre, the performers and the audience, is related to the experience of theatricality of which all spectators are aware outside the theatre.

In ordinary life each person is engaged in a constant endeavour to mark out his own role, his setting, his course of action and to distinguish between those who are to be fellow actors and those who are to be spectators. In the theatre where these demarcations have been anticipated involvement costs much less in anxiety or consequences. In the dramatic performance theatrical behaviour, legitimated and stylised, is organised in such a way that the possibilities of coherent chains of cause and effect, interrupted by accident or interference, can be grasped. The temporary reality of the theatrical world even at its most unrealistic is always in contact with the real world in the fringes of consciousness of the spectator.

The same consciousness that generates instrumental action recognises its composition and its elements of theatricality. And it is this recognition that can be painful and self-alienating. In their most highly valued relationships and preoccupations people like to think of themselves as free of all the attributes of an actor. It is, however, possible to preserve the necessary sense of authenticity if 'theatricality' is seen not as a mode of behaviour but as a mode of recognition. It belongs to the critical, judging, assessing 'I' that stands aside from the self—as conscience or 'ego'. But its function is enriched by theatrical awareness and theatrical insights that take into account the self as a social being. Just as drama is an enlargement of life, the theatrical view of life is also enlarging. Sartre treated fiction 'as deeply distrusted and humanly indispensable', and the same distrust and indispensability applies to the theatre and to the theatrical view that gives rise to it and arises from it. Without the ability to compose and to recognise the composition of our own actions and those of others, social and personal life would perhaps disintegrate. We might feel ourselves free but it would be a freedom that at our present state of development we cannot contemplate. It would call for a complete remaking of the self of each individual.

The dangers of 'theatricality', as it is perceived, lie only in rigidity or repetitiveness. There is often a sameness of view—an inability to generate or recognise new aspects of composition. Social behaviour can seem to be made up of empty rituals if we refuse to contribute the novelty of our own experiences—merely accepting the 'world-pictures' handed down to us through socialisation. Conventions,

[37] J. Duvignaud, *Sociologie du Théâtre* (Paris, 1963), p. 25 (my translation, E.B.),

whether rhetorical or authenticating, role playing and composition of action as plots and themes all depend upon the consensual and generative relationships of individuals in different social milieux. From a 'theatrical' viewpoint they are the paradigmatic grammar of the principles of thought and feeling that underlie social action.

Index of authors

Index of authors

General index

General index